Byte Wars

The Impact of September 11 on Information Technology

Selected Titles from the
YOURDON PRESS COMPUTING SERIES
Ed Yourdon, *Advisor*

JUST ENOUGH SERIES / YOURDON PRESS
DUÉ, Mentoring Object Technology Projects
MOSLEY/POSEY, Software Test Automation
THOMSETT Radical Project Management
YOURDON, Managing High-Intensity Internet Projects

YOURDON PRESS COMPUTING SERIES
ANDREWS AND STALICK Business Reengineering: The Survival Guide
BOULDIN Agents of Change: Managing the Introduction of Automated Tools
COAD AND MAYFIELD with Kern Java Design: Building Better Apps and Applets, Second Edition
COAD AND NICOLA Object-Oriented Programming
COAD AND YOURDON Object-Oriented Analysis, Second Edition
COAD AND YOURDON Object-Oriented Design
COAD WITH NORTH AND MAYFIELD Object Models, Strategies, Patterns, and Applications, Second Edition
CONNELL AND SHAFER Object-Oriented Rapid Prototyping
CONSTANTINE The Peopleware Papers: Notes on the Human Side of Software
CONSTANTINE AND YOURDON Structure Design
DEGRACE AND STAHL Wicked Problems, Righteous Solutions
DEMARCO Controlling Software Projects
DEMARCO Structured Analysis and System Specification
FOURNIER A Methodology for Client/Server and Web Application Development
GARMUS AND HERRON Measuring the Software Process: A Practical Guide to Functional Measurements
HAYES AND ULRICH The Year 2000 Software Crisis: The Continuing Challenge
JONES Assessment and Control of Software Risks
KING Project Management Made Simple
PAGE-JONES Practical Guide to Structured Systems Design, Second Edition
PUTNAM AND MEYERS Measures for Excellence: Reliable Software on Time within Budget
RUBLE Practical Analysis and Design for Client/Server and GUI Systems
SHLAER AND MELLOR Object Lifecycles: Modeling the World in States
SHLAER AND MELLOR Object-Oriented Systems Analysis: Modeling the World in Data
STARR How to Build Shlaer-Mellor Object Models
THOMSETT Third Wave Project Management
ULRICH AND HAYES The Year 2000 Software Crisis: Challenge of the Century
YOURDON Byte Wars: The Impact of September 11 on Information Technology
YOURDON Death March: The Complete Software Developer's Guide to Surviving "Mission Impossible" Projects
YOURDON Decline and Fall of the American Programmer
YOURDON Modern Structured Analysis
YOURDON Object-Oriented Systems Design
YOURDON Rise and Resurrection of the American Programmer
YOURDON AND ARGILA Case Studies in Object-Oriented Analysis and Design

Byte Wars

The Impact of September 11 on Information Technology

160201

Ed Yourdon

PRENTICE HALL PTR
UPPER SADDLE RIVER, NJ 07458
WWW.PHPTR.COM

Library of Congress Cataloging-in-Publication available

Editorial/production supervision: *Kathleen M. Caren*
Executive Editor: *Paul Petralia*
Editorial Assistant: *Rick Winkler*
Director of International Sales and Marketing: *Michael Vaccaro*
Marketing Manager: *Debby van Dijk*
Manufacturing Manager: *Alexis R. Heydt-Long*
Cover Design: *Nina Scuderi* and *Anthony Gemmellaro*
Cover Design Director: *Jerry Votta*
Series Design: *Gail Cocker-Bogusz*

© 2002 Prentice Hall PTR
Pearson Education Inc.
Upper Saddle River, NJ 07458

The publisher offers discounts on this book when ordered in bulk quantities.
For more information, contact
Corporate Sales Department,
Prentice Hall PTR
One Lake Street
Upper Saddle River, NJ 07458
Phone: 800-382-3419; FAX: 201-236-7141
E-mail (Internet): corpsales@prenhall.com

Printed in the United States of America

10 9 8 7 6 5 4 3 2 1

ISBN 0-13-0046594-1

Pearson Education LTD.
Pearson Education Australia PTY, Limited
Pearson Education Singapore, Pte. Ltd.
Pearson Education North Asia Ltd.
Pearson Education Canada, Ltd.
Pearson Educación de Mexico, S.A. de C.V.
Pearson Education—Japan
Pearson Education Malaysia, Pte. Ltd.
Pearson Education Inc., Upper Saddle River, New Jersey

CONTENTS

Chapter 2
STRATEGIC IMPLICATIONS OF 9/11 17

Chapter 3
SECURITY 79

Chapter 5
EMERGENT SYSTEMS. 155

Chapter 6
RESILIENT SYSTEMS 189

Chapter 7
GOOD ENOUGH SYSTEMS 221

Chapter 9
CONCLUSIONS 279

To my first grandchild, and
to the generation that will grow up
without ever having seen the
World Trade Center.

PREFACE

This is not a book I expected to write.

Indeed, it's highly unlikely that I would have written *Byte Wars*, had it not been for the awful events of September 11th. But even without the attacks on the World Trade Center and the Pentagon, someone should have been writing about the disruptive, chaotic changes we face in the coming years—changes enabled and facilitated by technology. As it turns out, many scientists, pundits, and gurus *have* been writing such books in recent years, including some about terrorism and bio-warfare to which we should have been paying much more attention. But most of the recent books dealing with the future of computers and the field of information technology (IT) have focused on the glamorous future of e-commerce and the Internet; ironically, *that* future appears much less glamorous than it did just a short while ago.

One of the themes in *Byte Wars* is that a number of changes—not just gentle, incremental changes, but massive, paradigm-shift changes—have actually been underway for the past several years. The events of September 11th have crystallized those changes, forcing us to confront and acknowledge some new realities that we have ignored for too long. For example, anyone who accesses the Internet is aware of the rash of computer-based viruses and worms that have proliferated since the "Love Bug" episode a couple years ago. But we may not have faced up to the terrifying threat of "zombie armies" of powerful home computers with high-speed, always-on Internet connections, computers that can be invaded by hackers and reprogrammed to launch denial-of-service attacks on businesses and government agencies.

It doesn't take a rocket scientist to see that computer technology is going to play a central role in the war on terrorism being formulated by the U.S. government as this book goes to press. Not only are we likely to see billions of dollars invested in a new generation of laser-guided missiles, computer-assisted weapons, but we'll see a vast array of scanning devices, face-recognition devices, and other computer technologies to enhance identification and tracking of suspect individuals. We'll see the development and integration of public-sector and private-sector databases, which will raise a plethora of privacy issues and concerns. And we'll see an enormous increase in the techniques and technologies for protecting telecommunication networks, Web sites, Internet portals, and other computer-dependent aspects of the nation's "critical infrastructure."

Even so, many IT professionals may be predisposed to view these activities as nothing more than a "political" response to September 11th, much like the Cold War was a response to the actions of the former Soviet Union after World War II. As such, the reaction to September 11th is obviously a much less upbeat and cheerful response than that caused by the fall of the Berlin Wall, the reunification of Germany, and the collapse of the Soviet Empire in the late 1980s and early 1990s. Americans—including not only IT professionals, but everyone else, too—must now confront the discomforting reality that they are no longer protected by two vast oceans. They must confront the reality that some conflicts, especially those that involve deep ethnic and religious disputes, can go on for generations and centuries. And they must confront what they've heard for years, but never really accepted: not everyone appreciates or approves of Coca-Cola, McDonald's, Disney World, MTV, Hollywood, and various other trappings of the American way of life.

I don't have much advice to offer when it comes to politics, religion or ethnic disputes. And the only observation I'll make about Coca-Cola, McDonald's, and Disney World is that our corporate executives might be well advised to re-examine their built-in assumptions that globalization is *always* a good thing. Perhaps we don't need the same corporate logo on every office building around the world; perhaps we shouldn't be attempting to impose the same standardized payroll and inventory control system on every regional office around the world; perhaps not everyone wants to see the same MTV video clips and the same Hollywood movies. Maybe what our technology has done for us, as *Clue Train Manifesto* co-author David Weinberger suggests in the title of his forthcoming book, is to make it possible for peaceful coexistence in a global environment consisting of "small pieces, loosely joined."

Or maybe not. The point is that technology *is* a factor in these choices and decisions. Thus, while many IT professionals may prefer to think about September 11th as nothing but a terrorist attack, and while they may believe that the enormous response to that attack is nothing more than politics and military saber-rattling, their crown jewels—the most advanced and most sophisticated computer technology that they create—will be at the heart of that response. And that will be true not just for the next few weeks or months; I fully agree with the predictions that September 11th has ushered in an era that will last as long as the Cold War lasted. The fact that it will almost certainly last to the end of my life is only a trifle troubling to me; the fact that it may be the dominant influence on the lives and careers of my children, and *their* children, is something I don't feel I can ignore—particularly if that future is influenced significantly by the computer-based technologies that we IT professionals create.

So it's important for us to think about the topics in this book—not just the obvious topics of security and risk management, but also the somewhat less-understood topics of emergent systems and resilient systems, as well as the controversial concepts of good-enough systems and death-march projects. Not everyone will agree with the themes and recommendations I've offered on the following pages. That doesn't particularly bother me, but I do think it's important to remind the relatively young, idealistic IT professionals that existing power structures in corporations and government agencies may do little more than pay lip service to concepts such as emergent systems and resilient systems. Resiliency almost always implies redundancy, and the creation of enough "slack" in a system to withstand unanticipated disruptions; that's hard to justify in today's super-efficient, cost-conscious, lean-and-mean business environment.

And the notion that ad hoc, grass-roots systems can emerge on their own (supported, in many cases, by the peer-to-peer communication technologies that we IT professionals supply) and do a better job of responding to unplanned, disruptive threats is an anathema to traditional top-down, hierarchically managed organizations. It's worth remembering that the U.S. military, with all of its awesome resources, was unable to prevent two commercial airlines from crashing into the World Trade Center, nor a third plane from crashing into its very nerve center in Washington, DC. From that perspective, it's sobering indeed to realize that the only hijacked plane that *was* prevented from reaching its target on September 11th was United flight 93, in which a group of utter strangers, with no preconceived strategy and no top-down leadership, managed to create an ad hoc, grass-roots plan to take matters into their own hands.

It's customary, in a preface like this, for the author to acknowledge and thank the individuals who provided assistance in the creation of a book. But for me, that would require thanking almost everyone I've known since childhood; I am nothing more than the product of friendship, love, advice, guidance, and mentoring from thousands of friends, family members, business colleagues, former bosses, co-workers, and students.

But my wife and children deserve special thanks for tolerating periods when I would "tune out" in mid-sentence and
begin thinking about the chapter I was working on. And my
colleagues at the Cutter Consortium deserve special thanks,
too, for many provocative and thought-provoking discussions about the future of computer technology. Numerous
individuals, including anonymous Internet denizens from
all over the world, provided valuable feedback and suggestions as I posted chapters of the manuscript online. And
Steve Heller, who always loves to remind me of my 1975
prediction, in *Techniques of Program Structure and Design*, that
"unless you're very rich or very eccentric, you'll never have
your own computer," deserves special thanks for reading
every word of every chapter, critiquing and challenging
everything I wrote. Finally, a high-powered "death-march"
team at Prentice Hall, headed up by Kathleen Caren and
Paul Petralia, worked valiantly to bring the book out in
record time. Of course, any mistakes that remain are my
responsibility alone.

—Ed Yourdon
New York, NY and
Taos, New Mexico
February 2002

INTRODUCTION

September 11, 2001

During the late 1980s and early 1990s, I made several busi-
ness-related trips to Japan to work with some of the leading
computer companies in the country. One of those trips took
place in early December 1991; at the end of a long, busy
work-week, I awoke in my Tokyo hotel room on a Saturday
morning, and realized with a shock that it was December 7th.

December 7th—a date, as my parents had been informed
by a somber President Franklin Delano Roosevelt, that
would forever live in infamy. And this was not just any run-
of-the-mill December 7th, but the 50th anniversary of the
attack on Pearl Harbor that launched America into the second World War. I am one generation removed from that
event, and was not even born when it occurred; but I
couldn't help feeling tense and nervous as I left my hotel
room to stroll around the streets of Tokyo on that quiet, gray

1

Saturday morning. *How will people behave?* I wondered. *What will they say to me? How will I respond?*

I tried to anticipate a number of different attitudes and interactions from Japanese citizens that I expected to encounter in the hotel lobby, on the streets, and in the shops. I anticipated seeing thoughtful editorials in the newspapers, and earnest spokesmen on the television news programs; and I tried to sort out my own feelings about a date that had taken on mythic proportions throughout my entire life. But the one attitude and reaction that I did not expect, and that I saw consistently throughout the city of Tokyo that day, was: *nothing.* No remorse, no belligerence, no moment of quiet reflection, no jingoistic speeches of pride for the Japanese military forces, no mention whatsoever. Nothing. Nada. Zip. Everywhere I went, I was surrounded by a young generation of earnest, well-groomed, polite Japanese men and women who were completely preoccupied with the day-to-day tasks of shopping, or taking their children to the park, or (as they do so often in Japan, even on Saturday) hurrying into their offices to put in a full day of work. Pearl Harbor, for all its significance to me, apparently meant nothing to them.[1]

And perhaps a grandchild of mine, 50 years from now, will have the same experience—and perhaps that experience will be magnified, as it was for me, by the unexpected coincidence of celebrating the 50th anniversary of September 11, 2001 on the streets of Kabul or Kandahar. But as I write these words, just a few short weeks after the attack on the Pentagon and the World Trade Center, it's hard to imagine that anyone could ever forget the horror, and also the

---

1. Of course, one could argue that Pearl Harbor meant little or nothing to Americans younger than my generation, at least prior to Hollywood's release of the *Pearl Harbor* movie in the spring of 2001. As I learned from reading Morris Berman's *The Twilight of American Culture*, a 1998 survey by the National Constitution Center found that 42 percent of American adults (not students, but adults!) could not locate Japan on a world map, and that 15 percent could not even locate the United States! Even worse: 41 percent of American teenagers can name the three branches of government, but 59 percent can name the Three Stooges. So perhaps my expectations about the memorable impact of Pearl Harbor and September 11th are unrealistic.

significance, of that Tuesday morning in New York City and Washington. It was, as Obe Wan Kenobee remarked in the original *Star Wars* movie, when he sensed that one of the rebel planets had been obliterated by Darth Vader's Death Star, a "disturbance in the Force."

More than just a disturbance in the Force, September 11th represents a *paradigm shift*—a fundamental transformation in our understanding of how things work, and why things happen. Part, though by no means all, of that paradigm shift will involve the field of information technology (IT); and the details of the IT paradigm shift are the subject of this book.

The paradigm shift

The term "paradigm shift" was popularized by the late Thomas Kuhn in a classic book, *The Structure of Scientific Revolutions*. My Microsoft Word dictionary says that one of the definitions of "paradigm" is "a generally accepted model of how ideas relate to one another, forming a conceptual framework within which scientific research is carried out." And a paradigm *shift* occurs when the existing framework requires so many exceptions and special cases, and when it fails to address so many important problems, that it literally collapses under its own weight and is replaced by a new, simpler, more persuasive paradigm.

It's reassuring to know that, in the aftermath of September 11th, the paradigms of the physical sciences, which we all learned in high school and college, still seem intact; even though I feel disoriented and confused much of the time these days, I know that the law of gravity still holds. Indeed, even though most of us were so astounded by the real-time experience of watching the World Trade Center collapse that we whispered, in awe and terror, "This can't be happening!", the architects and engineers who replayed those awful videos over and over again have convinced themselves that the buildings *did* obey the laws of physics and thermodynamics—and that, in many ways, they did exactly what they were intended to do, when subjected to a sudden and catastrophically violent shock.

But in addition to paradigms of physics and astronomy and mechanical engineering, there are also *business* paradigms and *political* paradigms and *social* paradigms that we've become accustomed to. And those political/social paradigms have a great deal of influence on the plans, strategies, and—without meaning to overuse the word completely—the paradigms of the information-technology (IT) profession to which I've devoted my career. Those paradigms have indeed shifted; and while we may need to wait for several more months or years before our politicians and philosophers can understand and articulate the quantity and quality of the social/political paradigm shift, we should start doing our own thinking about the IT ramifications.

For example: Many of us were gratified by the success of the ad hoc communication networks that were stitched together by desperate family members and business colleagues in the hours immediately following the WTC attack; they were grass-roots, bottom-up, and *emergent* (as opposed to pre-planned, and hierarchically managed) in nature. Independently of what corporations and their IT departments might plan, by way of an effective post-9-11 environment, I firmly believe that individual citizens and corporate employees will put more and more faith in these ad hoc networks in the coming months, as they continue to cope with the sluggish, ambiguous, contradictory, and sometimes untrustworthy flow of information from "official" channels.

If things like this were *only* taking place at the individual level, it might not be worth writing about. But it's not just individuals, and not just corporate IT departments, who might be thinking about such issues: the military is taking it seriously, too. In an article by Leslie Walker entitled "Uncle Sam Wants Napster!" (*Washington Post*, Nov. 8, 2001), we learn that the Pentagon is looking at peer-to-peer (P2P) file-sharing and collaboration tools like Napster and Groove— not because they want to download pirated music, but because the classic top-down, hierarchically-developed communication systems often turn out to be incompatible (e.g., Navy communication systems can't talk to Army communication systems), and too cumbersome to cope with the chaotic, fast-moving world of terrorist warfare.

If this is relevant for the military community, could it be relevant for corporate IT environments too? And even if corporate executives think it isn't, is it possible that their front-line workers—the sales reps, and field-service technicians, and work-at-home telecommuters—might disagree? Is it possible that the urgent, time-critical need to communicate will cause them to completely abandon and ignore their company's high-security, firewall-protected email systems, and resort instead to SMS-messaging on their cell phones, and AOL instant messaging on their Palm Pilots? Even if it's against company policy, is it possible—perhaps even likely—that they'll do it anyway? And if they're going to do it anyway, because they believe they absolutely *have to*, does it make sense for companies to design their systems to support ad hoc, emergent, P2P communications in the first place? Apparently, the U.S. Defense Department thinks it's worth considering; perhaps other companies should, too.

In addition to thinking about communication networks, there are numerous other paradigm shifts that IT organizations will have to accommodate in the coming years. For example, within a week after September 11th, IT industry journals reported that Ford Motor Company was seriously rethinking the lean inventory system that its IT organization worked so hard to enable;[2] after all, the likelihood of chaotic disruptions necessitates a more resilient supply chain, with more "buffers" and more inventory. In the weeks since then, I've heard about numerous other companies which are also re-thinking their inventory systems, and re-thinking the assumptions upon which their entire supply chain is based.

Similarly, the whole notion of globalization is being called into question: If tensions increase and various parts of the world become more hostile and isolationist in nature, it might be far too risky to present a homogeneous corporate image in a hundred different countries. But if there is a strong move, within today's multinational companies,

---

2. See "Ford Starts Stockpiling," by Steve Konicki, *InformationWeek*, September 21, 2001.

towards autonomy and heterogeneity, what does that imply for the integrated Enterprise Resource Planning (ERP) systems that our IT organizations have been grappling with for the past decade?

Interestingly, some of these paradigm shifts were already underway *before* September 11th; after all, terrorism was already a fact of life, and many corporations were already concerned about security. And beyond the obvious and direct threat posed by terrorism, more and more companies have been realizing that change—competitive change, regulatory change, technological change, market-preference change, etc.—is occurring at an ever-increasing speed, and in ever more disruptive forms. To cite just one non-terrorism example, consider Napster: Without any warning or fanfare, one individual college dropout was able to create an Internet-based music-sharing technology that threatened to wreak havoc upon the mammoth music industry.

Napster and the September 11th terrorists share a characteristic that corporations and government agencies are likely to see more and more often in the future: disruptive threats caused by "stateless actors," whose technology makes them disproportionately powerful. In the past, nations expected to face threats from other nations; corporations expected competition from other corporations. But now, if the official reports are accurate,[3] a handful of individuals, armed with box-cutters and funded with less than a million dollars in "seed money," has managed to wreck four commercial airplanes and cause over a hundred billion dollars in physical destruction. And one college student,

---

3. Many of the so-called "facts" in this chapter, and throughout the book, should probably be prefixed with a disclaimer of this kind. I walked the circumference of Ground Zero a few weeks after September 11th, so I have the direct, physical, *personal* experience that twisted rubble has replaced the twin towers whose constructions I personally observed in the late 1960s and early 1970s. Beyond that, everything is second-hand, third-hand, or even further removed from my ability to provide direct, physical, personal corroboration. Thus, it would be more accurate to use the long-winded disclaimer one occasionally sees in newspaper articles: "Information from several independent sources, normally deemed credible and accurate, indicates that…" For the sake of brevity, I'll omit such caveats and qualifiers from subsequent "factual" statements in this book, but the reader may wish to keep them in mind.

whose only objective seems to have been the achievement of a "cool" technology for sharing music with his friends, nearly brought the recording industry to its knees. This is indeed a new world.

As it turns out, Napster has probably been put out of business by the legal counter-attack posed by the recording industry; but the battle may go on for years into the future, as rebellious teenagers use Gnutella, LimeWire, and a dozen other derivative technologies to circumvent the "legitimate" practice of buying CDs and tape cassettes in stores for their listening pleasure. As for the World Trade Center attack: The President, the Secretary of Defense, the Secretary of State, and numerous other high officials have told us that we are engaged in a war that will go on for years, and possibly decades. The established order of things has been upset by new paradigms, and we're being told that we should expect them to *continue* being upset for years into the future.

There is one other aspect of the paradigm shift that is exemplified in a particularly stark fashion by the World Trade Center attack, but also by the Napster phenomenon and many of the other disruptive changes we're facing today: The war is no longer "over there," it's *here*. In the past, our military forces expected attacks upon the United States to emanate from other parts of the world—e.g., in the form of Russian ICBM missiles flying over the North Pole to attack us via Canada, or by enemy submarines popping up in the middle of the Atlantic and Pacific Oceans and lobbing missiles at our cities. Meanwhile, our publishers typically expected their copyright threats to emanate from China, or Russia, or Third-World countries where copyright laws were ignored, or flouted openly. But Napster was created by an American student at Boston University; and the World Trade Center, along with the Pentagon, was attacked by commercial U.S. airlines piloted by individuals living in the U.S. on student/tourist visas.

IT will be one of the likely battlefields of the future

The battlefield between Napster and the recording industry was the courtroom; and, as this book is being written, the battlefield in the war against terrorism exists largely in Afghanistan. But in a larger sense, information technology (IT) is the battlefield upon which many of the conflicts are likely to be fought in the next several years.

Some of these conflicts will be obvious and direct, in terms of their association with IT; "cyber-warfare" is the catch-all term that's being used to describe various forms of hacking, viruses, physical attacks on computer centers or the Internet backbone, etc. In some cases, the attack may not be on the computers per se, but on the ability of computer systems to support such critical functions as telephone switching centers, stock-market trading systems, air-traffic control, etc.

It's also important to realize that IT is involved *indirectly* in almost every other aspect of hostility we're likely to face in the coming years—including the "hostile competition" that private-sector organizations face, even without the terrorism associated with September 11th. One of the stumbling blocks in implementing a more comprehensive air-travel security system, for example, is the lack of adequate information systems to identify potential terrorists before they get on the airplane. And one of the concerns that the health-care community has, in the face of potential anthrax/smallpox attacks, is that it lacks the kind of real-time tracking systems that UPS and Federal Express use to monitor the movement of packages through their organizations.

On a somewhat more subtle, philosophical level, information technology determines the degree to which we live in an "open" versus a "closed" society. It may seem overly melodramatic to suggest that the September 11th attack launched a war between the "open" society of the United States and the "closed" society of the fundamentalist Taliban movement. But it definitely *is* true that a large dimension of the American response to that attack has been a reassessment of the very openness that allowed terrorists to enter the country and board civilian airlines with little or no trouble. Now we find ourselves discussing and debating such questions as: what information does the government have a right to know about citizens and visitors to this country? What information is it obliged to disclose, when it monitors and eavesdrops upon citizens and visitors, and when it arrests them for suspected terrorist activities? What information are citizens allowed to access and publish on the Internet? What rights do we have to encrypt the private messages we wish to send our personal friends and business colleagues? What obligations do our banks, our hospitals, our tax-collection agencies, and numerous other private-sector and public-sector organizations have to maintain the security and privacy of personal information they collect about us?

Obviously, questions like these are not going to be answered exclusively by IT professionals or computer companies like IBM and Microsoft. On the other hand, IT professionals are likely to have a more realistic assessment of the feasibility and practicality of various privacy and security policies and regulations being contemplated by government authorities. Furthermore, government and the legal profession tend to be *reactive* rather than proactive; and their time-frame for reacting to problems and opportunities is measured in months or years. Meanwhile, the private sector—and, in particular, the high-tech startup companies in places like Silicon Valley—is proactive, opportunistic, and fast-moving. If you're concerned about issues of privacy and security, you'd better start talking about it with IT professionals *now*, because companies like Microsoft and Sun and Apple are likely to do something *tomorrow* to exploit whatever opportunities they see available.

What Assumptions Does the Book Make About You? _____

As you may have gathered from the comments above, this book discusses the impact of September 11th on the IT profession. As such, I assume that you, gentle reader, are involved in, affected by, or interested in the IT-related aspects of the terrorist attacks, and whatever consequences flow from those attacks. I can't imagine that anyone would *not* be interested in this perspective—but I'll admit that I'm biased, having worked in the IT field for over 35 years. I realize that there is more to life than computers, and that some people will prefer to focus on other aspects of the post-9/11 world—e.g., the economic, military, social, or religious aspects, as well as the possibilities of bio-terrorism, chemical and nuclear attacks. The fact that I don't dwell on these other areas extensively in this book does not mean that they should be ignored or de-emphasized; it simply means that I'm going to focus my comments, in this book, on the areas I know best.

While I do assume that you have a significant degree of interest and concern about IT-related aspects of the war on terrorism, I do *not* assume that you necessarily have the power or authority to change the situation in your company or your community. Obviously, if you're a "C-level" officer in a company (CEO, CIO, CTO, CFO, etc.), you do have such power; and if you're a mayor, a city-council member, a state legislator, or a governor, you can exert some degree of influence on public policy. But most of us barely have enough power and authority to influence our own lives, and that of our family and immediate friends; so why bother talking about cosmic issues and significant changes that are likely to take place in the coming years?

Well, even if you're only a humble citizen, you can still vote. And even if you're only a humble employee in a large bureaucratic organization, you can vote with your feet. If you don't like the way our public officials are responding to the high-tech and low-tech terrorist threats, you can vote for someone else at the next election. And if you feel that your company's senior executives are ignoring the threat to their IT infrastructure, you can look for a job in some other better-prepared and better-managed company.

Obviously, your single vote is unlikely to sway the outcome of an election; and elections occur at such infrequent intervals that disastrous crises could occur before the current set of officials is voted out of office. Similarly, my suggestion that you "vote with your feet" as a response to an unacceptable work environment is a rather glib one, in today's recessionary economy; the practical reality is that it might take months to find an equivalent job in your field, and/or your geographical area. And this touches on a theme that I'll elaborate upon later in the book: Our traditional "response time" to perceived risks and problems may not be fast enough to cope with today's fast-moving, chaotic disruptions.

In any case, one of my assumptions is that you want to have a better (and earlier) understanding of IT-related issues that could put you—and your family, your friends, your company, and your community—in harm's way in the months and years to come. To whatever extent you can act to reduce the chances of harm, by means of better information, so much the better. But it's also possible that you may conclude that your current situation (job, lifestyle, residential location) is untenable—and that because those who *do* control/influence your life (your boss, your elected leaders, perhaps even your bank or your hospital or your grocery store) are unwilling or unable to change, you're going to take matters into your own hands.

Much of this discussion would be moot if we assumed that the September 11th attacks were a "singular" event—i.e., an aberration, consisting of a single attack by 19 crazed terrorists. And some people *do* believe this to be the case; understandably, their reaction to September 11th is, "Yes, it was awful, and the after-effects may go on for a while. But fundamentally, it's over and done with, and our biggest priority is to get back to normal again." Such an attitude contradicts the publicly stated threats and warnings from terrorist leaders in the weeks following September 11th; and it contradicts the warnings of top officials from the FBI and other government spokesmen. But everyone is free to draw their own conclusions, and to make their own predictions about the future. If *your* assumption is that there will never again[4] be a disruptive event of the scale and magnitude of the September 11th disaster, then this is probably not the book for you.

My assumption, which forms the basis for this book, is that there *will* be more events like September 11th. At least for the next few years, it's reasonable to expect that such events won't consist of commercial airplanes flying into office towers; after all, there is far too much scrutiny for such attacks to take place easily. But as we've all seen and heard from the endless commentaries in the media, we could find ourselves dealing with equally devastating attacks on bridges, dams, nuclear reactors, and other prominent sites. Or we could find ourselves coping with biological attacks, chemical attacks, nuclear attacks, or cyber-warfare attacks. Meanwhile, in the normal course of events on this planet, we could find ourselves coping with environmental "attacks" in the form of earthquakes, floods, hurricanes, drought, or pestilence. There is no obvious reason to suggest that such environmental crises would be any more likely, or less likely, as a result of September 11th; but some of us are more sensitive about the consequences of a major environmental crisis than we would have been before.

---

4. "Never again" is a phrase that we use casually, but it's more useful to think in *relative* terms than in *absolute* terms. Those who were directly involved in the 1993 World Trade Center attack might have been almost as badly shaken as the rest of us were on September 11th; and they might have vowed to take appropriate steps to prevent, or at least mitigate, the effects of any subsequent attack. But would those vows have been as earnest if those individuals had been told that the next attack would be far worse, but would not occur until eight years later? We'll never know; but what we *do* know is that, after a year or two of relative peace and quiet, many of the vows and policies, the laws and the regulations, that were enacted by the government in the aftermath of the 1993 attack, atrophied and died away. It's a sobering thought in today's environment; notwithstanding the government's vow that September 11th has unleashed a war against terrorism that will last for decades, there is always the possibility that after an initial flurry of activity, things may gradually revert to some semblance of the way things were before.

Who Is This Book Aimed At?

Because this is a book that discusses the IT-related issues associated with the post-9/11 world, I'm writing it primarily for people who know something about computers, software, and information technology. Thus, it should be particularly suitable for programmers, software engineers, database designers, network architects, and people with similar titles in the IT industry.

Indeed, some of what will be happening in the IT field in the coming years will be entirely technical in nature—and will thus be of concern primarily to the technical people who make it happen. How will we go about building more robust, more secure, and more resilient systems? How much redundancy do we need to build into our systems, so that they continue running, or at least exhibit a suitable "fail-soft" behavior, in the face of massive attacks and disruptions? Are today's programming languages, database packages, and configuration-management tools adequate for a new world that demands substantially higher levels of security?

On the other hand, none of these technical issues will be addressed and implemented unless some management decisions are made first. So, a number of the issues discussed in *Byte Wars* will be particularly relevant to project managers and team leaders; and the "strategic" issues will be on the agenda of meetings between the CIO, CFO, CEO, and other senior executives who ultimately provide the funding and policies for whatever IT systems are built and deployed within an organization.

So, if you're not a programmer or a business executive, does that mean you should put this book down and return to your Tom Clancy spy novels? Perhaps not: I believe that there are IT-related issues that will be relevant for politicians, elected officials, regulators and law-enforcement officers—and ultimately, for the millions of ordinary, average citizens who simply want to get on with their lives.

Obviously, it's the politicians, elected officials, and regulators who establish the laws and regulations that control the behavior of individuals and corporations. We've gotten a first taste of how the politicians have responded to September 11th, with a flurry of new laws of which the so-called PATRIOT bill is the most prominent; and it's reasonable to expect that there will be many more laws and regulations in the coming months and years. Some of these new laws and regulations may involve non-IT issues—e.g., the circumstances under which an individual can be tried by a military tribunal for suspected terrorist activities—and are thus entirely beyond the scope of this book. But other laws will involve issues of computer-related wiretapping, encryption, privacy, security, access to databases, and related technological issues; and I hope that *Byte Wars* will shed some light on what's realistic and practicable in those areas, and what's not.

Finally, the book is intended for the "man on the street"—the ordinary citizen who simply wants to live an ordinary life. If the September 11th attacks had taken place in 1974, the first year that the World Trade Center opened for business, then the average citizen would expect to play a passive role in any discussion about IT-related consequences. But today, the average citizen has more computing power in his home computer than the entire MIT campus had in 1974; and the computing power of that home computer is augmented by the (computer-enabled) cell phone, Palm Pilot, pager, Blackberry, fax machine, MP3 digital-music player, and Tivo TV-recorder. Half of us have an Internet connection at home, in addition to the network access we have at work; and many of us have always-on, high-speed cable-modem access to the Internet. To further complicate matters, we citizens have access to *free* encryption packages (e.g., PGP) whose sophistication throws a serious monkey-wrench into the efforts of government agencies to eavesdrop on our private communications.

So what? Well, at the very least, the citizens of the U.S. and other advanced countries around the world are going to be pawns, if not victims, in the high-tech struggles that will take place in the coming years. But to the extent that they decided to participate in those struggles, they have some powerful tools (I hesitate to call them weapons), and they represent a potentially formidable force. To illustrate: I have some 35,000 files and documents on my personal computer; not a single one of them involves anything subversive or threatening to any government, but there *are* private and confidential files, databases, and spreadsheets that I will do my best to prevent anyone from seeing without my permission. I know how to do this reasonably well, as does any other IT professional; but the average citizen has probably never thought about such issues before, and may be shocked to learn how open and vulnerable his computer files are.

Even before September 11th, operating an Internet-connected home computer was like living in a frontier town in the Wild West of yore. But in the post-9/11 world, it's like living in a frontier town in the midst of a blazing gun-battle between an overbearing, intrusive sheriff and his busybody deputies, facing off against a gang of rapacious, heavily-armed outlaws.

Structure of the Book

As I've already noted, *Byte Wars* does *not* discuss germ warfare, chemical weapons, nuclear weapons, and several of the other threats posed by terrorists in today's stark new environment. Instead, it focuses on IT-related issues, and it begins with a summary of the IT-related "strategic implications" of the September 11th attacks.

Following that overview, I've chosen six major aspects of information technology to discuss: security, risk management, emergent systems, resilient systems, good-enough systems, and death-march projects. Each of these topics is covered in a separate chapter; and each chapter begins with a review of basic concepts and techniques, followed by a summary of the "paradigm shift" that has occurred since September 11th. And each chapter concludes with some guidelines and suggestions for appropriate strategies that should be discussed and evaluated by the various "communities" of readers mentioned above: IT professionals, managers, government leaders, and citizens.

There's no guarantee that I've identified *all* of the IT issues that we'll be facing in the new world. Indeed, it's highly likely that there will be second-order and third-order consequences of September 11th that will lead to new technologies, new ways of looking at the technical design and implementation of computer systems, and new social/political paradigms about privacy and security. As such, a book like this may need to be revised every couple of years to remain current and relevant; and some critics might argue that it would be better to wait for several years, until the situation has stabilized, before documenting a new "equilibrium" that may have been established.

But we won't achieve such an equilibrium unless we start doing things now; indeed, some things *have* begun happening already, as part of the "knee-jerk" reaction to September 11th on the part of citizens, corporations, and government leaders. We need to make the best decisions we're capable of making, with whatever information and tools we have available today. If *Byte Wars* can make a contribution to that effort, I will consider it to have been a success.

STRATEGIC IMPLICATIONS OF 9/11

No more prizes for predicting rain. Prizes only for
building arks.   ■

—Anonymous

When Franklin Delano Roosevelt told a joint session of Congress that December 7th, 1941 was "a date that would live in
infamy," at least one "strategic implication" was immediately clear: It provided the justification for a declaration of
war, the primary consequences of which could be anticipated—albeit incompletely—by anyone old enough to have
experienced World War I. But beyond that, there were other
strategic implications that were clear only to specialists, and
others that did not become clear until after the war ended.

Almost immediately, for example, economists and
national planners could see that the war effort would require
reductions in personal luxuries, and perhaps even rationing
of gasoline and certain food items. On the other hand, pre-
scient economists might have been able to predict that the
declaration of war would create a sufficient increase in
industrial output to help jump-start the economy out of a
decade-long depression. Historians and politicians might

have been able to predict that the war would hasten the decline of the British empire, and would launch America into a new role of global superpower. But it's unclear whether anyone would have predicted, on December 7th, that the Pearl Harbor attack would ultimately launch a massive research program that would culminate in the atomic bomb. Nor, for that matter, would anyone have predicted in 1941 that World War II would provide the incentive to calculate bomb trajectories more accurately, which led to the ENIAC computer and the birth of the modern age of computers.

So, too, there may be consequences of the September 11, 2001 terrorist attack that won't become clear until five, ten, or 20 years from now; and there are others that we might be able to glimpse now, like distant shapes in a fog. Still other consequences are already clear, though we may not be able to tell how long they will last, or how deeply they will penetrate into the social fabric of this country.

No doubt dozens of books will analyze the social, economic, political, and spiritual implications of September 11th, expanding upon the hundreds of articles, editorials, and essays that have already been written. My task is to focus on the impact of September 11th on the information technology (IT) industry and its workers; and while this is obviously a narrower, and more specific, perspective than that tackled by the television commentators and newspaper editorial writers, it is still fairly broad and comprehensive. Any discussion that involves the computer field, as a whole, is bound to be broad and comprehensive—but it's particularly true in this case, for the computer field will continue to experience substantial technological advances and improvements while the effects of September 11th play out over the next several years. Various IT experts have predicted, for example, that during the next five to ten years, we will be able to participate in mobile videoconferences from a hand-held computer; we will enjoy always-connected interactions with the global Internet via head-mounted or eyeglass-mounted displays; and computers will understand spoken language with near-100% accuracy. Computer power (memory, storage capacity, processing speed) will have increased by another hundred-fold; wireless machines will have shrunk to the size of a wristwatch, if not smaller; and e-commerce will have become the primary form of commercial transaction.[1] Indeed, some of these technological advances will be shaped and influenced by the immediate military/ political reaction to September 11th, as well as whatever ongoing military actions continue for the next several years; just as atomic weapons were created toward the end of World War II, IBM's Internet chief Irving Wladawsky-Berger suggests that we may see the current conflict producing even more powerful versions of today's supercomputers, and venture capitalist Steve Jurvetson suggests that biotechnology will make great leaps forward because of the political/military need to counter bioterrorism.[2]

Specific aspects of the IT impact of September 11th are covered in the subsequent chapters of this book, but we'll begin here with a brief overview of the *personal* consequences, the *corporate* consequences, and the *national* consequences that are likely to be experienced by IT professionals.

Personal Consequences

Across the United States—from sea to shining sea, as our nearly-forgotten patriotic song, *America the Beautiful* reminds us—everyone has been personally affected by the September 11th terrorist attacks in different ways. The victims, their family members and close personal friends were affected the most deeply, of course. The survivors who escaped from the WTC towers and the Pentagon offices, along with business-people, tourists, residents of nearby homes and apartments, and bystanders in the immediate vicinity of the attack, have also been affected more deeply than most of us can ever hope to understand.

---

1. See Jose A. Corrales, "An Asturian View of Networking 2015," *Communications of the ACM*, Sept. 2001, p. 47; see also "Technology Visionaries Scope the Future," by Mathew Schwartz, *Computerworld*, Oct. 8, 2001.
2. See "No telling what kind of technology this war will give birth to," by Kevin Maney, *USA Today*, Oct. 10, 2001.

But what about everyone else? What about the millions of people who sat transfixed in front of their television sets on that awful Tuesday morning, knowing that they and their family members were physically safe—but knowing, also, that their lives had almost certainly been changed forever? In this book, I've focused primarily on the national consequences, the corporate consequences, and the ramifications throughout the IT industry; but it seems appropriate to offer a few comments on the *personal* consequences that IT professionals are likely to face in the days ahead. Poets and philosophers will eventually record the deep, universal fears and hopes and anguish that we all feel; but on a slightly less cosmic level, many of us IT professionals will be experiencing some common reactions as we trudge into our offices and cubicles, and as we sit in front of our computer workstations to create our software systems. Here are some actions for you to consider:

- Reassess your priorities
- Recommit to the ones that matter
- Harmonize personal priorities with the corporate and national priorities we see around us
- Develop personal networks in preparation for any future disasters[3]

As a computer consultant, I visit dozens of IT organizations every year; as such, I often feel like an anthropologist observing primitive tribes as they go about their day-to-day rituals in a remote jungle. The rituals and games are often strange and mysterious; the petty bickering, back-stabbing political games, and intense power struggles are often depressing to watch. At the end of almost every consulting

---

3. A few of us—though probably only a very, very few—will ask ourselves whether we really want to live in the kind of post-9/11 society that is emerging. As we'll discuss later in this chapter, it appears to be one in which people are spied on, regulated, controlled, and interfered with, to an ever-increasing degree, in the name of "national security." It also seems to be one in which Washington politicians talked about "partnership" for about one week after the September 11th attacks, and then degenerated back into their old-fashioned behavior of inter-party squabbling, back-stabbing, and support for pork-barrel projects of dubious value.

assignment, I remind myself how lucky I am that I'm not permanently trapped in such a culture—because most of it appears to be not only un-productive, but counter-productive and utterly pointless.

Of course, the people who work as full-time salaried employees in such IT organizations may have an entirely different opinion—why else would they continue working there? But that question—*why do you continue putting up with this, day after day?* —is one that many IT professionals never seem to ask themselves. They stumble into a job shortly after graduating from college; and since the surrounding corporate culture seems to be reasonably stable, they assume that it's the way things were meant to be. They move on to another job, and discover that while the details of the new corporate culture are somewhat different—different rituals and different code-words to describe what's going on—the fundamental reality remains: People are devoting most of their time and energy to things that simply don't matter. If this weren't the case, I firmly believe that *Dilbert* cartoons would not enjoy such enormous popularity among IT professionals.[4]

Arguably, none of this really mattered very much when times were good—and with rare exceptions, times have been pretty good since I first started working in the computer field in 1964. Many of today's IT professionals had not yet entered the work force when the recession of 1990-91 came along; and for the most part, the only ones who were affected by that recession were the middle-aged COBOL programmers who were told that they were being replaced by twenty-something Visual Basic programmers. Similarly, most of today's IT professionals aren't old enough to remember the recession of 1982-83; and only a few remember the recession of 1973-74. Aside from these blips on the economic landscape, the outlook has generally been opti-

---

4. It's also worth remembering that the creator of the *Dilbert* cartoons, Scott Adams, worked in the IT department of a large utility company before deciding that there was a better way to spend his life. See "Scott Adams: An Idiot's Life: the *Dilbert* creator waxes philosophic on God, the universe, and the intense cruelty of the cubicle," by David Roos, *TechTV*, Oct. 12, 2001.

mistic and upbeat for IT professionals: Our salaries have
gone up every year, we've continued getting new toys and
gadgets to play with, and sometimes we even get enough
stock options to retire at a young age.

In this kind of environment, priorities and such philosophical abstractions as "ethics," often didn't seem very
important. In moments of candor, a lot of IT professionals
would tell you that if you paid them $75,000 per year and
gave them a pile of stock options, they would be willing to
work on doomed projects, and report to tyrannical bosses.
Why not? After all, if things got too unbearable, there was
always the option of quitting, and going to work somewhere else for a 20-percent pay increase—with the possibility that the next project would be slightly less doomed, and
the next boss would be slightly less tyrannical. And during
the manic period of the late 1990s, there was always the
hope that if one could put up with the nonsense for just a
few months longer, one's dot-com company would go public, and one could cash in all those stock options, and *then*
tell the boss to go to hell.

Well, that was then and this is now. Now it's a new
decade and a new recession—a recession that, at least for a
period in late 2001, has created higher unemployment levels
in the IT community than in the general workforce. It's particularly severe, of course, in the dot-com segment of the IT
industry; but things are pretty tough throughout the IT services companies, the hardware and PC manufacturing companies, and even the IT departments of staid old banks and
insurance companies. And in the midst of this gloomy economic situation, we've now experienced the terrorist
attacks of September 11th; as we'll discuss in the Corporate
Consequences section below, this has exacerbated the economic downturn in many companies, and is already causing a shift towards military, government, and security-
related computing activities.

Unless you're completely cut off from humanity (which,
unfortunately, *is* the case for some members of the IT community!), all of this has to have a personal impact. If nothing else, it forces some of us to ask the question that we've

often repressed in better economic times: *Why are we putting up with this stuff, day after day?* Horrific as it may have been, September 11th has been a wakeup call for people in all walks of life, in all professions and industries; there's nothing unique about the IT industry, other than perhaps the degree to which we were able to disavow the realities of the world during the dot-com euphoria.

So, if you haven't done it already, spend a few quiet moments asking yourself what your priorities really are. Ask yourself whether your job, your project, your co-workers, your boss, your company, and your country reflect those priorities. To the extent that you feel obligated to "do the right thing" with respect to your own sense of ethics, and the values you share with your family and your community, ask yourself whether your work environment reflects those ethics. If you have trouble figuring this out, ask your children; they tend to view the world in simple, black-and-white terms, and they can often help cut through the fog and ambiguity of our adult world. If you want some specific suggestions about appropriate ethics for members of the IT profession, take a look at the ACM code of ethics and the IEEE code of ethics; indeed, it's a sad commentary that most IT professionals are not even aware that such codified statements exist, or that they've implicitly pledged to follow them by virtue of belonging to these professional societies.

If the first step is reassessing priorities, then the next step should be a reaffirmation of and recommitment to the ones that really matter. For some of us in the IT profession, it may be a recommitment to "quality" in our work, or a reaffirmation that we only want to work on well-managed projects for end-users who really want high-quality, well-designed systems to be built for them. For some of us, it will mean remembering why we got into the IT field to begin with— e.g., for the intellectual pleasure of working on challenging development projects with new technology, rather than mind-numbing maintenance projects implemented with obsolete technology. And for some of us, it may require an admission that *nothing* about our current project, job, employer, or career really matters—and that some significant changes are called for. It's no surprise that, since September

11th, there has been an increase in the number of people who can be heard to mutter, "Life is too short..."—too short to get ulcers by working for a schizophrenic boss, too short to work long hours on a doomed project that nobody really wanted anyway, too short to participate in a low-quality, ethically dishonest project that the marketing department has managed to sell to a naïve, unsuspecting customer.

Indeed, what this really means is that we need to harmonize our personal priorities and ethics with those that are being articulated and practiced by our employer, and by the community in which we live. Of course, "articulate" and "practice" are two entirely different words: The values and priorities that one's boss and one's employer espouse (including such wonderful aphorisms as "quality is job #1") are sometimes different from the ones they practice. The differences may be occasional, minor, and accidental—in which case, most of us are willing to accept the imperfection of personal and corporate behavior, and to trust in the articulated desire to achieve a high ethical standard. But sometimes the differences are constant, pervasive, massive, and deliberate—in which case we have to decide whether we're going to continue being part of the lie. Again, this is the sort of thing that many of us repressed during the golden years of the 1990s and the 1980s: why ask embarrassing questions when we were making money, having fun, and dreaming of lucrative stock options?

Even today, the reality is that not very many people will be willing or able to accomplish a fundamental reassessment of their lives, their priorities, and their ethics. But if not now—in the aftermath of September 11th—then when? We can all find excuses for not having done this before, just like we find rationalizations for not living up to those New Year's resolutions that we make year after year. Those of us who are younger might complain that society never gave them the kick-in-the-butt required to make a serious commitment to whatever principles and priorities they pretended to believe in. And those of us who are somewhat older might look back ruefully on all of those tiny compromises that we've made over the years, and wonder what ever happened to the passionate idealism that energized our marches for civil rights, or women's rights, or an end to the Vietnam war, or a dozen other causes. But whatever the explanations, whatever the rationalizations, whatever the excuses, they're all behind us; this is a new time, and a new opportunity to reassess our lives and re-prioritize the many responsibilities, demands, and opportunities that confront us.[5]

In the late 1980s and early 1990s, when many companies were struggling with traumatic reorganizations, downsizing, and global competition, it was common for tough-minded leaders to stand before their workers—who were often frustrated, befuddled, hostile, and fearful for their jobs—and say, "Lead, follow, or get out of the way."[6] It's an apt statement for today's times, and it applies to IT professionals as well as business executives, political leaders, and citizens in all walks of life. Some of us will use September 11th as the inspiration to take on leadership roles in areas that we ignored, or treated casually, in the past—e.g., community service, computer security, improved emergency-response systems, and innovative business strategies for dealing with new forms of risk and uncertainty. Others of us will see new leaders to follow—e.g., political leaders like Rudolph Guiliani and George Bush, or managers and business executives in our own organization. Still others will decide that the post-9/11 world is so turbulent and danger-

---

5. This means more than simply re-ordering some items that are numbered one through ten on a list. Some things ought not to be on the list at all; and some of the things that currently aren't on the list *should* be. And instead of a linear, one-dimensional list, consider a two-dimensional grid, of the sort suggested by Stephen Covey in *First Things First* (Fireside, 1996), so that one can separate the dimension of "importance" from the dimension of "urgency." Consider, for example, the difference between something that is very urgent *and* very important, like a heart attack (if you don't do something about it right away, you'll die), and something that is very important but not very urgent (regular exercise and diet, which rarely has a deadline or someone nagging you to get it done). And that's different from things that are urgent, but not very important (most email, phone calls, and similar interruptions), which is also different from the things that are neither important nor urgent (like most television entertainment).

6. According to *Simpson's Contemporary Quotations*, the slogan is attributed to a sign on the desk of media mogul Ted Turner, and was pictured in the Jan. 5, 1987 issue of *Fortune* magazine.

ous that the best thing to do is hunker down and stay out of the way.

To "stay out of the way" does not necessarily mean fleeing the cities and moving to a farm in the countryside, though it is an increasingly attractive option for many knowledge-workers who can "tele-commute" to big-city offices via the Internet. But it does mean maintaining a lower profile in potentially dangerous situations; and it may mean avoiding potentially dangerous situations such as crowded shopping malls or sports events. As a corollary, it means developing protective mechanisms—on a personal level—in order to maintain contact with friends and family members in the event of any future crisis. What instructions and advice do we give our children, in the event that a crisis occurs when they are in school while we are at work? What kind of instructions should we give our family members about "hunkering down" and avoiding danger if there is a terrorist attack that shuts down public transportation (as was the case for subway transportation in New York City on September 11th) and disrupts telephone communication? These are issues that confront all American citizens, as well as citizens in many other countries susceptible to terrorist attacks; but they are likely to be more relevant to urban dwellers (where high-visibility attacks are more likely to occur) and to "road-warriors" who may find themselves stranded in a strange locale and cut off from their office and families. Quite a few IT professionals found that the only practical way of coping with the September 11th situation was to hunker down in their hotel room, or in the airport, or in a client's office, and use a combination of cell phones and wireless instant-messaging devices to stay in touch; and as analyst Craig Mathias observed in a post-mortem of the September 11th attack, this means that some road warriors will begin "traveling with more than one network."[7]

Corporate Consequences

Since most of us spend the majority of our waking hours in a corporate environment, and since we depend on that corporate environment to provide our income, it's important to anticipate the implications of September 11th on that environment. Though the details will differ significantly from one company to another, there are some common themes that managers, senior executives, and Boards of Directors are already beginning to grapple with; they include:

- Recognizing the unpredictability of today's world
- Developing an "early warning" system of impending disruptions and crises
- Recognizing the importance and vulnerability of information assets

There are also IT-related corporate implications in several specific areas, which will occupy the next several chapters of this book: IT security, risk management, emergent systems, resilient systems, good-enough systems, and an "extreme project management" approach for dealing with the growing phenomenon of death-march projects.

Recognition of the unpredictability of today's world

In the months following the September 11th attacks, commentators and pundits have remarked that "business will never be the same."[8] Such comments might be appropriate even if we could be absolutely certain that the terrorist attacks on that day were a singular event, never to be repeated. But repeated warnings from high-level American government officials, coupled with veiled threats from terrorist spokesmen, suggests that such attacks could be—

---

7. See "Users, analysts: Companies need alternate networks when disaster hits," by Bob Brewin, *Computerworld*, Sept. 20, 2001; also, see "Staying connected in a postattack IT world," by Matt Hamblen, *Computerworld*, Sept. 18, 2001. Interestingly, on the day of the attack, America Online recorded 700 million messages from non-AOL subscribers on its free AOL Instant Messenger (AIM) service, plus another 500 million AIM messages generated by AOL subscribers. See "Internet messaging keeps businesses, employees in touch," by Jennifer Disabatino, *Computerworld*, Sept. 17, 2001.
8. See "Business will never be the same, Gartner says," by Cara Garretson, *Network World Fusion News*, Sept. 12, 2001.

indeed, probably *will* be—repeated in the not-too-distant future, though probably not in the same fashion.

Thus, when Compaq Chairman and CEO Michael Capellas explained why his company suffered lower revenues in the quarter ending September 30, 2001, he said that "I think the only way that describes it is 'the perfect storm.'"[9] In addition to the immediate consequences of the September 11th attack, Compaq's business was also disrupted by a severe typhoon in Taiwan and the announcement of its intended merger with Hewlett-Packard—thus, the combination of the three events might be analogous to the fabled "storm of the century," in which several severe factors converge.

While the merger had presumably been planned for some time before it was announced, the marketplace reaction to the announcement may have been unexpected. And while typhoons are not an unusual phenomenon in Taiwan, the one that occurred in September 2001 was so severe that it disrupted some manufacturing operations upon which Compaq depended. And apparently, nobody but the terrorists expected the attack on the World Trade Center. Still, it would be a mistake to expect that such a "perfect storm" will not—and cannot—happen again for another century. Despite whatever public assurances Mr. Capellas and other corporate CEOs might be offering to investors and Wall Street analysts, the stark reality is this: Not only will business never be the same again, but business executives will never again assume that they can predict the future with confidence.

To some extent, this is not an entirely new concept: Businesses in California never know whether tomorrow will bring a devastating earthquake, and businesses in Florida never know whether the next hurricane will be a killer or not. Thus, some companies have responded to the September 11th attacks by simply reviewing and updating their disaster recovery plans[10] and their Y2K contingency

---

9. See "Compaq warns of Q3 revenue drop, blames 'perfect storm' of
    events," by Ken Mingis, *Computerworld*, Oct. 1, 2001.
10. See "Users urged to revisit disaster recovery plans," by Lee Copeland,
    Carol Sliwa, and Matt Hamblen, *Computerworld*, Oct. 11, 2001.

plans—indeed, some organizations were lucky enough to be able to put these plans to work as they coped with the September 11th attacks.

But in some important ways, life *has* changed forever. Weather-related and environmental disasters may be unpredictable, but they are "neutral" in their choice of targets. And as John Koskinen, former head of the government's Y2K effort, remarked recently, "Unlike the Y2K phenomenon, today's terrorist threat to IT is undefined, the response is difficult, and there is no known time frame."[11]

While most of us would argue that terrorists are uniquely malevolent and evil, Koskinen's remarks could just as well be a description of the "disruptive" competitive threats faced by large businesses in today's fast-moving, high-tech, global economy. Michael Hammer, the management guru who initiated the "business process reengineering" movement in the early 1990s, argues in a new book, *The Agenda*, that business executives must prepare for a world that they can no longer predict. Written before the September 11th attacks (though published slightly afterwards), Hammer reminds us that the five-year strategic plans created by large businesses in the 1990-1995 period generally did *not* anticipate or "plan" for the Asian financial crisis, the emergence of the Internet/Web, the introduction of integrated "enterprise resource planning" (ERP) systems, the emergence of supply-chain integration, the creation of the Euro currency, or the consequences of deregulation in the energy industry (culminating in the bankruptcy of Enron in late 2001)—events that had enormous, and often devastating, consequences in the late 1990s and early part of the current decade.

Thus, the bottom line—which we should have acknowledged years ago, and which September 11th has reinforced indelibly—is that change is now too fast, too chaotic, too disruptive, and sometimes too cunningly malevolent for us to be able to "plan" for.

---

11. See "Businesses eye Y2K effort as model for terrorism fight," by Patrick Thibodeau, *Computerworld*, Oct. 2, 2001.

Developing early-warning systems of impending change

If we can't plan for an orderly unfolding of events in the future, what *can* we do? One option, popularized nearly 30 years ago by the Royal Dutch Shell company at the beginning of the 1973-74 Middle East oil embargo, is *scenario planning*—i.e., identifying and categorizing a wide range of possible "scenarios" that might or might not occur in the future. In the most extreme case, this means "thinking the unthinkable": identifying and acknowledging the possibility of worst-case scenarios,[12] with the understanding that such scenarios might be *exactly* what terrorists and hostile competitors might be planning.

Of course, scenario planning assumes that we're creative enough to imagine the kind of scenarios that might plausibly occur, including the worst kinds of scenarios. It sounds easy enough for senior executives to issue an edict to their managers, strategists, and planners to begin indulging in such creative speculation—though it's likely to be a severe culture shock in an organization where contingency planners were ridiculed as "gloom-and-doomers," and where the prevailing corporate culture was "if it ain't broke, don't fix it." Unfortunately, even if senior executives can overcome the natural reluctance of their employees to contemplate catastrophic risks, that doesn't guarantee their employees are *capable* of contemplating such things. Of the 40,000 people who worked in the World Trade Center towers, how many were intellectually, emotionally, and psychologically capable of contemplating the possibility that a suicidal terrorist would turn a commercial airplane into a guided missile?

Thus, while it's obvious that companies across the country and around the world will be ramping up their emphasis on contingency planning, risk management, and disaster-recovery planning, it's also likely that companies will begin focusing on "first alert" and "early warning" sys-

---

12. See "U.S. Recovery: Companies Rethink IT Strategies," by Ashlee Vance, *Infoworld.com*, Sept. 20, 2001.

tems, in order to provide at least a brief period of time to prepare for an oncoming disaster—regardless of whether that disaster takes the form of a tornado, terrorist attack, or marketing blitz from a hostile competitor. IT will obviously play a crucial role in any such effort, for it involves getting the right information to the right people at the right time— i.e., credible information about the impending threat, delivered to decision-makers and affected individuals, *before* the threat manifests itself, not the day after.

In addition to creating their own internal early-warning systems, it's also possible that we'll see more collaboration between companies, as well as collaboration between the private sector and government, in order to share information about various threats. A good example of this kind of collaboration is the collection of vendors and research organizations who monitor and track computer viruses and worms when they first appear on the scene; in today's globally connected world, it behooves everyone to share information about such cyber-attacks. But in a broader sense, many organizations are reluctant to share information with each other, because they don't want to give sensitive information to competitors; indeed, it's illegal to do so in some cases, for it violates anti-trust regulations.

Thus, one of the strategic implications of the September 11th attacks is likely to be a renewed effort on the part of the government to encourage and enable companies to share information more openly than they have in the past. One example of such an effort is a public-private collaborative effort called *Infragard*, which was created in January 2001. It is coordinated by the FBI and its members include representatives from companies that run the nation's water, electricity, medical, communications, and transportation systems.[13] It has set up an email list that allows people to report potential problems, even anonymously. Of course, it's possible that efforts like this will get bogged down in bureaucracy; but if the participating organizations believe they are facing a common threat—and that the threat is a clear, present, and

---

13. See "Alert System Sought for Internet Attacks," by Ariana Cha, *Washington Post*, Oct. 25, 2001.

immediate danger—then there is at least some chance that they will cooperate. In any case, efforts like this will be part of the corporate agenda in the coming years, at least until there is a consensus that the risk of disruptive threats has faded into the background.

Beyond that, it remains to be seen how much of an impact the "early warning" concept has on the day-to-day operation of large businesses. Remember: the federal government employs thousands of people in the CIA, NSA, FBI, and other agencies in order to gather this kind of information. Many private-sector organizations have no comparable "intelligence" group; and the ones who do typically focus their efforts on a high-tech marketing group, analogous to the analysts at the CIA's Langley headquarters.

In *The Agenda*, Michael Hammer argues eloquently that the corporate equivalent of CIA field-agents are the front-line employees who have direct, day-to-day contact with customers, competitors, suppliers, vendors, and partners. These people are not the Vice Presidents sitting in their comfortable offices in the executive suite at Corporate Headquarters; they are the sales representatives, the customer-service technicians, the order-entry personnel, and the field-service people who visit the customer site to install and repair photocopiers, dishwashers, and cable-TV systems. As Hammer puts it,

> "The powerless know more than the powerful in virtually all organizations. During periods of intense change, this paradox can be fatal."

The reason that the paradox is fatal is simple; as Hammer explains,

> "anyone looking for signs of change is almost certainly guilty of not keeping his or her mind clamped on the formal job."

While this might be characterized as "common sense," it remains to be seen whether corporate executives will recognize it as such, and whether they'll do anything about it. It's interesting that the federal government has asked the public to be watchful, and to report suspicious incidents; for example, the top-level page of the FBI Web site provides separate links for reporting tips about anthrax and terrorism. I have not yet seen an equivalent link on any corporate Web sites, which makes one wonder just how effective these organizations were when creating their early-warning systems. We'll elaborate this point further in Chapter 6, in the discussion of *resilient* systems

Learning to change and adapt much more quickly than ever before

It's one thing to acknowledge the essential unpredictability of today's world; and it's one thing to create an early-warning system to learn about disruptive threats before they occur. But neither of these steps will be relevant if the organization is unable to respond quickly enough. The U.S. military learned this lesson on September 11th: Although the air-traffic controllers deduced that the four airplanes had been hijacked, the Air Force was unable to scramble its fighters and get them to the scene until *after* the terrorists had hit the World Trade Center and the Pentagon.

Of course, one could argue that a tragedy like this means that the "early warning" system has to be improved; if the terrorists' hostile intentions had been discovered and reported within, say, a minute after the flights had taken off, perhaps there would have been enough time for the Air Force to get its fighters into position. In the meantime, it appears that one of the government's short-term responses to the terrorist attacks has been to schedule military patrol flights over major American cities so that they *can* respond more quickly.

While certain kinds of threats will involve early-warning periods and response-time periods measured in minutes, or possibly even in seconds, one of the biggest difficulties facing organizations will be speeding up changes that currently take months, if not years. The government's response to airport-security problem—which was widely known prior to September 11th, but evidently not considered a high-priority issue—is a case in point. Despite the publicity and the obvious urgency of the problem, it took the House and Senate *ten weeks* to pass legislation to provide a level of airport security that many experts still feel is inadequate, but is at least cosmetically better than before. But even more amazing: The legislation stipulates that within 60 days after passage, short-term measures must be implemented to scan checked passenger baggage for bombs or other dangerous items; and within *one year*, the 28,000-person airport security staff who operate the metal-detectors at security checkpoints must be federalized and reorganized, and a full-scale baggage-scanning system must be implemented. But almost immediately, bureaucrats and pundits began predicting that the government would fail to meet its own deadline unless it embarked upon the equivalent of a "Manhattan project";[14] and within a week after the legislation was passed, Transportation Secretary Norman Mineta announced that his department would be unable to meet the 60-day deadline for the short-term baggage-screening system.

Cynics might argue that all of this is irrelevant, since terrorists would probably use some other mechanism for launching a major attack in the near future. But the point remains: If the attack of September 11th could be regarded as some kind of horrendous early-warning sign about the vulnerability of American airports (and, by extension, trains, buses, subways, and other forms of public transportation), then a year is too long to wait for the problem to be rectified. If a particularly stubborn and persistent group of terrorists did decide to commit mayhem by loading their suitcases full of bombs, and then detonating the bombs upon takeoff, it would be only incrementally more difficult to accomplish now than it would have been on September 10th.

Business managers and IT professionals might argue that, while they are concerned and sympathetic about the airport security situation, they don't have to worry about such awful, life-and-death issues. On the other hand, any managers of *Fortune* 500 companies who aren't worrying about the threat of physical attacks on their corporate headquarters, or public place of business (e.g., Disney World or Yankee Sta-

---

14. See "Baggage screening deadline looks doubtful," by Alan Levin, *USA Today*, Nov. 29, 2001.

dium) are living in dreamland. And any IT managers who aren't worried about the threat of a massive, persistent cyber-attack on their IT systems and networks need to have their heads examined—or, at the very least, consider the aspects of vulnerability summarized in the following section.

Bottom line: One of the strategic implications of the September 11th attacks will be a realization that organizations have to respond much more quickly to threats, once they have become known. For IT managers, this will mean asking such questions as:

- How long does it take us to plug a security hole in our servers and firewalls, throughout the organization, when we become aware of it? How can we reduce that time from hours or days, down to seconds or minutes?

- How long would it take us to reconfigure our network and our external Internet Service Provider (ISP) if a terrorist attack (or an environmental disaster) disrupted our primary network and ISP? How can we speed that up, so that our employees are not cut off from the outside world, and so that our customers are not cut off from us, for hours at a time?

- How long would it take for us to switch from our current ERP vendor (e.g., SAP, Peoplesoft, Oracle) if our existing one went bankrupt, or if their products and services were effectively rendered unusable by some kind of cyber-attack?

Recognizing the importance and vulnerability of their "information assets"

While the attacks of September 11th vividly demonstrated that airplanes, airports, office buildings, and other public places were vulnerable to deadly attack, they also forced many businesses to examine their computer systems and telecommunication networks for signs of vulnerability. Indeed, the increasing number of malicious computer viruses had made this a high-priority issue even before September 11th; but the deadly nature of the airplane attacks made it clear that future attacks could have much more devastating consequences.

Or, to put it another way, September 11th has forced IT managers, corporate executives, and government leaders to acknowledge and confront the importance and vulnerability of their "information assets," rather than just treating them as background problems. If you believe the pain in your head is a migraine headache, you try to ignore it, or take a couple of aspirin tablets; but if you believe it's a brain tumor or an aneurism, you hustle down to the hospital to get it taken care of.

Interestingly, it was an entirely different kind of threat—the much-ballyhooed Y2K bug—that made IT managers, business managers, public officials, and ordinary citizens realize just how dependent on computer systems our businesses, our government, and our society have become. Whether we should have been more confident about the ability of computer programmers to successfully repair the "non-compliant" computer programs before the inexorable 1/1/2000 deadline is a matter of ongoing debate; but during the "assessment" period in which companies studied the implications of Y2K on their day-to-day operations, virtually every Chief Information Officer, and most Chief Executive Officers (CEOs) became convinced that *if* their mission-critical computer systems stopped or misbehaved at the stroke of midnight on December 31, 1999, their business would be grievously damaged.

It has been less than two years since Y2K came and went; thus, most senior executives and most senior government officials still remembered their assessment of the importance of their "information asset" when the attacks of September 11th took place. Not only that, they still had their Y2K contingency plans available, and those plans proved invaluable for many companies in the immediate aftermath of September 11th. But what most organizations had *not* learned from their Y2K preparations was that their information systems were vulnerable to attack; and the awareness and acknowledgment of that vulnerability will be a major consequence of September 11th.

Almost immediately after the attack, consultants and research firms and government agencies began publishing dire assessments of the nation's IT vulnerability. The management firm of KPMG, for example, published a survey of 500 executives in mid-November 2001, in which almost four out of ten believed that their company was vulnerable to security breaches; the author of the report, KPMG's Stuart Campbell, argues that "until more executives regard information security as a strategic business issue, organizations will remain vulnerable."[15] And the Computer Emergency Response Team (CERT) Coordination Center reported in mid-October 2001 that it had counted nearly 35,000 attacks and probes into corporate computer systems during the first nine months of 2001; CERT estimated that the total figure for 2001 would be slightly more than 46,000, which is more than double the 22,000 incidents reports in 2000.[16]

When non-technical people hear the term "information asset," they're likely to think of desktop PC's, telecommunication networks, Web servers, and other familiar items of computer technology. But the horrific nature of the World Trade Center attack emphasized that information assets take other forms, as well, and reside in other places besides the corporate computer room. Remember those millions of scraps of paper that could be seen floating in the air as the towers collapsed? Many of them were old-fashioned legal documents—contracts, mortgages, wills—that had *not* been stored in a computer database, because the documents have legal significance only if they exist in hard-copy form, with ink signatures of the relevant individuals and entities.

But more important than the scraps of paper were the people. The Wall Street trading firm Cantor Fitzgerald lost nearly 700 of its traders; and while it's difficult to think of anything beyond the enormous loss of human life in such a statistic, there's an "information asset" issue, too: The company lost vast quantities of facts, rumors, names, phone numbers, wisdom, knowledge, and tidbits of information stored in the heads of those 700 people. Other companies experienced similar tragedies, even if smaller numbers of people were involved; and this experience is likely to have a

---

15. See "Report: Business fails on global security," by Robert Lemos, *ZDNet News*, Nov. 14, 2001.
16. See "Feeling Insecure," by Dan Luzadder, *Interactive Week*, Oct. 22, 2001.

profound impact on the way corporations operate in the
years to come.

In simple terms: Companies had already concluded, as
part of their Y2K contingency planning efforts, that it made
sense to distribute and decentralize their computer hardware and computer systems. And now, after September
11th, they're beginning to do the same with their employees—especially the "knowledge workers" who can carry
out their intellectual activities from almost anyplace that
has a connection to the Internet.[17] The very fact that 40,000
people were crammed into two high-rise office towers is an
anachronism that no longer makes as much sense as it did
when the World Trade Center was constructed in the early
1970s. Investment banking firm Morgan Stanley, whose
3,700 WTC-based employees all escaped safely on September 11th, has apparently come to the same conclusion: The
firm has decided not to move into the Manhattan central
office that it had prepared shortly before the attack.[18] As
Chuck Wilsker, executive director at the Washington-based
International Telework Association & Council says, "A lot
of people are going to want to telecommute more, and this
is going to be a permanent change."[19]

The emphasis in Mr. Wilsker's comment should be on
more: there are already 28.8 million teleworkers,[20] according
to a recent survey by the International Telework Association
and Council; but the events of September 11th are likely to
boost that figure significantly—and, as Wilsker observes,
it's likely to be a permanent change. And for the companies
who aren't ready to embrace full-scale telecommuting,
there's another obvious strategy to help reduce the risks
associated with air-travel, and congregating in large build-

---

17. See "Aftermath: Rethinking 'Place' in Business," by Bob Tedeschi,
    Smart Business, Nov. 2001.
18. See "Companies Moving Away From Centralized Offices," by Amy
    Harmon, *New York Times*, Oct. 29, 2001.
19. See "Worried workers turn to telecommuting," by Stephanie Armour,
    USA Today, Oct. 17, 2001. See also "The Sept. 11 attacks put telecommut-
    ing on the front burner for some companies," by Marianne Kolbasuk
    McGree, *Infoworld.com*, Oct. 22, 2001.
20. See "Rethinking Where People Work," by Toni Kistner, *Network World*,
    Nov. 12, 2001.

ings: videoconferencing and teleconferencing, using a wide range of available technologies, products, and services. Again, this is a trend that was already underway, particularly as higher bandwidth and lower costs made videoconferencing a more practicable and economical alternative to "physical" meetings; but September 11th has added the element of security to the decision-making process. Thus, one of the virtually-certain corporate consequences of September 11th will be an increased investment in, and commitment to, video/teleconferencing; however, industry experts do not believe that such technologies will replace traditional business travel completely, because the American business culture is one in which clients have always preferred to conduct deals on a face-to-face basis.[21]

National Consequences

In the days immediately following September 11th, pundits announced that the nation had suddenly lost interest in "reality" television shows. My reaction, upon hearing this cosmic news, was, "Who cares?" In a similar vein, it may turn out that the World Trade Center attacks lead to a national craving for chewing gum, or a sudden national disdain for pepperoni pizza—but who cares? Obviously, if you happen to work for a chewing gum company, or if you own stock in Pizza Hut, sudden changes like this could have dramatic consequences; but for the nation as a whole, it's a non-event.

I mention this point because it begs the obvious question: Why should we care whether the IT industry is affected by the events of September 11th? From a national perspective, does it even matter? Without meaning to denigrate the importance of chewing gum or pepperoni pizza, the answer is: Yes, IT *does* matter. According to a study released by World Information Technical and Services Alliance, global spending on information and communications technology

---

21. See "Videoconferencing: Companies Rethink Business Travel," by Kirstin Downey, *Washington Post*, Sept. 23, 2001.

was $2 trillion in 1999, and is expected to exceed $4 trillion by 2004.[22] So, while pundits and politicians may worry about the impact of September 11th on the consumer's desire to spend money on automobiles, homes, airplane trips, vacations, restaurant meals, and Broadway plays, it also matters whether they continue buying PCs, cell phones, and Palm Pilots. It also matters whether they continue spending money via the Internet; and it matters whether corporate America continues to buy products and services from IBM, Microsoft, Oracle, and thousands of other high-tech companies.

The *economic* consequences of September 11th on the IT industry are indeed important, and we'll explore them in more detail below; but as we'll also discuss, September 11th has emphasized the importance of IT as part of the nation's "critical infrastructure"; and IT will also play a critical role in the area of privacy and civil liberties, which are already undergoing drastic changes as a result of the September 11th attacks.

"Guns *and* butter" vs. "guns *or* butter"

Short-term impact on IT industry

Because so much of the U.S. economy is based on consumer spending, there is obviously a great deal of interest in encouraging the public to *continue* spending, even as a war effort is mounted and as the country grapples with a recession whose beginning has now officially been pegged at March, 2001. In the weeks following the September 11th attack, the President and several of his spokesmen have urged the American public to shop, fly, enjoy meals in restaurants, and generally go about their business as they did before; and in New York, both Mayor Guiliani and Gover-

---

22. See "Global IT spending to top $4 trillion by 2004," by Patrick Thibodeau, *Computerworld*, June 19, 2000. Of the global spending on IT and communications technology, North America represents approximately 53%, Europe represents 40%, and the rest of the world represents the remaining 7%. The top ten countries in terms of per-capita IT spending, ranging from approximately $2,000 to $3,250, were Switzerland, Japan, US, Sweden, Denmark, Singapore, Norway, Netherlands, UK, and Australia.

nor Pataki have filmed television commercials imploring tourists to return to what is, arguably, *still* the greatest city in the world. On the other hand, it's clear that tourism *has* dropped, airline traffic is down, reservations for holiday cruises have plummeted, and consumer spending overall has leveled off in almost all areas.

Meanwhile, preliminary estimates indicate that the military action launched against Afghanistan would cost the U.S. government approximately $1 billion per month; and the initial Federal outlay for the entire spectrum of anti-terrorist programs (including aid to New York City to recover from the WTC attack) will be approximately $40 billion. These are obviously big numbers, but they pale in comparison to the overall $6 trillion GDP of the United States, and the $2 trillion federal budget. Similarly, even though the Secretary of Defense called up some 50,000 National Guard reservists, there has been no discussion of reinstating the military draft, or creating the kind of 500,000-person military force that the U.S. fielded in Vietnam a generation ago. While all of this could change dramatically in the next few months or years, it's obvious that the current national situation is radically different than what our parents faced in World War II: Instead of making a conscious choice for (military) guns over (civilian) butter, the current strategy is to produce both guns *and* butter—indeed, the attitude in Washington seems to be that the more guns and butter we can produce, the more likely we are to spend our way out of the nascent recession.

So what does this mean to the IT industry as a whole? Bottom line: The feedback and data that were available as of December 2001 indicate that the events of September 11th have exacerbated a downturn in the IT industry that began sometime in the spring or summer of 2000; and the terrorist attacks will probably prolong that downturn by another fiscal quarter or two into 2002. In the short term, it has already caused the deferral or cancellation of various "discretionary" IT projects, but in the long term, IT will continue to be as important as it ever was. Indeed, the long-term outlook may include *more* money being spent on IT than before; but as I'll explain in more detail below, that will be caused by a shift in IT spending towards security, surveillance, contingency planning, and disaster recovery.

To the extent that IT is woven into the very fabric of the American economy, IT budgets will basically reflect the overall fortunes of the organizations they serve. Thus, airlines are currently struggling with the severe financial consequences of a 25-30% reduction in passengers; and in addition to the well-publicized layoff of airline employees across the board, IT budgets within many of the major airlines—which normally represent approximately 7% of gross airline revenues—are being tightened dramatically. American Airlines, for example, announced within weeks after the September 11th attack that it was examining which IT projects could be deferred, and was shifting the focus of its IT spending to systems that could improve security.[23] Similarly, United Airlines announced that it had put all of its future technology projects, including wireless check-in, on hold in the wake of the terrorist attacks.[24] The key point to recognize here is that *all* IT organizations engage in a certain amount of "discretionary" spending, which typically represents approximately 25% of their overall budgets. In the case of airlines, there was an immediate pressure to defer, or even cancel, things like the development of a wireless check-in service, for the simple reason that the marketplace wasn't demanding it anyway. In a similar vein, Delta Airlines announced in early October 2001 that it was reevaluating the installation of a high-speed, on-board Internet service, which would require retrofitting aircraft with Ethernet-type wiring and phased-array antennas to connect to a high-speed satellite service, so that airborne passengers could surf the Web while flying from hither to thither.[25]

Meanwhile, other organizations said that their IT projects (and thus, presumably, their IT budgets) were still on track in the aftermath of the attacks. For example, Federal

---

23. See "American Airlines looks to defer IT spending," by Bob Brewin, *Computerworld*, Oct. 4, 2001.
24. See "United Airlines puts tech projects on hold," by Bob Brewin, *Computerworld*, Oct. 2, 2001
25. See "Delta may delay airborne Web service," by Bob Brewin, *Computerworld*, Oct. 4, 2001.

Express and United Parcel Service—which obviously depend upon a functioning air-traffic control system, but do not carry passengers—indicated that they had *not* put any major IT projects on hold.[26] But overall, it appears that IT budgets *are* being trimmed, at least for the remainder of 2001, and probably for most of 2002 as well. For example, a CIO Magazine/Yardeni.com survey in September 2001 found that CIOs and managers expected their IT budgets to grow by 3.7 percent in the year ahead; a similar survey in August 2001 had found growth projections of 7.2 percent.[27] Similarly, a survey by Merrill Lynch, conducted during approximately the same period, found that 73 percent of CIOs said that their businesses had been harmed by the terrorist attacks, while 23 percent said that the attacks had affected their business directly; while a Merrill Lynch survey prior to the attack found that 45 percent of CIOs expected to increase IT spending in the second quarter of 2002, a post-survey attack found that only 32 percent still expected such an increase.[28] And a Morgan Stanley survey of 225 CIOs indicated that while 31 percent planned to adhere to spending strategies already in place before September 11th, another 33 percent felt that it was too soon to make any predictions on how their technology spending would be affected.

It's important to remember that many of these opinions were collected in the *immediate* aftermath of the September 11th attacks; and within a month or two, there was beginning to be some optimism about a return to normalcy. For example, an October 2001 survey of 231 top executives, conducted by CIO Magazine, indicated an expectation that IT budgets for 2002 would increase by 4.7 percent, compared to the 3.7 percent increase that had been projected in September.[29] And IT managers within the public-sector govern-

---

26. See "Major FedEx and UPS IT projects still on track," by Bob Brewin, *Computerworld*, Oct. 4, 2001.

27. See "CIO poll: Attacks shrink IT budgets," by Sam Costello, IDG.net, Oct. 1, 2001.

28. See "Survey: Attacks prompt IT spending gloom," by Larry Dignan, ZDNet News, Oct. 17, 2001.

29. See "IT Budgets Stabilize, CIO's Focus on IT Contingency Plans," by Lorraine Cosgrove Ware, *CIO Magazine*, Nov. 1, 2001.

ment organizations seem almost giddy with optimism; a recent survey by the Government Electronics and Information Technology Association reported that government IT spending was expected to increase by 15 percent in 2002;[30] however, as we'll discuss in more detail below, the *way* in which those IT dollars are spent will probably change significantly, with a much larger percentage going to security, disaster-recovery, and contingency planning.

Meanwhile, most of the gloom-and-doom attitude in the IT industry during the last quarter of 2001 is more closely associated to the economic recession than to the after-effects of the terrorist attacks. An October 2001 survey by outplacement firm Challenger, Gray & Christmas, for example, found that the job-cuts in the dot-com sector of IT had increased by 62%;[31] and while the terrorist attacks might have contributed to the cutbacks to some extent (e.g., Compaq Computer estimated that it lost $700 million in September because of shipment delays caused by the shutdown of the nation's air-traffic system), it was basically a continuation of a trend that had already been underway for all of calendar year 2001, and much of 2000 as well. And while the downturn has been especially severe in the dot-com companies, all of Silicon Valley had a tough year in 2001, as did the entire PC industry. As Sung Won Sohn, the chief economist for Wells Fargo & Co., pointed out in a recent article,[32] Silicon Valley corporate profits peaked in the spring of 2000, and have been going downhill ever since and are not expected to recover until the second half of 2002. Similarly, the PC industry as a whole has been suffering for the past year; even before the September 11th attack, the research firm of Gartner Dataquest forecast an 11-percent decline in PC sales for 2001; and the research firm of Giga Information estimated that the consumer PC sector would decline by as much as 30 percent for the year.[33]

30. See "IT spending to jump, survey says," by Patricia Daukantas, *Government Computer News*, Oct. 22, 2001.
31. See "Dot-com job cuts on rise since terrorist attacks," by Linda Rosencrance, *Computerworld*, Oct. 31, 2001.
32. See "Valley's recovery outlook is gloomy," by David A. Sylvester, *Mercury News*, Oct. 23, 2001.

Finally, it's worth noting that the attacks themselves—both at the World Trade Center, and also at the Pentagon—incurred substantial costs for replacement of computer hardware, software, databases, and communications systems. A study by Computer Economics estimated that it would cost as much as $15.8 billion to repair the IT-related damages to the World Trade Center alone, including $1.7 billion to replace critical equipment and maintain service continuity, plus another $8.1 billion to replace hardware that was lost in the attack. While this might be regarded as a boost in revenues for the IT industry, it's primarily a one-time phenomenon; and while $15.8 billion might seem like a large number, it's relatively small compared to the overall size of the U.S. IT industry (not to mention the overall financial impact of the terrorist attack on real estate, businesses, and jobs in the New York area).

Resources shifting into the military sector

While the September 11th attacks may have exacerbated an IT downturn that was already in motion, a much larger impact will be associated with the shift from civilian spending to military/government spending, and a shift from development of new IT applications to security[34] and protection of *existing* systems and infrastructures. Evidence of this shift was already becoming visible in the weeks after September 11th, and I believe that it will increase in 2002 and the years beyond. For IT firms with established markets and customers and profits, this may not be a significant event; but for companies that are scrambling to replace revenues and customers lost from the 2000-2001 recession, this shift will have a significant strategic impact. Similarly, for IT professionals trying to anticipate how their career will evolve in the coming years, it's important to take this shift into account.

---

33. See "Tech sector braces for tougher times after attack," *Siliconvalley.com*, Sept. 13, 2001.
34. For example, a recent survey conducted by Gartner and the SoundView Technology Group found that 48 percent of respondents said that security would receive a greater portion of IT budgets in 2002.

Consider the following analogy with the Cold War of the 1960s and 1970s: A college graduate with a degree in aeronautical engineering typically expected to find employment in companies like Boeing, Lockheed, or McDonnell-Douglas; and while those firms were obviously building airplanes for the commercial marketplace, a significant part of their revenues were derived from military applications. Similarly, scientists with a PhD in nuclear physics could have pursued a successful career in academia in the 1960s and 1970s, but if they wanted to venture outside the university environment, there was a good chance that they would be engaged in the design and development of nuclear weapons at institutions such as Los Alamos Labs.

In the 1990s, after the fall of the Berlin Wall and the collapse of the Soviet Union, the situation changed drastically: The nation's defense budget began shrinking, which forced aerospace firms and high-tech research labs to scramble for civilian/commercial customers and products. But what the IT industry is likely to find in the post-9/11 world is just the opposite: The combination of consumer-based recession and the war on terrorism is causing a shift towards products and services for the government/military marketplace. Obviously, this is not an "all-or-nothing" shift: The private sector *is* still building commercial IT systems, and the consumer marketplace *is* still buying cell phones, Palm Pilots, and home computers. But a shift of 10-20 percent in spending patterns can have dramatic consequences for firms with razor-thin profit margins; and such a shift can have significant consequences for investors and job-seekers, too.

One of the less-visible consequences of this shift is the money spent by IT firms on high-risk research for next-generation products and services. Companies with "deep pockets," like IBM and Hewlett-Packard, can continue investing large sums for R&D in the midst of a recession, in order to gain an even larger competitive advantage when the next economic upturn begins. But smaller companies often don't have this luxury; if they sustain significant losses for more than a few fiscal quarters, there is enormous pressure to cut back on any kind of research or investment activity that cannot demonstrate a credible, near-term return-on-investment (ROI). It's interesting to see that the Federal government has already begun filling the R&D vacuum created by the combination of the economic recession and the September 11th attack. But of course, government R&D sponsors like the Defense Advanced Research Projects Agency (DARPA) have their own agenda: rather than investing research money for the next generation of consumer gadgets, they're now investing in research that can assist the war on terrorism. For example, DARPA's Microsystems Technology Office spends up to $50 million per year on optical data network research that could be applied to next-generation weapons, as well as routers and servers for commercial networks.[35] DARPA is also working on directional antennas, with the hope of achieving faster data rates and a lower probability of detection and jamming by enemy forces; in addition to the military applications, such technology could also support improved vehicle communications for the next generation of Internet-equipped automobiles.

And DARPA is not the only organization providing this kind of R&D funding. A group called the Advanced Technology Program (ATP) within the government's National Institute of Standards and Technology (NIST) recently provided 43 grants totaling $100 million for research into such fields as nanotechnology and microsystems. Interestingly, President Bush indicated, prior to September 11th, that he wanted to eliminate new ATP grants, reduce the group's fiscal 2002 budget from $145.3 million to $13 million, and prevent NIST from spending $60.7 million that had already been earmarked for new projects. But the ATP funding was saved by the Senate, and it remains to be seen whether it will continue to play a larger role in the post-9/11 world.[36]

---

35. DARPA is best known for funding the research that led to the Internet in the early 1970s; in recent years, the agency has funded the development of numerous other technologies, such as wavelength division multiplexing and Gigabit Ethernet. DARPA was formed in 1958, and has a staff of 140 technologists who award matching grants to universities and corporate researchers; the agency's $2.2 billion annual budget includes $590 million for research related to advanced networking and high-performance computing, according to Federal Sources, a market research firm. See "Bigger role seen for defense R&D," by Carolyn Duffy Marsan, *Network World*, Oct. 15, 2001; see also "DARPA's Disruptive Technologies," by David Talbot, *MIT Technology Review*, Oct. 2001.

Another well-known organization, the National Science Foundation (NSF), recently awarded $156 million for IT research projects[37]; by contrast, NSF awarded only $90 million for IT research in 2000. It appears that much of NSF's funded research does *not* have overt military objectives, but recent grants have included such computer security, human/computer interfaces, information management, and research into new ways of verifying the reliability of embedded and autonomous systems. Along with NSF, the government has also begun establishing closer ties to the nation's scientific community through the 5,000 members of the National Academies of the United States; the new efforts include an anti-terror panel headed by Harvard physicist Dr. Lewis Branscomb, and increased scientific support for the Technology Support Working Group, a group founded in 1986 with representatives from the CIA, FBI, Secret Service, and the Departments of State, Energy, and Defense.[38]

While some of this government-related IT funding comes from long-established agencies like DARPA and NSF, it's also important to note that Congress is passing its own IT-related spending bills, in order to shore up what it sees as weak areas in the nation's defense against terrorism. Some of these spending bills were still being debated in Congress while this book was being written, others were being nego-

---

36. See "Government continues to fund high-risk, high-payoff projects," by Jeff Karoub, *Smalltimes*, Nov. 13, 2001. On November 14, 2001, the House of Representatives passed a "Commerce-Justice-State" (CSJ) appropriations bill that provided $184.5 million for ATP in fiscal 2002. At the time this book was being written, it was not clear whether the House CSJ bill would be approved by the Senate (which had earlier voted $204 million for ATP in 2002), or whether the President would sign the bill. See "House OKs Bill With Cyber-Security Funding," by Brian Krebs and Robert MacMillan, *Newsbytes*, Nov. 14, 2001.
37. See "National Science Foundation awards $156M for IT research," by Patrick Thibodeau, *Computerworld*, Sept. 25, 2001.
38. See "Government Reviving Ties to Scientists," by William J. Broad, *New York Times*, Nov. 20, 2001. Interestingly, Dr. Branscomb is quoted as saying that the developing bond between science and government promised to rejuvenate the partnership that built the atomic bomb, landed American astronauts on the moon, won the Cold War and cured many diseases. According to the *New York Times* article, Branscomb said that the whole scientific enterprise of the country might need to be different now that suicide jets and germ attacks had driven home the reality of new kinds of terrorism.

tiated in House-Senate conference committees in order to align them with similar bills approved by the Senate, and still others were awaiting Presidential approval or disapproval. And the budget cycle will begin anew in 2002, and every year thereafter; and regardless of the details, it's reasonable to assume that additional moneys will continue being allocated for some of the IT-related initiatives discussed throughout this book, as long as the President and/or Congress believe that the country faces a credible threat.

To illustrate the kind of legislation that is being introduced, consider the Computer Security Enhancement and Research Act of 2001, proposed by Representative Brian Baird of Washington.[39] It would establish a 10-year R&D initiative at NIST to bolster information security, starting at $25 million in the first year and growing to $85 million in its final year, by funding appropriate research projects at universities, in collaboration with private-sector companies engaged in security products and services. In addition to Baird's stated desire to generate improved technology to track people who attack Web sites, and cheaper ways of protecting databases that are accessed via the Internet, Baird's legislation would also provide funding to train new graduate students and postdoctoral research assistants. Baird explained the training aspect of the legislation by saying, "Right now, we don't have enough people doing research on protecting networked computer systems. At the same time, more and more of us relay on these systems for basic services like electricity and financial transactions."

Similarly, the House approved a 2002 appropriations bill in mid-November 2001[40] that not only increased the funding for the ATP program discussed earlier, but which also provided $10 million for U.S. attorneys to spend on cyber-crime and enforcement against intellectual property violations such as software piracy; $1.5 million for the Center for Rural Law Enforcement Technology, which includes funding for facial recognition devices and DNA research; $9.2

39. See "Rep. Baird Introduces Computer Security Legislation," by Robert MacMillan, *WashingtonPost.com*, Nov. 19, 2001.
40. See "House OKs Bill With Cyber-Security Funding," by Brian Krebs and Robert MacMillan, *Newsbytes*, Nov. 14, 2001.

million for computer equipment, forensic research and an instant background-checking system for the White Collar Information Crime Center; and $6.5 million for the Internet Crimes Against Children Task Force, a Justice Department program designed to beef up law enforcement investigations into child pornography. Chances are that most IT professionals, IT vendors, and ordinary citizens have never heard of these task forces, government agencies, or funding programs—but that's just the point. We're likely to see more and more of this kind of government-sponsored activity in the future, and it's likely that their budgets will increase as they begin persuading legislators that they need more money to pursue their stated objectives.

While much of this activity is being funded and directed in a conscious, organized fashion, it's also apparent that the government is asking for ideas, suggestions, and help from the private IT sector in its fight against terrorism. As reporter Caron Carlson notes in a recent article,

> The pattern of military-developed technologies evolving into commercial products has come full circle: As the Pentagon hastens to develop tools for battling terrorism and fighting treacherous foes in dangerous environments, it is looking closely at advanced IT products developed for the private sector in the recent high-tech boom.[41]

Thus, a computer visualization technology developed by Silicon Graphics, Inc. (SGI) for automobile manufacturers and filmmakers is now being used by the Department of Defense for its own purposes. This is not meant to suggest that the government/military organizations are unable to develop technologies on their own; but in most cases, high-tech companies in the private sector can innovate and develop new technologies much faster than the larger, more bureaucratic government organizations.[42] And since speed is of the essence in today's high-tech, fast-moving environment (a point which we'll discuss in much more detail in Chapters 5-7), it's often much more practical to give the pri-

---

41. See "Pentagon looks to civilian IT for clues," by Caron Carlson, *ZDNet News*, Nov. 19, 2001.

vate-sector organizations as much latitude as possible. For example, the Federal government recently published a 28-page request for proposals, which contained a "wish list" of some 38 technologies that it wants to implement in the next 12-18 months. One of the items on the list is computerized voice technology: The Pentagon is looking for an automated speaker recognition system that can distinguish between spoken languages, as well as a voiceprint identification system that can verify the identity of specific individuals such as suspected terrorists.[43]

As another example of the emerging partnership between government and private industry, the former deputy assistant Secretary of Defense for command, control, communications and intelligence, Art Money, is now a member of the Board of Directors of SGI. Speaking at a recent SGI "Defense Summit" conference, Money noted that IT is the cornerstone of the Pentagon's plan to achieve what it calls "information and decision superiority"—getting the right information to the right people at the right time and in the right format, something "that can only be achieved through a reaffirmation of the government/industry team."[44] Among other things, the Pentagon has an urgent requirement to integrate its many different databases, and

---

42. Indeed, not only are the government organizations slow-moving and bureaucratic, but many of the large, traditional defense contractors like Boeing, Lockheed Martin, and General Dynamics suffer from the same problem. Also, while the traditional defense contractors have expertise in a wide range of disciplines, they have often emphasized the development of hardware-oriented aircraft and weapon systems; in the emerging war against terrorism, software and communications technology are likely to be just as important. As a result, many of the smaller high-tech IT firms are beginning to realize that they have an opportunity to compete for the government's projects to detect and deter terrorist threats. However, while their corporate culture may be innovative and fast-moving, the small high-tech firms are also recognizing that they have one important weakness: a lack of Washington-based consultants and lobbyists who can help make contacts and introductions to the decision-makers within the vast government bureaucracy. See "Techies answer USA's call to arms—war on terrorism could hinge on computer, biotech firms," by Edward Iwata, *USA Today*, Oct. 30, 2001.
43. See "Security Might Be Just Talk," by Donna Howell, *Investor's Business Daily*, Nov. 15, 2001.
44. See "Private-sector IT key in war on terrorism," by Dan Verton, *Computerworld*, Nov. 5, 2001.

develop a conceptual data model that can facilitate the creation of interoperable databases. This may sound like an abstract, theoretical problem, but it's one of the reasons for the targeting errors that led to Red Cross food aid facilities being mistakenly bombed twice within two weeks in Afghanistan, as well as the U.S. Defense Department's accidental bombing of the Chinese embassy in Kosovo in 1999. Part of the problem is that objects identified as "unknowns" in one military database have been interpreted as "enemy" in another military database—an issue that becomes more and more serious as Air Force, Navy, Army, Marine, CIA, NSA, and other databases exchange information in real-time while a military engagement is underway.

One of the most ambitious and intriguing government proposals involves the creation of a National Emergency Technology Guard, otherwise known as NetGuard, that would consist of volunteer workers who could mobilize quickly in a national emergency, in order to secure the country's IT infrastructure.[45] The details have not been formulated, and Congress was planning to begin holding hearings on the concept in December 2001, as this book was being written; but the basic idea is to enlist members from top technology companies like IBM, Microsoft, Compaq, Oracle, and Hewlett-Packard. These volunteer members would attend periodic training sessions, much like the existing National Guard has monthly and annual practice sessions. Interestingly, the proposal has the support of industry leaders such as Intel's Andy Grove, and McCaw Cellular's Craig O. McCaw; but as Intuit Chairman Scott Cook suggests, NetGuard probably needs the kind of enthusiastic public support that John F. Kennedy gave to the Peace Corps in order to make it a reality.

In the meantime, many IT professionals are finding that their participation in the "regular" National Guard is much more demanding than ever before. While some IT professionals were called into active duty during the Gulf War and the Bosnian conflict, the urgency and immediacy of the

---

45. See "New Economy: Plans for Technology National Guard," by Amy Cortese, *New York Times*, Nov. 26, 2001, page C4.

September 11th attack has created an even greater demand for IT specialists with expertise in security, telecommunications, and related disciplines. Several of the IT specialists have been able to handle their new military duties while continuing to fulfill their civilian jobs in a "virtual" sense, via email, voice mail, and teleconferencing. But it's inevitable that some will find that it's impossible to do two jobs at the same time, and that will create some obvious challenges for both employee and employer. Interestingly, when a similar situation occurred during the Bosnian conflict, 75% of U.S. companies said that they would make up any gap between the military pay earned by reservists, and their ordinary salaries;[46] but a survey after the September 11th attack indicated that only 60 percent of U.S. companies would provide compensation for the pay disparity.[47] It remains to be seen how this situation will evolve over a longer period of time; the National Guard call-up may turn out to be a relatively short-term, one-time phenomenon; if it becomes an on-going, quasi-permanent mechanism for the Defense Department to obtain the skilled IT personnel that it needs, then we may see legislation guaranteeing that reservists maintain their pay parity, in order to avoid discouraging participation in the National Guard.

Similarly, it's difficult to tell, at this point, whether the proposed NetGuard will become a reality; my personal guess is that it will fade away and be forgotten unless there is a significant terrorist attack on the IT infrastructure, which we'll discuss later. But with or without NetGuard, it is already clear that the government's new emphasis on IT initiatives is having an impact on the high-tech work force in the United States. For example, many IT workers are applying for jobs with government IT contractors, in order to contribute their technology expertise to help the country; unfortunately, relatively few have the top-level security clearances that are needed for sensitive work on military projects and sensitive projects throughout the government,

---

46. See "IT workers get the call," by Deborah Radcliff, *Computerworld*, October 5, 2001.
47. See "Firms Wrestle With Effects of Reservists' Call-Up," by Donna Howell, *Investor's Business Daily*, Nov. 7, 2001.

including IRS, FAA, the Justice Department, and State Department.[48] For now, employers are scrambling to fill job openings—Northrop Grumman Information Technology, for example, had 800 job openings in November 2001—and are relaxing some of their demands for technical qualifications if applicants have the necessary security clearances; other firms are offering bonuses for new hires, or investing in training newly-hired recruits with appropriate technical skills while waiting for the security clearance applications to be processed. In the long run, though, we're likely to see much more emphasis on security clearances as one of the common qualifications for getting a good IT job in both private-sector and public-sector companies; this was a common and familiar occurrence in the early 1960s, when I applied for a summer job in the computer department of a defense contractor, but it obviously faded away in the 1980s and 1990s.

The sudden demand for cyber-security skills, along with contingency planning, security audits, and related high-tech skills, has also created a boom in training. Organizations ranging from the National Security Agency to the Defense Department, and non-profit organizations like the SANS Institute and International Information Systems Security Certification Consortium, have experienced a significant increase of interest in their security programs;[49] registrations for the SANS Institute's security courses, for example, have increased threefold in 2001, to 14,000 enrollees.

Recognition of *national* "critical infrastructure" issues

Within moments after the hijacked airlines slammed into the World Trade Center towers on September 11th, it became apparent that the terrorists had done more than just destroy buildings and lives: they had also wreaked havoc upon the *infrastructure* of New York City, and to some extent

---

48. See "Security Clearance Requirements Spark IT Talent War," by Gail Repsher Emery, *Newsbytes*, Nov. 12, 2001.
49. See "No Recession for Cybersecurity: Companies, Agencies Struggle to Meet Demand for Security Specialists," by Gail Repsher Emery, *Washington Technology*, Nov. 19, 2001.

the entire country, if not the entire world. Telephone calls became almost impossible throughout the city for several hours; subway and automobile traffic via bridges and tunnels was stopped. Television broadcasts that had emanated from the antennae atop the WTC towers were no longer possible. The list of interruptions and disruptions went on and on—though officials at Worldcom Inc. were quick to report that the Defense Department's Defense Information Systems Network (DISN) continued to function "normally," despite the suicide attack on the Pentagon.[50]

And as public officials contemplated the implications of the WTC attack, it became increasingly clear that other aspects of the nation's infrastructure—a vast web of electric utilities, dams, bridges, tunnels, telecommunication switching systems, reservoirs, roads, natural gas pipelines, refineries, Post Offices, and the Internet—might also be at risk. Some portions of the nation's infrastructure are vulnerable to bombs, radiation, chemical attacks and germ-warfare attacks; and many are vulnerable to cyber-attacks, since they are typically managed and controlled by computer systems of one kind or another.

As noted earlier in this chapter, business organizations began recognizing the importance and relative vulnerability of their IT assets as they grappled with the Y2K problem. At approximately the same time, federal and state government agencies began developing the same awareness—as well as the same vulnerabilities extended to terrorist attacks, which many government officials believed would accompany the world-wide New Year's Eve celebrations at the end of 1999.

As a result, the FBI formed a National Infrastructure Protection Center (NIPC), and the Commerce Department formed a Critical Infrastructure Assurance Office (CIAO) in 1998, though neither group had the kind of visibility or sense or urgency that we now see in the post-9/11 world. Meanwhile, a planning exercise known as "Black Ice" was conducted in November 2000 by a group of federal, state and local officials in Utah to explore the consequences of a

---

50. See "Defense Dept. command and control nets unaffected by terrorist attack," by Bob Brewin, *Computerworld*, Sept. 11, 2001.

possible terrorist attack during the 2002 Winter Olympics; and where the consequences of that simulated attack were indeed devastating, the details and conclusions of the exercise were closely guarded.[51]

As it turns out, the Bush administration had begun a consolidation and reorganization effort some four months before the September 11th attack, and the results were announced in mid-October 2001: a new entity, known as the President's Critical Infrastructure Board, has been formed, under the leadership of Richard Clarke.[52] And the Black Ice exercise has now received considerable publicity—which may stimulate more exercises and studies, in order to "think the unthinkable" and anticipate future attacks before they occur.

The September 11th attacks themselves could be regarded as "infrastructure" attacks, since they shut down the nation's air-transportation systems and stock-exchange systems for nearly a week. And in the days following September 11th, the nation began focusing on the possibility of additional forms of infrastructure attacks: Guards were posted on major dams, security was increased at nuclear power plants, and California citizens were warned of the possibility of an attack on the Golden Gate Bridge.

And almost immediately, the government began emphasizing that IT was a significant part of the nation's critical infrastructures, and that it too might be vulnerable. One day after the attack, the Senate Governmental Affairs Committee held a hearing to determine whether computer networks that provide vital services are vulnerable to terrorism. The answer, not surprisingly, turned out to be an emphatic "yes": Two government witnesses testified that government systems, in particular, were suffering from poor security, partly because they rely on buggy commercial software products, and partly because the government agencies are slow to receive security "incident reports" that could help them plug security holes.[53]

---

51. See "Black Ice scenario sheds light on future threats to critical systems," by Dan Verton, *Computerworld*, Oct. 18, 2001.
52. See "New focus on infrastructure protection emerging," by Dan Verton, *Computerworld*, Oct. 18, 2001.

And it wasn't long before pundits began predicting that the government would need to spend large sums of money to adequately protect the nation's cyber-infrastructure: At a mid-October 2001 conference, the President of the Information Technology Association of America (ITAA), Harris Miller, argued in favor of federal funding for cyber-security, and said, "I personally think $10 billion in federal spending, grants and loans is needed to get the job done."[54] Without committing to a specific dollar amount, the newly-appointed cybersecurity czar, Richard Clarke, echoed this basic message in a November 2001 speech in which he warned that cyberattacks on the nation's critical IT infrastructure could potentially cause "catastrophic damage to the economy."[55]

While the government was trying to decide what needed to be done to protect its own IT-related infrastructure, it was also warning private-sector companies that they are exposed to similar threats. In early October, for example, the FBI sent warnings to more than 27,000 corporate security officers at banks, railroads, telecommunication companies, water supply utilities, electric power facilities, and transportation companies.[56] Of course, one's first impression would be that such institutions would be primarily concerned with *physical* attacks, perhaps including biological or chemical weapons; but since computer systems and information technology are vital to the operation of these national-infrastructure organizations, the risk extends to IT as well. As if to emphasize this point, the FBI joined with the SANS institute to publish a list of the 20 top vulnerabilities of "Internet-connected systems"[57]—which, today, means almost *every* system of any significance.

53. See "Senate committee looks into IT vulnerabilities," by Patrick Thibodeau, *Computerworld*, Sept. 12, 2001. See also "Information security will be key with lawmakers," by Patrick Thibodeau, *Computerworld*, Sept. 14, 2001.
54. See "Billions needed for proper IT security, expert says," by Dan Verton, *Computerworld*, Oct. 18, 2001.
55. See "Cybersecurity czar urges more spending to protect IT infrastructure," by Maryfran Johnson and Deborah Radcliff, *Computerworld*, Nov. 8, 2001.
56. See "FBI warns infrastructure owners to brace for attacks," by Dan Verton, *Computerworld*, Oct. 8, 2001.

If there was any doubt that IT has now been identified as a critical part of the nation's infrastructure, it has been dispelled by President Bush's recent appointment of Richard Clarke (formerly a senior advisor to the National Security Council) as the new "cyberspace security czar"; in this new position, he reports both to the director of the newly-created Homeland Security Department, as well as National Security Advisor Condoleeza Rice.[58]

In addition to urging Congress to allocate more money for protection of the nation's IT infrastructure, Clarke has also proposed an idea that has generated a fair amount of controversy: development of a highly secure government-only voice/data communications network, known as GovNet, that would be operated separately and independently of the Internet. Govnet is often described as the "brainchild" of Mr. Clarke, and he had been developing some of the initial ideas prior to September 11th;[59] but the attacks, and the subsequent awareness of the Internet's vulnerability, have elevated the priority and political acceptability of the concept. But there are criticisms of the concept, and warnings of high costs and potential technical flaws, from both computer experts and bureaucrats as prominent as former CIA director George Woolsey.[60]

In addition to concerns about high cost and technical flaws, there are also widespread doubts that such GovNet can be developed within the rapid time-frame proposed by the government. The General Services Administration (GSA) issued a request for proposal in early October, and asked for responses by November 21, 2001. After selecting a contractor, GSA expects to complete GovNet within six months—an

57. This was an update of a "top-10" list that had been published by the SANS Institute a year earlier. See "FBI, SANS Institute: Internet 'not ready' for attack," by Patrick Thibodeau, *Computerworld*, Oct. 1, 2001.
58. See "For Clarke, a Career of Expecting the Worst," by Ariana Eunjung Cha, *Washtech.com*, Nov. 4, 2001. See also "Bush taps Clarke as cyberdefense chief," by Dan Verton, *Computerworld*, Oct. 1, 2001.
59. See "To Forestall a 'Digital Pearl Harbor,' U.S. Looks to System Separate from Internet," by Alison Mitchell, *New York Times*, Nov. 17, 2001.
60. See "Government Takes Security Lead," by Rutrell Yasin, *Internet Week*, Oct 23, 2001 and "GovNet concept flawed, former CIA director says," by Dan Verton, *Computerworld*, Oct. 26, 2001.

ambitious plan, to say the very least, especially considering that it will involve building an entirely new infrastructure, with new routers, and a heavy layer of security.

Though the outcome is unclear at the time this book is being written, it does appear that Mr. Clarke will continue advocating the concept of a separate network (or, to use the language that bureaucrats have adopted for this situation, a "bifurcated Internet"). And it is reasonably likely that one or more potential vendors will submit proposals that the GSA will evaluate favorably. But since the price tag for such a system is almost certain to be in the multi-billion dollar range, it will require approval by Mr. Clarke's superiors, and funding from Congress. Unless there are additional crises or terrorist attacks, the funding debate could drag on for several months; and the proposed legislation could disappear forever into one or more Congressional committees.

Meanwhile, it's unlikely that individual businesses will follow a similar strategy, simply because of the cost; on the other hand, it *is* conceivable that certain industries (e.g., banking) could decide to shift more of their activities to "private" networks, in order to avoid the risks associated with the public Internet. Most companies, though, are likely to take a more traditional approach, by investing more heavily in encryption, firewalls, virus-checking tools, security "awareness" training for employees, and a beefed-up staff of security experts.[61]

While most discussions about the nation's IT infrastructure are concerned with the *physical* components (e.g., routers, servers, telephone lines) and the operational capabilities of those systems, it's also important to recognize that a significant part of the "information asset" consists of the "bits" that comprise our databases and our libraries of "source code." The notion of protecting our databases is already a familiar one, since the news media provide a steady stream of stories about the theft of credit card numbers, medical information, and other valuable pieces of data; but it's amazing to see how few organiza-

---

61. See "Companies Stress Network Security," by Edward Iwata, *USA Today*, Oct. 2, 2001.

tions take any steps to protect the millions of lines of COBOL, C++, and Java code their programmers have written. That source code embodies the business rules, policies, strategies, inventions, and proprietary secrets with which the business is able to compete effectively; and protecting *that* part of our IT infrastructure will also be an important part of the post-9/11 world.

And while most discussions about the nation's IT infrastructure emphasize attacks *on* that infrastructure, it's also important to note that the Internet was part of the very infrastructure *used* by the September 11th terrorists (along with the nation's telephone system, credit-card system, student-visa system, car-rental system, etc.) in order to coordinate, organize, and facilitate their attack on the "physical" infrastructure of the World Trade Center, the "financial" infrastructure associated with the banking and stock-exchange activities headquartered in the area, and the military infrastructure headquartered on the Internet. Thus, we have to assume that one of the ulterior motives of a new infrastructure like GovNet will be to deprive future terrorists of the opportunity to "piggy-back" on government resources to accomplish their nefarious activities. And we may see additional legislation in the coming years, as governments attempt to limit the sale of high-tech computers, telephone systems, and software packages to rogue countries and terrorist groups.[62]

And this concept is beginning to "trickle down" to lower-level infrastructure resources: within days after the September 11th attack, both public-sector and private-sector Web sites began removing maps, checklists, descriptive manuals, employee directories, and other information that might conceivably have been valuable to terrorists. Companies concerned about "hostile" competitors have been doing the same thing for several years: If your Web server is clever

---

62. An interesting corollary is that even if a rogue country succeeds in purchasing high-tech computers, weapons, or military systems, those items are likely to become obsolete relatively quickly—and they are likely to require ongoing maintenance, service, and support by the vendors who built them. See "Can We Stop The Terrorist Tech Trade?" by Robyn Weisman, *NewsFactor Network*, Nov. 15, 2001.

enough (and your competitor is unsophisticated enough) to determine the IP address of a visitor, it can check that against a list of known competitors before allowing access to the catalogs, price lists, and other information that you *do* want your customers to see. Competitors can be simply blocked from entering the site, or (more deviously) can be directed to a "phony" site, where they will be subjected to whatever "disinformation" the security officials feel like doling out.

As we'll discuss below, such practices may create some significant challenges to our current concepts of privacy and civil liberties. If I'm running an airline, I don't want to sell a ticket to a terrorist—even if I was 100% certain that the terrorist had no intentions of blowing up airplanes, but merely wanted to fly from location A to B in order to blow up a bridge in location B. In the same vein, I don't want to rent a car, or provide telephone services, or sell a personal computer, or provide the ISP hosting services for a Web site,[63] to a known terrorist. But how do I "know" that an individual—someone whom I've typically regarded merely as a potential customer—really *is* a terrorist? What kind of information from law-enforcement agencies should I ask for, and how do I know that such information is credible and trustworthy? What obligations do I have to withhold products and services from known and/or suspect terror-ists? And what *rights* do I have, as a business person, to withhold such products and services? There will be difficult questions and debates about these issues, and the nation will be grappling with them for years to come; it's impor-tant to recognize that IT will play a central role in the debates, because much of what we claim to "know" about individuals is based on the data we have collected about them, and/or profiles about "similar" individuals.

Finally, it's worth noting that IT is likely to become an ever-greater part of the *offensive* weaponry used against ter-rorism and "enemy states" in the coming years, in addition to its unfortunate role of being part of the "vulnerable"

---

63. See "Why Every Terrorist Needs a Web Site," by David Rowan, *London Evening Standard*, Oct. 24, 2001.

infrastructure of the nation. Some aspects of the offensive weaponry are visible and obvious: Ever since the 1991 Gulf War, it has become increasingly evident that the bombs, missiles, planes, tanks, and hand-held weapons used by American military forces are filled with high-tech, computer-assisted gadgets. But a lesser-known aspect of that war involved disrupting the very same kind of IT infrastructure in Iraq that we worry about in our own country: communication systems, computer-controlled electrical power systems, and so forth. And while the opportunities for such offensive cyberwarfare may be limited in low-tech countries like Afghanistan, one can only assume that it's part of the overall military arsenal held in readiness for possible use against other, more sophisticated enemies.

Of course, the September 11th attacks demonstrated that not all "enemies" are full-fledged states or nations; they may consist of widely-dispersed groups, or even lone individuals. Thus, the offensive cyberwarfare weapons that we may have designed a decade ago to knock out an entire country's IT infrastructure may need to be refined and modified to focus on "stateless" enemies who, as mentioned earlier, piggyback on the existing infrastructure of the nation where they are operating. While political and military leaders are understandably reluctant to discuss such issues in detail, there is a general consensus among civilian hackers and computer experts that the government could use its technological prowess to withdraw money from terrorist bank accounts, impersonate a terrorist's voice on the telephone, disrupt voice/data communications completely, and disrupt GPS signals used by a terrorist's navigation equipment.[64]

---

64. See "U.S. could use cybertactics to seize bin Laden's assets," by Dan Verton, *Computerworld*, Sept. 20, 2001. A colleague who read a draft of this chapter observed that, in a pessimistic scenario, law-enforcement officers or politically-motivated government operatives could use the same technology to disrupt the communications of *non*-terrorist citizens who were felt to be excessively troublesome, disloyal, or unpatriotic. This might seem like the kind of conspiracy-theory scenarios one sees in movies like *Enemy of the State*, but it's only a slight variation on the old-fashioned strategy of asking the IRS to harass one's political opponents.

Coordination, improvement of existing systems

While *protecting* the nation's IT infrastructure is obviously going to have a high priority in the coming years, *improving* that infrastructure will also be important—so that it can function more effectively in the war against terrorism. We'll never know for certain, but it's a commonly held belief that the attacks of September 11th could have been prevented if the nation's law enforcement agencies had shared information and cooperated with one another more effectively.

Some of this involves old-fashioned politics and turf wars; more specifically, it involves *human* decisions to allow (or demand) that law enforcement agency X share its data with law enforcement agency Y; and some of it involves even murkier issues of sharing human "assets" such as spies and undercover agents. But a significant part of the problem involves the *technology* of sharing, integrating, coordinating, and communicating data between *computer* system X and Y. To the politician and the ordinary citizen, this may seem like a minor, humdrum issue; but IT professionals recognize that the problem is often overwhelming in terms of scope and complexity.

That doesn't mean the integration/sharing problem is impossible; but it does mean that a significant amount of money and people will have to be focused on solving it; indeed, the effort may spawn a bureaucracy of its own. As an example, the U.S. State Department has been working since 1998 to create a "collaborative knowledge management" system known as the Overseas Presence Interagency Collaboration System that would coordinate efforts to combat terrorism and manage crisis situations, across 40 federal agencies with overseas operations. A prototype version is expected to be launched in January 2002 at a cost of $17 million, and the final version is expected to cost somewhere between $30 million and $100 million.[65]

---

65. See "Terrorism Spurs Web Collaboration Effort," by Carolyn Duffy Marsan, *Network World Fusion*, Oct. 29, 2001.

Of course, this kind of collaborative sharing across multiple government organizations is not a new idea; over the past 20-30 years, there has been a gradual effort to coordinate the computer data bases of law-enforcement agencies, welfare and child-support agencies, tax-collection agencies, and numerous other government agencies at the local, state, and federal level. But in many cases, progress was hampered by the inevitable political turf wars and the lack of an overwhelming sense of urgency. The State Department's system, for example, was conceived in the wake of the 1998 embassy bombings in Tanzania and Kenya; one wonders why it wasn't initiated after the 1993 World Trade Center bombing, and why it wasn't finished and operational on September 11th.

In addition to integrating and coordinating the data that various public-sector government organizations already have, there is also a movement to encourage private-sector companies to share their security-related data—with each other, and with the government. Some of this can be mandated by law, and can be enforced relatively easily; for example, the government informed international airlines in late 2001 that it was determined to enforce a new policy requiring detailed biographical information about foreign visitors *before* the flights landed in the U.S., and that the deadline for initiating the policy was going to be moved up by several months. Other initiatives can be mandated legislatively, but are apparently not as easy to enforce; in the aftermath of September 11th, for example, we learned that government officials had been reluctant to demand that universities report on the attendance records of foreigners attending classes on student visas.

And since the mandated reporting requirements are likely to represent a minimal "lowest common denominator" of information, it's likely that any truly effective sharing of data between public-sector and private-sector organizations will have to be voluntary. And though most individuals and private-sector organizations are bubbling over with feelings of patriotism and civic duty in the aftermath of September 11th, there is a natural aversion to sharing truly sensitive information—if for no other reason than fear of disclosure to hostile competitors, gun-shy customers, inquisitive lawyers, and busy-body government bureaucrats. Thus, it's interesting that within a month after the September 11th attacks, Senators Robert Bennett and John Kyle introduced a bill called the Critical Infrastructure Information Security Act (mirroring a similar bill introduced in the House), which requires an amendment to the Freedom of Information Act, in order to hide information that private-sector organizations choose to share with the government. And for those organizations that choose to share security-related data with other private-sector organizations, the bill would eliminate the risk of violating traditional antitrust collusion laws.[66]

Much of the discussion about data-sharing involves the identification, authentication, and tracking of particular individuals who are known or suspected to be terrorists.[67] And some of it may involve studying *patterns* of behavior of individuals, or groups of individuals, which private-sector organizations have been doing more and more aggressively for the past decade: If you have technology that helps you spot the trend that customers who buy a six-pack of beer also buy lots of pretzels, then that same technology can help spot ostensibly unrelated customers who are all using the same credit card to buy one-way airplane tickets.

But the coordination of data will go beyond these obvious issues of tracking and identifying individuals. In the aftermath of anthrax-laced letters popping up around the country throughout the fall of 2001, it became increasingly apparent that the same lack of database integration and coordination was seriously hampering the government's efforts to respond to biological/chemical attacks. For example, in early October 2001, the Department of Defense had to confront the embarrassing reality that it cannot guarantee the availability and effectiveness of its inventory of chemical and biological warfare protective suits, because its military services and the Defense Logistics Agency use at least

66. See "Congress Eyes Bills to Bolster Security Data Sharing," by Patrick Thibodeau, *Computerworld*, Oct. 9, 2001.
67. See "Security Experts Say Antiterror Information Tools Flawed," by Dan Verton, *Computerworld*, Sept. 24, 2001.

nine different systems to manage their inventory—and all of the systems use different data fields, and contain records that cannot be easily linked.[68]

Unfortunately, the problem is often far more severe than simply integrating existing databases. In a devastating report issued in March 2001—six months before the September 11th attack, and the first anthrax attack on October 4th—the Centers for Disease Control (CDC) likened the nation's public health IT infrastructure to a "pony express" system. As of October 4th, only half of the country's 59 state and territorial health departments and 6,000 state and local health departments and boards had full-time Internet connectivity; and 20% of these organizations had no email. As Dr. Paul Weisner, director of the Board of Health in DeKalb County, Georgia (which includes the city of Atlanta) observed, "We need to get into the modern age of communications. UPS lets you track a package in real time, but I can't track my emergency room patients in real time. Instead, I have an icon on my desk here that only gives me an update every 24 hours.[69]

Though it appears nobody paid much attention to the CDC report for six months, things *are* slowly improving at this point—but the upgrading of systems and integrating of government/private databases will almost certainly take years to accomplish, and will thus represent one of the major strategic consequences of September 11th. A small example of this ongoing effort was announced by the U.S. Air Force in early December 2001: It will complete work on an $8 million infectious-disease early-warning system called LEADERS (an acronym for "Lightweight Epidemiology Advanced Detection and Emergency Response System"); the system will allow medical personnel throughout both the public and private health sectors to track symptom outbreaks as they are reported by hospitals in real time; and it will allow them to map geographic regions where outbreaks are occurring, and determine the response capabili-

---

68. See "Lack of IT integration hurts chem./bio warfare defenses," by Dan Verton, *Computerworld*, Oct. 8, 2001.
69. See "CDC calls public health IT a 'pony express' system," by Bob Brewin, *Computerworld*, Oct. 18, 2001.

ties of various medical facilities. Interestingly, LEADERS is built as a Web-based system on an ASP (Application Service Provider) model, so that hospitals and medical authorities can subscribe to the system without having to buy any additional hardware or software.[70]

Impact on privacy

In a perfect world, perhaps it's possible to achieve the level of security that American society demands for its protection, without sacrificing the privacy and civil liberties that are guaranteed by its laws and its Constitution, and that it has long taken for granted.[71] And perhaps, in a perfect world, it's possible to achieve the desired level of security by implementing laws and systems *inside* the country, without regard to the events beyond our borders.

Alas, we do not inhabit a perfect world, nor is it likely to become so in the foreseeable future. And the balance between security and privacy/liberty within our country *is* affected by events outside our borders, in addition to the various political events and debates within our borders. Thus, the events of September 11th have accelerated a number of privacy-related initiatives that were already underway, and have introduced a number of new ones. It was January 1999 when Sun Microsystems' Scott McNealy made the famous comment, "You have zero privacy anyway. Get over it."[72] It may have seemed an overly pessimistic and

---

70. It's also interesting to note that LEADERS was used in New York City shortly after the Sept. 11th attack, and within 24 hours had linked more than 250 hospitals to real-time symptom tracking. See "Bioterrorism fighters get ammo," by Dan Verton, *Computerworld*, Dec. 3, 2001.

71. Obviously, the same issue can be raised about the security-versus-privacy balancing act in Canada, England, France, Germany—and even Iran, Iraq, Saudi Arabia, and Afghanistan. But each country has its own laws and customs, its own culture and expectations. I'm not competent to judge whether my comments make any sense whatsoever in countries like Iran or Iraq; and while I assume that the "basics" are the same in Canada, England, France, and Germany as they are in the U.S., the nuances and details are different. Thus, my comments are limited to the situation in the U.S.; hopefully there will be thoughtful discussions and debates about the same issues in other countries around the world.

72. See "Sun on Privacy: 'Get Over It'," by Polly Spenger, *Wired News*, Jan. 26, 1999.

cynical statement at the time; but hardly anyone would disagree if McNealy were to repeat his comments again; if there was any doubt that privacy was already being attacked by computer-supported bureaucrats, books like Simson Garfinkel's *Database Nation* (O'Reilly, 2000) spelled out the details for all to see.

For the record, I am one of those who believes that our privacy *has* been encroached upon for many years, and that the encroachment continues to escalate as both private-sector and public-sector organizations enhance their database capabilities. And while I appreciate the government's need to track down terrorists who may have infiltrated American society, I am also one of those who believes that existing laws, technologies, and databases should be fully exploited and integrated (in the sense described in the previous section) before any new privacy-encroaching laws are introduced. But my opinions are unlikely to have any impact on the initiatives that are already underway, and the new ones that are likely to emerge in the coming months and years. In the meantime, I'll be doing the same thing that most other citizens will be: monitoring the general areas of privacy intrusion, and doing my best to minimize that intrusion in my own life.

Corporations are also monitoring the situation. In the immediate aftermath of the September 11th attacks, it appears that some companies handed over electronic files and email archives to authorities without proper warrants and court orders. And it also appears that businesses are reassessing their existing privacy policies with regard to consumer-related information, in order to allow exceptions for cases of national security.[73] On the other hand, it appears that Internet companies that had refused the pre-9/11 requests to install monitoring technologies like the FBI's Carnivore system are now eager to help the government track down terrorist-related usage of their systems.[74]

---

73. See "Companies rethink Net privacy after attacks," by Stefanie Olsen, *Cnet*, Oct. 2, 2001.
74. See "Privacy Trade-Offs Reassessed," by Ariana Eunjung Chan and Jonathan Krim, *Washington Post*, Sept. 13, 2001.

Meanwhile, it appears that there are two primary areas of government activity that we will be facing in the short-term future: greater use of "smart cards" for national identification, and greater surveillance of activities of, and communications between, citizens.

The "smart card" concept has received a great deal of attention since the September 11th attack, partly because of the much-publicized offer by Oracle CEO Larry Ellison to provide the government with software to implement a database of national identity cards; indeed, Oracle followed through with that offer by delivering the software in early December 2001.[75] In addition, Sun Microsystems Scott McNealy, whose earlier-quoted remarks suggest that he has already abandoned any hopes for personal privacy, announced at a major computer conference "I'm a huge proponent of a national ID card."[76]

As this book was being written, the Federal government had offered numerous public assurances that it had no intention of pursuing a national ID card;[77] and numerous Congressmen and Senators indicated that they would oppose any plan that might be introduced. But government officials have been known to change their minds, and even the most ardent defenders of privacy might be pressured to compromise their ideals. In the meantime, what most people seem to have missed is that a national identity card already exists: it's called a Social Security card. And while it's optional, there's a more detailed national identity card called a *passport*; while it doesn't have a computer chip or embedded biometric data, it does provide a photo-ID of the bearer, and it does imply that the federal government considers the bearer to be a citizen in good standing.

---

75. See "Oracle donates ID software U.S. government," by Douglas F. Gray, *Computerworld*, Dec. 5, 2001.
76. See "McNealy calls for smart cards to help security," by Matt Hamblen, *Computerworld*, Oct. 12, 2001. And if a national ID plan offends you, you'll be thrilled to learn that a United Nations official has proposed that every human in the world should be fingerprinted and registered. See "Refugees meeting hears proposal to register every human in the world," smh.com.au, Dec. 14, 2001.
77. See "White House nixed national ID notion," by Jennifer Jones, *Computerworld*, Sept. 27, 2001.

Also, the debate about a *national* ID card presumes that the only relevant issue is whether it will be accomplished in a coordinated top-down fashion by the Federal government. While the debate continues, it's far more likely that numerous bottom-up initiatives will be introduced.[78] Even before September 11th, numerous states across the country were growing increasingly frustrated by the use of fraudulently-obtained drivers' licenses for identification purposes. And while the proposals to add fingerprints and other biometric data to a "smart" driver's license will draw similar objections from local legislators that the national ID plan has drawn from Congressional representatives, it's much more plausible that various levels of "intelligence" could be added to such licenses, little by little. One could imagine a state insisting that a record of past traffic violations be embedded into a driver's license, so that authorized law enforcement authorities could check it whenever they stop a motorist for speeding. And then the next step could be a law requiring that a driver's criminal record be embedded into the card. And then the next step …

While the timetable and details of such regulations are far from clear, the trend seems fairly clear: Little by little, such initiatives are likely to be introduced and eventually passed. And at some point, if enough states have introduced such smart-card mechanisms, then it's likely that the Federal government will attempt to introduce and enforce common standards, to ensure interchangeability of a New York license with a New Mexico license. And the next step beyond that will be a smart *national* card, perhaps in the form of a greatly enhanced Social Security card.

Meanwhile, local authorities have already begun introducing their own form of smart cards; for example, the "EZ-Pass" card, attached to the inside windshield of a car and capable of being automatically scanned by a camera, that allows New York City residents to pass unimpeded through bridges and tunnels, was originally designed as an automated-payment system, so that the city could reduce costs

---

78. This is a concept we'll explore in much more detail in Chapter 5, in our discussion of *emergent* systems.

by eliminating old-fashioned payment of tolls with coins and paper money. But since it *is* automated, it means there is a computer system that keeps track of the date and time that a particular automobile is located at a particular bridge or tunnel; and privacy advocates warned that this information could be mis-used by overly zealous bureaucrats and law-enforcement agencies. What the privacy advocates missed, though, and what the average NYC citizen is *still* blissfully unaware of, is a *much* more pervasive use of the EZ-Pass card: It can be, and *is*, being monitored by cameras installed at traffic intersections throughout the city, ostensibly to help gauge traffic patterns. Even though this is completely unrelated to the original purpose of the cards, such monitoring is apparently *not* against the law; and because some bureaucrat believes it's useful, that practice continues. Thus far, I'm unaware of anyone who has had such information used against him in a court ("Isn't it true, Mr. Jones, that you drove your car through the intersection of Broadway and 42nd Street at 12:07 PM on the date of the crime?"), but I believe it's only a matter of time.

Interestingly, IT magnates Larry Ellison and Scott McNealy have emphasized their belief that such smart cards should be voluntary. But of course, a Social Security card and a driver's license are voluntary, too. The problem is that, even if you're not retired and don't drive a car, the lack of these two familiar items makes it difficult to carry out a number of other functions that most of us find quite important, if not downright necessary. Since the driver's license is the only kind of "government-issued, photo-ID" identification the average citizen is likely to have, it's necessary in order to board an airplane flight (something that was already true, well before September 11th). And as most adults have long since learned, it's virtually impossible to open a bank account, obtain medical insurance, or obtain a job without a Social Security card—which, as most middle-aged adults are keenly aware, was initially issued with stern instructions, printed on the card itself, that it was *not* to be used for identification purposes.

But most of us have long since abandoned that fight; for better or worse, we've accepted Scott McNealy's advice to "get over it," and simply muddle on with our lives. And while the average citizen might agree that the pervasive requirement to identify oneself with a Social Security number is a nuisance and an intrusion into one's privacy, it doesn't cause very many *practical* problems in day-to-day life. The problem is trying to anticipate the point at which it *would* be a practical problem, and then deciding how far one should go to resist such identification demands on the part of the government. For example, suppose the government mandates that a "smart" national-ID card will carry a record of every citizen's sexually-transmitted diseases (STDs), in order to prevent STD-carriers from donating blood; and suppose the government justifies this action by announcing that the STD-related information will only be "visible" to qualified medical authorities. Given the nature of ever-encroaching laws and regulations, a skeptical citizen might well wonder how long it will be before his STD-related information is visible to a policeman when he's stopped for a traffic violation, or an employer when he's applying for a job, or a bank officer when he's applying for a mortgage. History suggests that those who claim that such scenarios "can't happen" are highly optimistic, or extremely naïve.

In addition to the notion of national-identification smart cards, the government has ratcheted up its efforts to monitor the movement and activities of individuals, as well as wiretapping and eavesdropping on their communications. Within a week after the September 11th attack, Congressional and Justice Department proposals called for greater electronic surveillance rights, easing of computer wiretapping restrictions, increased video monitoring, and increased Internet surveillance.[79] By late October 2001, the House and Senate had passed a compromise antiterrorism bill that will allow law enforcement officers to tape multiple suspected telephones, open voice-mail messages, capture email addresses, and view online account information of suspected terrorists; in addition, the new law expands the court's authority to order a warrant for broader communi-

---

79. See "Technology's Role to Grow in a New World of Security," by William Glaberson, *New York Times*, Sept. 18, 2001.

cations gathering that may extend beyond their traditional jurisdictions.[80] And by early December 2001, the CIA was asking Congress to give it the same legal authority that the FBI now has to gather data on foreign intelligence targets from telephone providers and Internet ISPs; at the same time, the Justice Department asked Congress to rescind the key legal provisions of the Foreign Intelligence Surveillance Act, which would thus enable wiretapping of suspected parties even if they were not connected to a foreign power or international terrorist group.[81]

In addition to new laws, and new surveillance activities, the September 11th attacks rejuvenated earlier surveillance initiatives—which, ironically, had been de-railed by privacy-sensitive Congressmen just a few months earlier. For example, within hours after the airplanes smashed into the World Trade Centers, FBI representatives began showing up at email/network providers and Web-based firms, asking them to accept the placement of Carnivore-like surveillance systems. And within a week after the attack, the Senate had approved expanding the permissible uses of Carnivore to include the investigation of acts of terrorism and computer crimes.[82]

The FBI has also begun developing its own version of the computer "virus" attacks that have floated around the Internet with such intriguing names as Code Red, Nimbda, BadTrans, and Sircam. The FBI virus, known as Magic Lantern, is intended to be planted surreptitiously (either by physical means or via email) on the computers of suspected criminals and terrorists; instead of deleting files and broad-

---

80. See "Net Surfing, E-Mail Targets of New Antiterror Law," by Cara Garretson, *PC World.com*, Oct. 25, 2001. See also "Ashcroft has immediate plans for antiterrorism tools," by Cara Garretson, *Computerworld*, Oct. 25, 2001.

81. See "Bush Team Seeks Broader Surveillance Powers," by Jim McGee *Washington Post*, December 2, 2001.

82. Carnivore is the name given to an FBI email surveillance system; it has since been renamed DCS1000. More information about Carnivore can be found at the Electronic Privacy Information Center's "Carnivore FOIA Documents" site; details about the post-9/11 FBI and Senate activities can be found in "Anti-Attack Feds Push Carnivore," by Declan McCullagh, *Wired News*, Sept. 12, 2001, and "Senate Oks use of Carnivore against terrorism," by Sam Costello, *Computerworld*, Sept. 17, 2001.

casting annoying messages like the better-known viruses, MagicLantern is intended to log the keystrokes of its victim when he or she invokes encryption programs like Pretty Good Privacy (PGP).[83]

No doubt there will be other eavesdropping and surveillance systems developed in the coming years—such as the face-scanning systems that have been prototyped in various parts of the country, and recently installed at the Oakland, California airport.[84] Interestingly, the current version of the Oakland system is used to scan the face of suspected criminals when they are arrested and booked in the Oakland city jail; the police department is installing a high-speed T1 communication line to the airport so that airport security officials can be connected to the jailhouse database. But as privacy advocates would no doubt argue, future versions of such a system might include photographs of *anyone* that the local law enforcement agency regarded as "suspicious."

One of the most contentious areas of debate in recent months has been the right of citizens to combat the intrusions on their privacy by using publicly available encryption programs. I think it's fair to say that most American citizens are unfamiliar with the details of encryption, and are probably blissfully unaware that (a) the e-commerce transactions that they carry out when ordering, say, a book from Amazon, are protected by moderately strong encryption, or that (b) government authorities have been attempting for well over a decade to create a "back-door" into the common encryption tools, so that they could access the communications of terrorists.

All of this was part of a bitter debate between government officials and privacy advocates in the late 1980s, revolving around the government's efforts to introduce a back-door-equipped "Clipper Chip" encryption device into

---

83. See "FBI Software Cracks Encryption Wall," by Bob Sullivan, *MSNBC News*, Nov. 20, 2001. In mid-December 2001, the FBI acknowledged that Magic Lantern was "under development," but claimed it had not yet been put to use. See "FBI confirms 'Magic Lantern' exists," *MSNBC News*, Dec. 12, 2001.
84. See "Oakland airport to install face-scan technology," by Jennifer Disabatino, *Computerworld*, Oct. 18, 2001.

commercial products.[85] The Clinton Administration eventually abandoned the fight, but during the height of the controversy, a free-spirited privacy advocate named Phil Zimmerman effectively destroyed the government's ability to impose control over civilian encryption when he surreptitiously released a "freeware" program called Pretty-GoodPrivacy (PGP) on the Internet.[86] While most commercial encryption technologies—such as those used by Netscape and Internet Explorer for e-commerce transactions—typically involve encryption "keys" of either 40-bits or 128-bits in length, PGP allows keys as long as 4096-bits. While the numbers are not meaningful to the average citizen, it's fair to say that a competent individual, using the full capabilities of PGP, could create an encrypted message that would be extraordinarily difficult, if not downright impossible, for government authorities to crack.

And while the relevant government agencies had, at least temporarily, accepted the reality of this road-block, the events of September 11th changed the political climate immediately. Shortly after the attack, Senator Judd Gregg said (in remarks that were published in the *Congressional Record*), "We have electronic intelligence of immense capability. It needs to be improved, especially in the area of encryption."[87] Gregg's remarks were interpreted as a call for mandatory encryption back-doors, which set off a furious round of criticism reminiscent of the old Clipper Chip debates.[88] But perhaps more significant, security experts quickly began advising law-makers like Senator Gregg that

85. For more details, and a long list of articles, about the Clipper Chip, see the Electronic Privacy Information Center's Web page on the topic.
86. Zimmerman's "amateur" activities were eventually transformed into a commercial enterprise, which was eventually acquired by McAfee.com, a division of Network Business Associates. Free copies of PGP, for Windows and Macintosh computers, are still available from McAfee; in addition, it can be obtained from MIT and various other organizations in the U.S., as well as numerous sources outside the U.S.
87. See "Encryption advocates resist legal limits," by Rick Perera, *Computerworld*, Sept. 17, 2001. See also "Disputes on Electronic Message Encryption Take on New Urgency," by John Schwartz, *New York Times*, Sept. 25, 2001.
88. See "High Tech Leaders Slam Encryption Back Door Bill," *Newsbytes*, Oct. 4, 2001, and "New Encryption Laws for E-Mail Unlikely," by Carrie Kirby, *San Francisco Chronicle Online*, Oct. 6, 2001.

his legislation was effectively like closing the barn-door after the horses, cows, chickens, and pigs have already left; or to use another metaphor, Phil Zimmerman let the encryption cat out of the bag a decade ago, and it's not coming back. Encryption technology is now too widespread *around the world* for the U.S. to control, and the task of recalling all of the "legacy" non-back-door encryption programs installed on the tens of millions (if not hundreds of millions!) of existing computers is virtually impossible.[89] In any case, Senator Gregg announced in mid-October that he had decided not to pursue his proposed legislation, and the matter appears to have been put to rest, at least temporarily.[90]

Even if some other Senator or government official decides to renew the battle for back-door access into encrypted messages between private individuals, there is a lesson to be learned from the ongoing exploits of computer hackers around the world: No matter how thorough and determined the law enforcement agencies might be, the technology changes so quickly that a nimble, and equally determined, individual can usually stay one step ahead.

But the average citizen is neither nimble, determined, or technologically savvy when it comes to encryption. At the same time, the debate over encryption of private messages is analogous to the debate over gun control: Regardless of one's political opinions on the matter, the reality is that average citizens have no desire to own guns, and no desire to encrypt their messages. At the other extreme, dedicated criminals will acquire guns and rifles regardless of how strict the gun-control laws are, and dedicated terrorists will find increasingly sophisticated means of encrypting or hiding[91] their messages. The debate is most difficult for the group in the middle—i.e., the law-abiding citizens who believe it is their Constitutional right to bear arms, without restrictions, and who also believe it is their Constitutional

---

89. See "Experts Say Encryption Can't Be Limited, A Setback for Lawmakers Seeking Change," by Lee Gomes, *Wall Street Journal*, Sept. 26, 2001. See also "Opening encryption 'back door' is problematic, experts say," *SiliconValley.com*, Sept. 25, 2001.

90. See "Senator Backs Off Back Doors," by Declan McCullagh, *Wired News Online*, Oct. 17, 2001.

right to communicate privately with their friends, without intrusion.[92]

Conclusion

This chapter has covered a broad range of topics—and in many ways, I have only skimmed the surface of each individual topic. Not only that, what I have written here is based almost entirely on the *actual* events that have occurred in the three months following the terrorist attacks of September 11th. If my discussion has been superficial, my excuse is that the full range, and the full depth, of the strategic implications of September 11th probably won't be fully known and understood for many years.

But some things *are* known: We already know, as discussed in the previous section, that the war on terrorism will accelerate the invasion of privacy that had already been underway for many years. We know that it will cause more emphasis to be placed on the IT-related components of the country's "critical infrastructure," and that it will shift government resources away from peacetime projects (like paying down the national debt, and funding Medicare and Social Security) to military projects. We know that it will have similar effects on business organizations, and we can make some plausible predictions about the personal impact that each citizen will feel.

And while all of this will be discussed and debated in the years to come by poets, musicians, preachers, and politi-

---

91. One of the high-tech ways of *hiding* messages is a techniques known as "steganography," in which coded messages are embedded within the bits and bytes of digitized graphic images, in such a way that the message is "invisible" when the image is printed in a normal fashion. For more details, see "Veiled Messages of Terrorists May Lurk in Cyberspace," by Gina Kolata, *New York Times*, Oct. 30, 2001.

92. In case you're curious about the Constitutional basis for such a claim on privacy, consider Amendment IV of the United States Constitution: *"The right of the people to be secure in their persons, houses, papers, and effects, against unreasonable searches and seizures, shall not be violated, and no Warrants shall issue, but upon probable cause, supported by Oath or affirmation, and particularly describing the place to be searched, and the persons or things to be seized."*

cians, it's particularly important for IT professionals to take part in those discussions and debates—because IT is the common theme, and the common "enabling technology," of all that is to come. Unless the nation, in a moment of techno-frenzy, elects Bill Gates as President, IT people will not be the ones to determine the answers to the many difficult questions we face in the years ahead. But if we want our leaders, our colleagues, our friends, and our family members to make wise, thoughtful, and informed decisions, then we must be sure to tell them everything we know about the technology we know so well—not just the benefits and strengths and opportunities, but also the threats and the weaknesses and the risks. To do anything less would not only be unethical and immoral, it could well be deadly.

SECURITY 3

> "Security is mostly a superstition. It does not exist in nature, nor do the children of men as a whole experience it. Avoiding danger is no safer in the long run than outright exposure. Life is either a daring adventure, or nothing."
>
> —*Helen Keller*

Basic Concepts

As we discussed in Chapter 2, it is rapidly becoming apparent to political leaders, as well as corporate executives, that computer networks and information are an important asset—and as such, need more protection than we have typically provided in the past.

Of course, this isn't news to the IT professionals who specialize in computer security, nor is it "new news" to most business managers. As far back as the 1960s, Vietnam-war protesters managed to bomb an occasional computer center; and it was common to see corporate computer centers buried underground or hidden in secret, nondescript locations. While there have been fewer and fewer overt attacks on computer centers in the past 20 years, hacking and computer viruses have increased dramatically. Meanwhile, most of the computer technology that we depend on is no longer kept in air-conditioned rooms the size of a football field; today's laptops, desktop PCs, and servers can operate in a normal household or business environment, which are *not* protected by thick walls and armed guards.

It has also become apparent that the information contained within our computer systems is as valuable, if not *more* valuable, than the hardware itself; after all, we can replace computers and switching centers lost in a disaster like September 11th, but if the data is lost, it may be lost forever. And while it may cost a lot to replace computer hardware—indeed, billions of dollars in the case of the WTC attack—the cost of lost data can be much higher, precisely because it often cannot be recreated at all.

The possibility of computer damage and lost data is not a new concept, of course: companies have spent billions of dollars over the years to maintain backup copies of their databases, as well as redundant computer centers, to help cope with the possibility of floods, fire, earthquakes, hurricanes, and other natural disasters. But aside from military organizations, which presumably have to worry about the possibility that their computer centers could be attacked by enemy missiles or bombs, very few private-sector or public-sector organizations have done much preparation for deliberate human attacks on their computers. In the aftermath of September 11th, that has obviously changed.[1]

Before the advent of the minicomputer in the 1970s and the PC in the 1980s, *physical* computer security basically consisted of placing the behemoth mainframe computers in a well-guarded room with thick walls and a guarded door. Television cameras, motion sensors and other high-tech gadgets have been introduced more recently, though September 11th taught us that most of these gadgets and strategies cannot cope with the impact of a fully-loaded airplane flying at 500 mph. As we'll see later in the Paradigm Shift section, the ongoing miniaturization of computers has

---

1. It is still too early to tell whether the increased attention to computer security is a short-term or long-term phenomenon. See "Companies Prepare for Data Disasters," by Dina ElBoghdady, *The Washington Post*, Oct. 19, 2001.

caused a paradigm shift in the field of physical computer security; and while we'll discuss the current aspects of physical security in more detail at that point, we won't dwell any further on the old-fashioned, but nevertheless still-important issues of protecting mainframes (and, in more modern terms, large "server farms" providing Internet access to thousands of people) in guarded rooms.

While protection of computer hardware is certainly important, computer *data* is far more vulnerable than a hardware "box," because it can be altered, corrupted, erased, or copied from afar, without the visible aspects of a physical attack. Thus, one of the immediate reactions to the September 11th attacks was the decision by government agencies, as well as some private-sector firms, to remove sensitive public data from their Web sites in order to reduce the risk of such data-oriented attacks. In retrospect, it's quite amazing to see how much information is still accessible to anyone in the world with a Web browser and an Internet connection; but now, information about chemical storage, air-quality readings, well-water contamination, and airport security violations are locked more carefully in the computer systems of their respective owners.[2]

Similarly, business organizations have already begun focusing on the security of their financial data, medical data, proprietary data about their products and services and customers. And this is causing both internal and external conflicts: Much of the past decade has been spent "opening up" databases to internal corporate employees through the creation of "data warehouses,"[3] and opening it up to corporate customers, suppliers, and partners through the

2. See "Public Data Gets Pulled Off Web," by Steve Johnson, John Wool-folk, and Mary Anne Ostrom," *SiliconValley.com*, Oct. 27, 2001 for details. Note that removing information from a publicly-accessible Web site does not guarantee that it is safe from unauthorized remote access. After all, the computer upon which the data resides might have a variety of Internet connections; and if security measures have not been properly implemented, a clever intruder may be able to access the computer and scan *all* of its files (as well as determining all of the other computers to which the compromised computer is connected).
3. See "Guarding the data warehouse gate," by Deborah Radcliff, *Computerworld*, Oct. 1, 2001.

creation of Internet-enabled "business-to-business" (or "B2B") exchanges. It's already evident that terrorists can buy a plane ticket with a credit card, via Internet travel sites; on a larger scale, the chemical industry is now examining its B2B exchanges to ensure that their security systems and business practices will prevent terrorists from using such "anonymous" marketplaces to purchase materials for chemical or biological attacks.[4]

Computer security is such a complex, fast-changing high-tech field that it almost represents an industry and a profession of its own, separate from the rest of the computer field. Dozens of books have been written on the topic in recent years, and it would be impossible to provide a comprehensive coverage of the topic in one chapter. Instead, I'll provide a summary of the basic techniques and technologies associated with computer security, along with a list of recommended books and Web sites for the reader who wants to explore the topic in more detail.

In the aftermath of September 11th, though, what's most important to understand—for IT professionals, corporate executives, government leaders, and ordinary citizens—is the paradigm shift that has slowly emerged during the past decade, and that is likely to accelerate in the years to come. This is more than an abstract, academic issue: The problem is that many, *many* companies and government agencies are still pursuing security strategies as if we were back in the mainframe era of 1975. Not only that, we're now living in a world with literally millions of powerful personal computers with high-speed, "always-on" cable/DSL connections to the Internet, owned and operated by technologically naïve consumers; as we'll discuss later in the Techniques and Technologies section, this creates a dimension of computer security that simply didn't exist as recently as the mid-1990s.

---

4. See "Chemical exchanges put security under microscope," by Michael Meehan, *Computerworld*, Sept. 28, 2001.

Techniques and Technologies_____

While a full discussion of the techniques, strategies and technologies of computer-related security would fill several volumes, there are five key areas that are likely to be the primary focus of attention in the coming years:

- identification of users of a system
- authorization and access control
- protection of data in transit
- audits of activities and accesses to information
- monitoring of potential intruders

Identification of users

A wonderful cartoon in the July 5, 1993 issue of the *New Yorker* shows two dogs sitting in front of a computer terminal, with the "alpha" dog explaining to the "beta" dog, "On the Internet, no one knows you're a dog." Over the years, we've gradually learned just how universal that statement is: In all too many cases, nobody knows whether a message on the Internet is coming from a man or a woman; a teenager or an octogenarian; a priest or a child molester; a police officer or a terrorist. Indeed, the recent spate of computer viruses has illustrated that we don't even know whether the message is coming from a human or a computer.[5]

Thus, all of the details about access to computer hardware, networks, programs, and data must begin by asking *who* (or what) is attempting to make that access. During the past decade, a related issue has become increasingly impor-

---

5. If we have the opportunity for open-ended, unconstrained interactions with the "entity" at the other end of an Internet connection, some individuals may not be able to determine whether it's human or machine. I'm not trying to promote the optimistic visions of artificial intelligence with such a statement, but merely pointing out that it's not too terribly difficult for a cleverly-written computer program to fool the average, unsuspecting human. MIT Professor Joseph Weizenbaum illustrated this in the mid-1960s with his "Eliza" program, and it remains impressive even today (indeed, there is a free, Web-based version available at www-ai.ijs.si/eliza/eliza.html). This is a relevant issue for computer security professionals who worry that their computers might be "tricked" into granting access to sensitive information.

tant, as we use the Internet for e-commerce and banking transactions; for mortgages, contracts, and legal documents; and for any other situation where "denial" or "repudiation" is relevant. If a person (or computer) is identified as a user or participant in a computer-related activity, we would like it to be a "non-deniable" identification—to avoid the unpleasant experience of getting an irate phone call (or personal visit, or even an email) from someone who says, "I don't know who you sold that $100,000 Rolls Royce to, but it wasn't me! Someone must have been impersonating me— it wasn't me who sent you that purchase order, and I've never seen the Rolls Royce that you claim to have shipped to me!"[6]

For the past several decades, the vast majority of computer systems have identified would-be users by asking their name, account number, email address or equivalent "user-id," which is then authenticated by asking the would-be user for a password. The weaknesses and potential misuses of such an approach have existed since computers were first built, and they will continue to exist as long as computer users are busy, bored, sloppy, untrained, and/or unconvinced that security is worth the time and effort required. And it should be emphasized that hacker/criminal/terrorists are extremely familiar with these weaknesses; they exploit the weaknesses in order to gain access to information that would otherwise be protected.[7]

---

6. Of course, problems like this occurred long before e-commerce became popular. Someone who discovers that his or her credit card or cell-phone has been stolen and used fraudulently must go through a process of persuading the authorities that it really *was* someone else who incurred the fraudulent charges.

7. Most IT professionals are also aware of the many weaknesses of the standard user-id/password approach, but a few examples may be helpful for the computer novice. It's common for users to select a user-id consisting of their first name, or their last name, or the concatenation of their last name and the first letter of their first name (e.g., "eyourdon" or "e.yourdon" or "yourdone" or "yourdon.e". Passwords chosen by a typical bored/busy/naïve user consist of the same characters as their user-id (for simplicity), or such things as their spouse's name, their children's name, their birthday, their dog's name, or their favorite four-letter curseword. To make matters worse, they write the user-id and password in large letters and tape them to the side of their computer terminal.

To the extent that we wish to increase the overall level of security of our computer systems, we will have to increase the effectiveness and credibility of the user-identification process. Indeed, drastic improvements could be made by simply enforcing *current* identification policies more rigorously (e.g., choosing non-obvious passwords, changing passwords frequently, etc.), but even in the best of cases, the old-fashioned approach is too vulnerable. While many alternative strategies are possible, it appears more and more likely to that *biometric* identification—i.e., systems that use fingerprint, voice-print, retinal scan,[8] or some other biological identification—will become the norm.

Authorization and access control

Once we know who (or what) has accessed a computer system, the next question is what that user will be allowed to do. While the details will vary considerably from one computer system to another, the authorization process usually involves such things as:

- What networks and/or servers is this person allowed to access?

- What programs are the user allowed to use, operate, or execute? Certain commands and functions within a program might be authorized, while others might be forbidden—e.g., a particular individual may be allowed to enter new orders, but not to delete orders.

- What data is the user allowed to access, and in what manner? Certain databases, files, records, or even fields within a record (e.g., an employee's salary) might be accessible, while others might not be. And the authorized access might consist of permission to read, write, delete, and/or append data.

- During what time periods is the user allowed access to the various components of hardware and software in the system? Some users might be granted access 24

---

8. For an example of technology that was already being developed in 1997, see "Eye-Dentification—Mission Impossible Depicts Hollywood-Style High Security—The Eye Scan," by Johanna Powell, *INFO-sec.com*, Sept. 27, 1997.

hours a day, 7 days a week; others might only be allowed to access the system during normal business hours.

- From what location, and from which "accessing device" is the user allowed to access the system? Some users might be allowed to "log in" from any computer terminal, anywhere in the world; others might be restricted to using a particular terminal/PC, from within a particular physical location.

All of these criteria sound obvious and straightforward; but the devil is in the details. And the details change from day to day, as technology changes, as security weaknesses and flaws in existing arrangements are discovered, as employees and personal relationships change, as business alliances and international treaties change, and so forth. A set of policies and procedures for authorization and access control might remain relatively stable within a small corporate environment; but for large multinational organizations, everything is in a state of flux all of the time.[9]

Protection of data in transit across "exposed" areas

In the good old days, an organization performed all of its computing activities on a single mainframe that was locked

---

9. You can read the glossy corporate brochures for a large *Fortune* 500 company (or simply visit their Web site and download it as a PDF file), and see the impressive numbers about how many thousands of employees they have in how many dozens of countries. But consider this as well: It's not unusual for the large organizations to have upwards of 100,000 PCs and 10,000 servers scattered across hundreds of offices in different geographical locations. While the systems administrators and IT managers might yearn for the day when every single employee has exactly the same configuration of hardware and software programs on his or her desk, the more common situation is a Tower of Babel: hundreds of variations on half a dozen different Windows operating systems (at least one Luddite is still running Windows 3.1, a few are running Windows 95, most are running Windows 95, 98, or Me, some are running Windows 2000 or Windows NT, and a few brave souls are running Windows XP); dozens of different variations on "office" software (word-processors, spreadsheets, etc.); and thousands of mysterious programs that inquisitive users have downloaded from the Internet because they look "cool."

within a heavily-protected building. If data had to be transported to or from the mainframe, it was stored on large reels of magnetic tape—which could be physically carried from place to place, under heavy guard. Unfortunately (for security professionals), those days have disappeared, along with the Hula Hoop and the Pet Rock; now we live in a world where vast amounts of data are transmitted from one (potentially secure) place to another (potentially secure) place, across large regions of open, unprotected, potentially hostile space. As the data moves from A to B, there is a risk that it may be blocked, deleted, intercepted, or subtly altered; all of these possibilities are obviously of concern to security professionals

Again, there are many strategies for coping with this problem—including the relatively new strategy of *steganography*, in which messages are encoded within the digital bits-and-bytes of graphic images, musical files, and other "concealing" data. But the primary technology used here is encryption: encoding of messages so that it will be unintelligible to anyone other than a person with the "key" required to decrypt the message into its original form. The world of encryption has changed dramatically in the past decade, with the introduction of so-called "public-key" mechanisms, but the viability of an encryption strategy still boils down to computer "horsepower": Unless I make some stupid mistakes, it's now easy to acquire a standard PC with enough computing power to encrypt my message so thoroughly that it will take years, if not centuries, for someone else to decrypt—even if they have a far more powerful computer.[10]

"Stupid mistakes" will continue to be a key element in the ongoing contest between those who encrypt their messages, and those who attempt to decrypt them. If I choose an encryption key that's very long but non-random—such as the first 20 digits of pi—it's only a matter of time before a persistent code-breaker will figure it out. If I leave the encryption key stored in my laptop or desktop computer, then (assuming that we don't have additional biometric protection mechanisms attached to the computer), it merely requires the code-breaker to access my computer when I'm not around.[11] If I write the password on a piece of paper and tape it to the side of my computer, I've made things even simpler for those who are determined to decrypt my messages.

Audit of activities and accesses to information

How does a company know that its accountants and book-keepers aren't skimming money from the corporate reve-nues, and then "cooking the books" to hide their theft? The starting point, as discussed above, is *identification*: Hire known people, and conduct a background check to ensure that they really are who they say they are, and that they don't have a criminal record. And then give them the finan-cial equivalent of passwords, and devise a financial system of checks-and-balances so that unauthorized financial trans-actions will be prevented.

All of this tends to reduce the likelihood of embezzle-ment and theft, but it doesn't eliminate it altogether. Thus,

---

10. Generally speaking, the longer the "key" (roughly equivalent to a pass-word) used to encrypt a message, the more thorough and unbreakable that encryption is. Throughout the mid-1990s, most commercial encryption products used a 40-bit key—i.e., 40 binary digits long. That's sufficient to keep casual observers and amateur criminals from decrypting your messages, but it won't take long for a dedicated, knowledgeable hacker (not to mention a government organization like the National Security Agency) to overwhelm it. Many of the e-com-merce systems in the early 2000s are using a 128-bit key for their encryption; that's sufficient to discourage even a moderately competent hacker, but it will merely slow down the efforts of the dedicated hack-ers and government officials who have obviously acquired far more powerful code-breaking computers than they had in the mid-90s. Meanwhile, though, publicly-available encryption packages like PGP allow the most casual end-user to create encryption keys of 1,024 bits, or 2,048 bits, or even 4,096 bits—which, for all practical purposes, are utterly unbreakable. (Unless, of course, new technologies such as "quantum computing" produce a way to factor large numbers rapidly, as indicated in "An Introduction to Quantum Computing and its Con-sequences for Cryptography," by Peter Fordham and Stephen Perrott, *ISE 2*, June 2000, in which case we will need new encryption methods).
11. As mentioned in Chapter 2, the FBI has developed a technology known as "Magic Lantern," which makes it possible (either through a hard-ware device surreptitiously attached to one's computer, or through a software virus injected into the computer) to capture the user's key-strokes as he or she types a password into an encryption program.

the next stage of protection, universally employed by pub-licly-traded companies, is an *audit* of the financial records, carried out by someone other than the people who actually perform the day-to-day financial transactions. As we know from the occasional scandals reported in the newspapers, audits are not entirely foolproof either—but they substan-tially reduce the risk of embezzlement and theft, partly because they remind the accountants and bookkeepers (and all the other employees as well) that someone is watching.

The same concept holds true with most aspects of com-puter security. A properly designed computer system will keep a record (variously known as a "log" or an "audit trail") of the relevant activities and transactions performed by the users of that system—including the action of logging in and logging out; reading, writing, deleting, and append-ing to records and files in the database; sending and receiv-ing of email messages; and accesses to both internal and external Web sites.[12] Alas, not all systems *are* properly designed; thus, one often finds systems in which only a sub-set of the users' activities is logged for possible analysis and auditing; and once such a system is developed and put into operation, it may not be easy to retro-fit it with appropriate logging mechanisms.

There is a conflict between security and privacy through-out almost every topic discussed in this chapter; but it is particularly evident in the area of logs and audit trails. As a privacy-minded citizen, for example, I may object to the very notion that I'm required to identify myself when I use a "public-access" computer system—such as an information retrieval system at a public library. But it's only relevant if my identity, and my subsequent activities on the system, are logged; it's at that point that I begin worrying that some bureaucrat will begin looking at the selection of newspaper

---

12. For just this reason, one of the common strategies of a hacker is to cir-cumvent or alter the log itself, so that a subsequent review will not show any unauthorized or suspicious activity. Some computer systems, for example, are designed to allow a "super-user" (sometimes known as "root") to override most, if not all, of the password and authoriza-tion controls that are imposed on all other users; and in the extreme case, the super-user has the ability to disable the log, so that he effec-tively becomes a "ghost" on the computer.

and magazine articles I've chosen to read on that system. Another familiar example of this conflict is the use of "cookies" on one's Web browser; I can appreciate the need for the *New York Times* to force me to identify myself as a subscriber before it displays any articles on my Web browser, but I don't want it to keep track of the navigation path that I follow from one article to the next.

As we suggested in Chapter 2, the likely consequence of the September 11th terrorist incidents is that privacy will be diminished even more aggressively by government and corporate policy-makers who argue that the need for security outweighs the right to privacy. Thus, we're likely to see *more* logging and monitoring of the activities of users on computer systems of all kinds. And that raises an interesting question: What do we do with all of the data thus accumulated?

To return to the financial metaphor for a moment, it's worth noting that most companies only conduct *partial* audits of their accounting and bookkeeping activities. Criteria are established for monitoring "critical" accounts and transactions (e.g., all checks greater than a million dollars, all purchases and sales of the company's stock by its officers and directors); and everything else is subjected to a "random sampling" to ensure that things are in order. Anything beyond that is impractical—for the time, effort, and cost of conducting a *full* audit would be monumental.

Similarly, imagine that the computer security group at XYZ company maintains a log of all email messages and all Web-site visits associated with all 10,000 of its employees. One can imagine some of the criteria that might be used for selective examination of the massive amount of data that would be collected: email traffic of selected employees might be monitored closely (thus creating another conflict between privacy and security), visits to pornographic Web sites might be monitored, etc. But beyond that, the analysis of the audit-trail data would almost certainly be done on a random-sampling basis, given the limited resources of the security group.

Inevitably, this will lead to greater emphasis on spotting *patterns* of behavior and activity, in order to spot security threats either after they have occurred or (ideally) before they have occurred. Is it significant, for example, that an employee received an email message from his stockbroker on Monday, and then sold a thousand shares of the company's stock the next day? Is it significant that four different employees in the company's marketing department visited the same page of a competitor's Web site on the same day, and then bought a thousand shares of the competitor's stock?

In many ways, this kind of analysis is similar to the "trend analysis" and pattern-matching efforts that companies are constantly performing with their products and customers. Amazon.com, for example, probably has a pretty good idea whether people who like Tom Clancy novels are likely to enjoy John Grisham's novels; and even more important, they're likely to know whether a particular individual—you or I or any one of its millions of individual customers—has such a preference. Perhaps you do, and perhaps I don't; in that case, Amazon will send you an email about John Grisham's latest work when you buy a Clancy novel, and they'll spare me.

One of the likely results of the effort to coordinate various government-agency databases and intelligence efforts will be to perform just this kind of trend analysis. And it's likely that we'll see greater efforts to combine public-sector/private-sector trend analysis efforts, as well as efforts entirely within the private sector to increase the effectiveness of their security by conducting more thorough trend analyses.

Monitoring of suspected security threats

A traditional strategy for law-enforcement officers and security professionals is to monitor the activities of individuals or groups who are either known to be, or suspected to be, future security threats. This obviously overlaps the "analysis" activity described immediately above, but it's slightly different. In the corporate finance metaphor, for example, some individuals and transactions and accounts are monitored simply because they are "sensitive," *not* because anyone has an overt suspicion that something improper is going on. But we also monitor transactions and accounts that would otherwise be considered innocuous and uninteresting *if* they are associated with an individual whom we know to be, or suspect to be, intent upon doing something improper.

Obviously, this is another area where security creates a conflict—not just with the notion of privacy, but with the even more fundamental notion of civil liberties. That conflict is likely to be a major one for politicians, lawmakers, and philosophers in the coming years; and computer technology will play a significant role in that conflict. For example, a trivial form of "profiling" can be carried out without computers: Law enforcement officers may suspect that someone of a particular race, nationality, or religious background is more likely to be a security threat than others. But what if—to conjure up a hypothetical example—the FBI publishes a demographic profile indicating that 95% of all terrorists have a college degree in one of three fields, *and* carry between three and five credit cards, *and* were born in either April or August, *and* were born in one of nine countries around the world? Identifying and locating such suspects, among all college students in the country or among all tourists coming into the country or among all citizens in the country, could only be done with computers.

Another familiar strategy for monitoring (and ultimately apprehending) "suspicious" individuals is based on entrapment. We're all familiar with this in the traditional law-enforcement field: A suspected criminal is enticed into buying illegal drugs, or offering a bribe to a government official, while law-enforcement officers secretly record the event. Interestingly, a variation on this concept is beginning to be used in the computer security field, by creating a Web site, file server, or other computer resource known as a "honey pot" to entice hackers to break into it.[13] Military and government agencies have been creating honey pots for the past few years; in the future, we're likely to see more and

---

13. See *Know Your Enemy: Revealing the Security Tools, Tactics, and Motives of the Blackhat Community*, by the Honeynet Project (Addison-Wesley, 2002).

more private-sector security departments doing the same thing.

Paradigm Shift

IT systems are part of the "critical infrastructure"

As we discussed in Chapter 2, one of the sobering realities today is that IT systems and networks are part of the nation's "critical infrastructure"—and as such, require a much more thorough and robust form of security than was typically expected in the 1970s or 1980s. The scope and pervasiveness of today's computer systems are breath-taking: They control the so-called "iron triangle" of telecommunications, banking, and electrical power without which the nation would come to a screeching halt. They control the nation's air-traffic system and the vast network of trains and railroad tracks; and they are a vital part of the day-to-day functioning of schools, corporations, government agencies, water and sewage systems, and highway traffic-control systems.

It did not take the attacks of September 11th to reveal the role that computers play in our national infrastructure; that awareness gradually took shape during the mid-1990s, and accelerated significantly during planning and implementation of Y2K repairs in the late 1990s. Government and military planners may have felt that they knew, all along, how important the nation's computer systems were; but it was an "intellectual" understanding, as opposed to the *visceral* understanding that came from "what-if" simulation exercises conducted in the months preceding January 1, 2000. Meanwhile, many corporations—including the very largest—were shocked by the sudden awareness, during their Y2K activities, of just how vulnerable they really were to the loss of electrical utilities, or a serious disruption in the nation's computer-controlled banking and telecommunication systems. And that shock was translated into action in most of the large organizations: Infrastructure suppliers were scrutinized to ensure that they really would be finished with their Y2K repairs in time, redundant suppliers were found for some of the most critical infrastructure services, and contingency plans were developed for coping with disruptions in those services.

When September 11th arrived, all of those plans for coping with possible infrastructure disruptions were already becoming a half-forgotten memory; and because no serious infrastructure disruptions did materialize on January 1, 2000, many corporate executives wondered if perhaps their fears had been exaggerated. But for better or worse, the plans *were* made, the redundant backups were established, and the unprepared infrastructure providers were replaced. Thus, it's probably fair to say that a serious terrorist-related disruption of the nation's critical infrastructure would be handled much more effectively today than would have been the case during the first half of the 1990s.

So why talk about it? Because one of the less-recognized aspects of the Y2K problem was that roughly one-third of the nation's small businesses and government agencies (i.e., agencies operating at the town and county level) made no preparations at all for potential problems; another one-third began making various plans and preparations, but never finished them. Interestingly, some of these small organizations *did* suffer moderate-to-severe Y2K problems in the days and weeks following January 1, 2000: Their computer systems stopped working altogether, or generated incorrect results, corrupted vital databases, etc. But there was very little awareness of this in the media; and meanwhile, the national infrastructure continued to operate with only minor hiccups. Thus, even though the Ma-And-Pa Bakery might have lost all of its computer files, and even though the Podunk school district couldn't issue paychecks for its teachers, and even though the Gruntville medical center found that all of its patient records had been corrupted, *the lights stayed on, and the phones worked.*

So, all of the small organizations that failed to make any contingency plans for coping with disruptions in electrical power, banking services, and telecommunications were no worse off for their lack of preparations. Those who waited for the Millennium Eve rollover with some trepidation may have wondered, just like their big-company colleagues, whether their fears had been exaggerated; and those who *deliberately* avoided making any preparations may well have uttered a smug, "I told you nothing would happen!" to anyone who would listen.

Y2K was not about terrorist attacks;[14] it was about coping with a quirk associated with the representation and manipulation of dates within computer systems. But while Y2K has come and gone,[15] other threats still remain. Hurricanes, floods, earthquakes, and other natural disasters are still with us. And, as we were reminded so forcefully on September 11th, terrorism is likely to be with us for several years to come.

For all practical purposes, everyone in the United States had access to electricity, telephones, banking (including ATM machines), air-travel, and other familiar components of the nation's critical infrastructure long before September 11th, and long before the nation's Y2K repairs began in the latter half of the 1990s. But there are at least two new components of the infrastructure that have emerged in the latter half of the 1990s and early 2000s: cell phones and pervasive use of the Internet. Though per-capita usage of cell phones in the U.S. still doesn't match that of Europe and parts of Asia, there were approximately 30 million units in use by 2001. And while there may not have been universal agreement that cell phones were a *critical* component of the nation's infrastructure prior to September 11th, there would be far less of an argument today.

Meanwhile, roughly half of the nation's households have Internet access; and an ever-increasing percentage of the

14. As noted in Chapter 2, large corporations and government agencies did worry that terrorists might synchronize their attacks with the rollover, in order to exploit the presence of large crowds of revelers, and also to exploit whatever disruptions might have occurred because of computer failures. While there were a few sporadic attacks on oil pipelines by disgruntled individuals, and while some full-scale terrorist attacks were thwarted in the waning days of December 1999 by government agencies, the public's perception was that the Y2K rollover phenomenon came and went *without* the presence of terrorists.

nation's businesses and government agencies are utterly dependent on the Internet for their day-to-day business—not only for e-commerce transactions with their customers and suppliers, but also for email communication with their own employees. As a result, the Internet poses an inviting target for terrorists attempting to disrupt activities across the entire country.[16] Particularly for large businesses, a very effective form of Internet disruption is a "denial of service" (DoS) attack that prevents anyone from accessing the company's Web site, email servers, and other Internet access points.[17]

Thus, the paradigm shift, for which some large organizations and most small organizations are not prepared, is that computer systems, networks, and databases are part of the nation's critical infrastructure—which was arguably *not* the case a decade ago. And most technology experts warn that the phenomenon will continue for the foreseeable future—as the nation becomes increasingly "wired," increasingly automated, and increasingly dependent on highly reliable computer systems. For example, individuals and organizations are now augmenting their email and cell-phone communications with instant messaging (IM), such as AOL's Instant Messenger service; while it's currently used prima-

15. Actually, Y2K has *not* "gone," though the lingering manifestations of the date-related rollover problem probably won't get any national attention in the years to come. While the vast majority of computers using Western-based calendars experienced a rollover from 1999 to 2000 on the same day, various other rollovers will be occurring in 2038 (for Unix-based computer systems), 2046 (for Tandem computers, if they're still running at that point), etc. Far more significant is the fact that many companies "fixed" their computer systems by re-programming them to interpret a two-digit "year" field as a 100-year "window" that straddles part of the 20th century and part of the 21st century. Thus, company X may have programmed its computers to interpret the two-digit year field as a year between 1910 and 2009; company Y may have chose a window of 1920-2019, and company Z may have chosen 1950-2049. When those computers move beyond their window—e.g., when company X's computers attempt to cope with the date of January 1, 2010—they'll experience the same kind of problems that *everyone* worried about on January 1, 2000. But it will only be company X's problem, and if it thoroughly disrupts X's computer systems, the rest of the country presumably won't care.

16. See "Securing the Lines of a Wired Nation," by John Schwartz, *New York Times*, Oct. 4, 2001.

rily for social chit-chat among a relatively small percentage of the population, there is every reason to believe that it will eventually permeate most of society (at least most of the people who have cell phones, Internet connections, pagers, and/or wireless Personal Digital Assistants [PDAs]).[18] And while social chit-chat may continue to be the primary usage of IM, many of those involved in the September 11th attack will vouch for its value in times of crisis, too.

The other part of the paradigm shift is that the attacks on the computer-related components of the nation's infrastructure have changed from infrequent and amateurish, to frequent and persistent and increasingly malevolent. And most security experts warn that this trend will continue, for several reasons:

- The Internet is a vast, mostly-open, hodge-podge of computers and routers and "root servers"[19] and communication lines that are riddled with vulnerabilities—which the hacker community can exploit more quickly than security experts can repair. For example, an anti-virus software company called Sophos reported in late November 2001 that the Nimda worm was the most extensive virus to be seen during the entire year—and yet it was only introduced in Sep-

---

17. In simple terms, a DoS attack involves flooding a victim's computer system with thousands, if not millions, of spurious messages—thus making it impossible for anyone else's message to get through. By analogy, imagine that a company had only one phone number that could be called to place an order, make a payment, lodge a complaint, or talk to the company's employees. If you could arrange for 10,000 of your closest friends to call the company's phone number repeatedly, around the clock, then it would be constantly busy—and nobody else would be able to get through. Computers don't need an army of humans to generate the equivalent of 10,000 phone calls; but as we'll discuss later in this section, clever hackers could conceivably co-opt the home computers of 10,000 naïve individuals into generating massive numbers of spurious messages. See "CERT/CC: Internet infrastructure targeted for DoS attacks," by Sam Costello, *Infoworld*, Oct. 24, 2001 and "Hack Attacks Become Deadlier: Is There a Defense?", by Tim McDonald, *NewsFactor Network*, Nov. 28, 2001 for more details.

18. Unfortunately, hackers like IM too, for it can often be used to propagate messages even more quickly than by email. See "Instant Messaging: hackers like it too," by Peter Henderson, *Total Telecom*, Nov. 29, 2001.

tember 2001.[20] And lest you think that we're facing a
mere two or three well-publicized viruses, Sophos has
a database of some 70,000 known viruses and worms,
of which 11,600 were detected in 2001.

- Hackers use the Internet itself to communicate with
one another, and to post popular hacking tools for one
another to share.

- New technologies are constantly being introduced and
grafted onto the Internet. Again, hackers are usually
able to find ways to exploit security weaknesses in the
newly-introduced technologies faster than the security
experts can figure out what the vulnerabilities are, and
how to eliminate them. Wireless devices and instant-
messaging are good examples of this phenomenon,
and it is almost certain to continue.[21]

19. The Internet standards group, ICANN (an abbreviation for Internet
Corporation for Assigned Names and Numbers), warned in mid-
November that the Internet was susceptible to terrorist/hacker attacks
via the 13 "root servers" that translate mnemonic Internet addresses
(such as www.yourdon.com) into numeric computer "IP addresses".
ICANN also warned that 10 central computers that hold top-level
domain registrations (e.g., a list of all the Web sites that end in ".com"
or ".edu" or ".gov") could be attacked. See "ICANN forum warns of
Web vulnerability," by Vern Kopytoff, *San Francisco Chronicle*, Nov. 17,
2001.

20. See "Deadly Viruses Set to Grow," *BBC News*, Nov. 28, 2001. A good
example of this can be seen in Congress' recent activities. In early
November 2001, House Science Committee Chairman Sherwood Boeh-
lert announced that his committee was planning to introduce a cyber-
security bill intended to shore up the known vulnerabilities in the Internet (see "Cyber-Security Bill Planned by House Committee," by Robert
MacMillan, *Newsbytes*, Oct. 31, 2001 for more details). But by the time
such a bill is drafted, debated, approved, funded, and implemented,
months (if not longer) will have gone by. Hackers won't wait that long.
And this assumes that Congress and the Federal bureaucracy actually
do act at all; after all, security experts have been publicly bemoaning the
vulnerability of the Internet for years, and very little substantive
progress has been made to cope with those vulnerabilities. September
11th was obviously a serious "wake up call" for the government
bureaucracy, but there is always the danger that an extended period of
relative peace and quiet may encourage the bureaucrats to fall fast
asleep once again.

Threats exist from various levels of players

In the good old days, computer security personnel typically expected the "bad guys" to fall into a relatively small number of categories, all of whom were technologically sophisticated. Some were thieves, some were corporate spies, some were "geeks" who considered it an intellectual challenge to outsmart the firewalls, passwords, and encrypted files they encountered. The military services had their community of "players," too: government spies from the KGB, computer geeks attempting to disassemble and reverse-engineer American computer systems. And by the early 1990s, as the military began refining its own concepts of "information warfare" for use in the Gulf War and other campaigns, it became evident that hostile nations might have entire armies of computer programmers, whose sole purpose was to probe and attack and exploit not only U.S. military computer systems, but the entire "critical infrastructure" of the country.

All of these players remain active in today's security battles. But there is another paradigm shift underway, involving the activities of three new groups of players:

- technologically naïve end-users
- Script kiddies
- Stateless terrorists

The technologically naïve end-users sometimes fall into the category of "disgruntled insider" who decides to steal money, delete files, or wreak some form of havoc. If you're a payroll clerk at XYZ Corp., you don't have to know very much about computer technology in order to enter payroll transactions into a system; the same is true for airline reservation clerks, customer service personnel, and a thousand other categories of administrative personnel who spend the entire day typing mundane transactions into a computer system. If they have a user-id and a password, they may have the ability to give someone a raise, or a free airline

---

21. See "Motion Sickness," by Nancy Gohring, *Interactive Week*, Oct. 29, 2001.

ticket, or three years of free maintenance on a newly-purchased automobile. But this has been a problem since the days of the first mainframe computer systems, and security professionals have devised various strategies for minimizing such attacks.[22]

But what's new is the technologically naïve end-user who has no evil intentions of his own, but who inadvertently and unknowingly allows his computer to be infected and—in the worst case—turned into a "zombie" that can participate in massive DoS attacks on other computers. Most of the day-to-day work carried out by administrative workers could still be performed with the first generation of PCs that we gave them 20 years ago; but for various reasons, we've now given them machines with more computing capacity than the entire MIT campus had when I was a student. We've then connected their computers to every other computer in the corporate environment; and we then connected them to the Internet, with high-speed connections that allow them to upload and download vast quantities of information in a matter of seconds. And because these technological naifs are using only a small percentage of the computing resources at their disposal, and since they typically have no idea what's going on "under the hood," they may be completely unaware that *while they are doing their work*, their computer is *also* being used by a remote hacker to wreak havoc.

A specific form of this problem is now apparent to millions of befuddled end-users, as a result of the rash of viruses and worms that have propagated across the Internet during the past year. Beginning with the LoveBug virus, and continuing on with such fanciful names as AnnaKournikova, CodeRed, Sircam, Nimda, BadTrans, and others, these viruses (often developed by script kiddies, whose antics we'll describe in more detail in a moment) infect the victim's machine through some relatively innocent action (after all, who wouldn't want to gaze lovingly at a digital picture of tennis star Anna Kournikova?); they then send copies of

---

22. See "Users are the weakest link, security experts warn," by Dan Verton, *Computerworld*, Nov. 15, 2001.

themselves to everyone they can find in the victim's email address books—and *then* they start deleting files and making the victim's computer more-or-less unusable.

In theory, companies and government agencies could minimize, if not eliminate, this problem by unplugging their users from the Internet, administering firewalls and security patches more vigorously, and informing end-users that they will be *instantly* fired if they cause the corporate computing environment to be infected because of a virus on their machine. And some large corporations have done exactly that, with a "zero-tolerance" attitude toward security infractions that even goes so far as to charge the negligent user for the cost of repairing any computer damages associated with his viruses.

Small companies, as we suggested earlier, are not so diligent about such matters; nor are they as technologically proficient. And no matter how bad the small-company environment might be, from a security perspective, it pales in comparison to the *home* environment, where powerful PCs are being operated by well-intentioned consumers who can barely find the power-on switch for their computer. To some extent, this has been a problem ever since the first Radio Shack and Apple II computers invaded the household. But for a long time, there weren't very many such computers; and for a long time, they weren't connected to the Internet, except by occasional dial-up connections to download email.

Today, half of America's households are equipped with computers; and these are not the wimpy, old-fashioned Apple IIs of the 1970s. For under a thousand dollars, a middle-class family can acquire a machine whose speed, power, and storage capacity would have made the most techno-savvy geek drool with envy a decade ago. Thus, like the modern office worker, the typical Homer Simpson is likely to be using only a tiny fraction of the computer's full capabilities—and may be blissfully unaware that his computer is simultaneously being controlled and manipulated by a hacker in Beijing, Moscow, Boston, or Silicon Valley.

Why would a hacker bother taking over, controlling, and manipulating the average home-user's computer? In a few rare cases, a home user might have some information worth stealing—e.g., credit-card numbers, or some confidential work-related material. But an increasingly common strategy is for the hacker to inject an autonomous virus into the victim's computer, which (a) replicates itself and spreads to anyone it can find in the victim's email address book, in the same fashion as CodeRed, etc.; and (b) unleashes a DoS attack on a pre-specified computer system. It might be the hacker's former employer, or the IRS, or eBay, AOL, or any other corporate/government "symbol" towards which the hacker feels ill-disposed. Such an attack from one computer would be a tolerable nuisance for such a large company; but if the hacker can create a "zombie army" of several hundred home-computers, each operating on a high-speed cable-modem Internet connection, it can be a devastating attack.[23]

More and more often, the people who initiate such attacks are not the old-fashioned high-tech hackers, but a new and younger breed of individuals who have come to be known as "script kiddies." Mostly high-school and college-age students, the script kiddies have learned enough about computers to be dangerous; in particular, they have learned where to find pre-written viruses, programs, and "scripts" (another form of computer program) that can be downloaded onto their own computer, modified and customized, and then unleashed. The romanticized version of a script kiddy was Matthew Broderick's character in the 1983 movie *War Games*; but in reality, the script kiddies exhibit personality traits that show up in every generation of teenagers: bored, sullen, rebellious, hostile, and looking for a cheap thrill. But instead of spraying graffiti on public buildings, or indulging in minor vandalism or shoplifting, the script kiddies use the powerful home computers their indulgent parents bought them, and surf the Internet looking for opportunities to create viruses and hack into computers.

---

23. See the Gibson Research Web site (www.grc.com) for a detailed and chilling report on one such attack, as well as some excellent advice on how to reduce the chances of such an attack.

It's important to realize that the script kiddies are *not* members of an organized, focused group; while they may collaborate in small groups, and communicate with a handful of other script kiddies on the Internet, they essentially work alone. And they can be found almost anywhere in the world where there are accessible computers and access to the Internet. There may be a preponderance of such individuals in America and Western Europe; but they also exist in Russia, China, Australia, Japan, Pakistan, India, Indonesia, South Africa, Brazil, and dozens of other countries. From what little we've learned of the Al Qaeda terrorist group, it appears to be highly focused and organized, in cells located in roughly 60 countries around the world; by contrast, the script kiddies are *not* an army of jihad warriors, but rather a motley collection of "rebels without a cause." Obviously, this makes it all the more difficult for law enforcement officers to track down and stop them.[24]

Finally, there is a third group of hackers which has joined the original ranks: the stateless terrorists who believe that cyber-warfare can be as effective a form of terrorism as blowing up buildings. Obviously, we've heard a great deal about groups like Al Qaeda in the aftermath of September 11th; but there are dozens of other terrorist groups in the Middle East, northern Ireland, Pakistan, Japan, and other parts of the world. Because they do not constitute traditional nation-states, we can't bomb them into oblivion and make them surrender in the traditional sense; at the same time, we can't ignore them the way we might ignore a lone hacker, because they do represent an organized, disciplined "force." Interestingly, some of these groups illustrate the

---

24. As an example, a Dutch court sentenced the originator of the Anna Kournikova virus, 21-year-old Jan de Wit, to 150 hours of community service (or 75 days in jail if he chooses not to perform the service). See "Kournikova worm maker sentenced to community service," by Joris Evers, *Computerworld*, Sept. 27, 2001. During the trial, De Wit claimed that he didn't know what he was doing when he created the virus, and didn't realize the consequences of posting it to an Internet newsgroup. But the court noted that De Wit worked in a computer store, and had collected some 7,200 viruses, which he kept on a CD. In the verdict, the court noted that the CD would not be returned to the hacker; but he could probably recreate it from scratch within a matter of days, if he was stubborn enough.

kind of "emergent" behavior that we'll discuss in Chapter 5: instead of following a rigid, top-down hierarchical management approach, they have individuals and small groups (or cells) whose strategies and behaviors can adapt, on an ad hoc basis, to local circumstances. And one of the consequences of such a structure is that eliminating the top leader is unlikely to cause the rest of the organization to stop functioning.[25]

Operational security vs. software development security

The familiar paradigm of computer security assumes that computer systems are developed by "insiders" who are considered trustworthy and benevolent; and attacks are perpetrated by "outsiders" whose skills may vary, but whose intentions are presumed to be bad. Thus, most security strategies consist of enlisting the aid of various insiders to help build protective mechanisms to keep the outsiders out.

But the reality is that, ever since the earliest days of the computer industry, a large percentage of unauthorized attacks and intrusions into computer systems are perpetrated by, or at least assisted by, "insiders"—e.g., computer operators, programmers, systems administrators, and other technologically literate individuals who have day-to-day access to access codes, user-ids, passwords, and other critical information. That continues to be true today; as a result, many government agencies have begun carefully reviewing the security clearances and background investigations of their programmers and high-tech employees. While all of this sounds like "déjà vu all over again," the situation has been complicated by the influx of large numbers of foreign computer personnel throughout the 1990s, from India, Pakistan, Russia, China, and many other countries around the world.

---

25. Of course, one could make a similar argument about the United States: If the President is eliminated or incapacitated, his role is then taken over by the Vice President, followed by the Speaker of the House, and so forth. But what if all of Washington, including the Pentagon, was eliminated instantaneously, before its inhabitants could scurry off into their bomb shelters?

But there is a more subtle paradigm shift that is beginning to concern security experts in the critical-infrastructure organizations (i.e., the banks, airlines, telephone companies, electric-power companies, etc.) and government agencies: a shift from concerns about *operational* vulnerability to a more all-inclusive concern that includes *developmental* vulnerability. Traditionally, it has been assumed that computer systems are designed and developed in a "safe" way, and that when placed in operational status, they carry out the functionality they were programmed to carry out—nothing more and nothing less.[26] The security problems were assumed to be external attacks upon a properly functioning system—or, in rare cases, an attack perpetrated by, or enabled by, an "insider."

Of course, there were always exceptions to this simplistic scenario. A disgruntled programmer could introduce "rogue code" to transfer funds from dormant bank accounts into his own, or print embarrassing messages on the monthly invoices sent to customers, or display nasty messages on the CEO's computer monitor. There have been numerous apocryphal stories of programmers who have been fired, or disappointed with their annual salary review, and who have programmed "time-bombs" into the computer system for which they were responsible; at least a few of these stories are true, and they usually result in a moderate amount of chaos and mayhem when the software time-bomb goes off.

But events like these have typically been perpetrated by individuals or small groups; and they are usually motivated by relatively straightforward emotions of greed or revenge. Even more important, they usually have a short-term time-frame: They are designed to accomplish their nefarious purposes within a matter of days or weeks, after which the rogue programmer usually does his best to disappear from view.

---

26. Of course, experience tells us that such an assumption is optimistic at best, if not downright naïve; to help emphasize that point, my word-processing program crashed three times while writing this chapter. Nevertheless, the perspective of the security professional tends to be focused on "after-the-fact" threats, once the system (bugs and all) has been put into operation.

The situation changes entirely when we consider the possibility of organized groups of terrorists, whose motives are far more deadly, and whose time-frame can be much longer. If you're part of a terrorist group that wants revenge for injustices incurred in the Middle Ages, you may be patient enough to plant a software time-bomb that doesn't go off for a year, or two years, or a decade; and you may be patient enough to behave innocently for a year, or two years, or a decade in order to gain the trust required to provide access to sensitive software code. And rather than merely stealing a million dollars and then retiring to a Caribbean island, why not program a software time-bomb into a process control system that runs a chemical plant or a nuclear reactor or an air-traffic control system?

I have not been personally involved in any computer projects at nuclear reactors, chemical plants, or the FAA, so I can't say whether such a scenario would be easy or difficult to accomplish. But I have been involved in financial systems for Wall Street firms and major *Fortune* 500 companies where it would be relatively simple to accomplish this kind of insidious longer-term damage. I have also been involved in numerous dot-com companies and high-tech firms throughout the country where *nobody* but the original programmer ever sees the computer code that gets installed in the final system. This is not a new phenomenon; it dates back to the time I entered the computer field in the mid-1960s, if not earlier.

Physical security has changed because of miniaturization

This next paradigm shift is an obvious and familiar one—but having visited several high-security installations during the past several decades, I can report that many organizations are simply unprepared to cope with it.

I'm talking about the phenomenon of *miniaturization*, which has been one of the many remarkable aspects of technology improvement in the computer field for the past few decades. Thirty years ago, security experts might have worried that terrorists would break into a computer center, or even blow it up; but they didn't worry about someone walking out of the computer room with the mainframe on their back. Twenty years ago, PCs began showing up in unprotected office environments; and though they were far larger, heavier and "clunkier" than today's computers, they nevertheless began disappearing from offices, as old-fashioned thieves found that they could break into the office at night and carry the computer out to their car. However, at least security guards basically didn't have to worry that a hacker or terrorist would carry a full-sized desktop PC *into* an office, in order to connect it to the corporate network and wreak havoc.

Then came laptops, and the game began to change. The laptop that I'm using to write this book is only an inch thick; nestled among file folders in a typical cluttered briefcase, it's easy for a careless security guard to overlook it—either on the way into the office, or on the way out. Until recently, I often carried *two* laptops in my briefcase, and when a bored airport security guard asked me if I was carrying a laptop, I would say "yes," and remove *one* of the laptops for inspection. *Never* did it occur to the security guards that I might be carrying more than one such machine; if it had, they might have changed their question to ask, "Are you carrying one *or more* laptops?"

Then came PDAs and cell-phones, and miniaturized digital cameras and video camcorders, and a seemingly endless succession of ever-smaller, ever-smarter devices; along with the devices themselves, we have an equally dizzying array of storage media, ranging from old-fashioned floppy disks to CDs to miniaturized hard disks that store 5-10 gigabytes on a device roughly the size of a pack of cards.[27] Obviously, it becomes easier and easier for people to sneak such devices in and out of the office, and harder and harder for security personnel to spot them. And to some extent, all of this is minor compared to the new "dimension" of security created by the miniaturization: the desire, both legitimate

---

27. For the mathematically and technically challenged, a gigabyte is a billion "bytes" or characters of information. 5-10 gigabytes of textual information is equivalent to the information contained in approximately 15,000 300-page books.

and illegitimate, to operate these devices entirely outside the protective environment of a corporate office or government agency. It's hard enough for diligent security professionals to protect all of the devices inside the corporate offices; how do they protect the laptop and its 20 gigabytes of storage when it's carried into an employee's home, or into the airport, train station, or automobile?

We began to see indications of this problem a decade ago, when newspapers carried the story of an embarrassed British military officer whose laptop computer, containing confidential files about the Gulf War, was stolen from his automobile. By the late 1990s, the problem had escalated: the FBI had to admit that dozens of laptop computers had been stolen from its own offices. One can only imagine how many Palm Pilots, cell phones, and other high-tech gadgets have been lost, stolen, or accessed inappropriately.

Obviously, this is a problem that will get worse before it gets better; as I pointed out in Chapter 1, technology forecasters expect the trend of computer hardware improvements to continue for the next several years. Thus, by the end of this decade, we can reasonably expect to see computing devices that are not only 10-100 times cheaper and/or faster, but also 10-100 times smaller and with 10-100 times more storage capacity.

Using the Internet as indirect weapon to support terrorism

A classic strategy of jiu-jitsu and other martial arts is to use an opponent's strength against himself; properly exploited, it allows someone who is smaller and ostensibly weaker to conquer a larger and stronger enemy. Familiar though this concept may be, it was nevertheless a shock for Americans to watch the technology that they had created—modern jet airliners—used as a weapon against themselves by a small band of individuals armed with only the most primitive of hand-weapons.

Similarly, IT professionals are beginning to realize that the very tools and technologies they have created are being used to help organize and coordinate terrorist attacks. This is something separate from the usual concern of "direct" attacks on one's computer systems; for example, the Internet search engines, which are such a boon to researchers, scientists, business professionals, and ordinary men and women, are also being used by hackers and terrorists to track down crucial information and security flaws.[28] This is not the fault of the search engines themselves; nor is it practical, given the proliferation of Internet technology, to restrict the use of search engines to a limited number of privileged individuals. It merely reminds us that we have created technology that not only allows "good" people to track down vast amounts of information on the Internet for legitimate purposes, but also "bad" people who can track down information, which may have been carelessly placed on the Internet, for illegitimate purposes. Indeed, many security experts believe that much of the necessary information about the type, location, and vulnerabilities of critical-infrastructure systems needed to organize and launch a serious attack is already available on the Internet.[29]

Of course, we've long known that drug smugglers, terrorists, and criminals of every kind have access to the "basic" technology of personal computers, word-processing programs, spreadsheets, database management systems, Web browsers, and email programs. But that's like saying criminals have cars and telephones and access to electricity; there's not much we can do about it.

But security experts have long been concerned that these same groups could also exploit the technologies of encryption, steganography, and firewalls to render their own communications impervious to snooping by law-enforcement agencies.[30] And while law-enforcement agencies have certainly encountered the use of encryption by cyber-criminals and drug-smugglers before, it's fair to say that the general public was oblivious of the issue, and corporate security professionals gave it little attention—because *they* weren't

---

28. See "Search Engines as a Security Threat," by Julio Cesar Hernandez, Jose Maria Sierra, and Arturo Ribagorda, *IEEE Computer*, Oct. 2001, p. 25.
29. See "Terror's Next Target?", by Erik Sherman, *Newsweek*, Oct. 15, 2001.

being attacked. But now that *everyone* is vulnerable to attack, everyone is paying attention to it.

No doubt criminals and drug-smugglers and terrorists will continue finding new ways to use information technology and the Internet to their advantage, thus turning our own creations against us in stronger and stronger ways. But the paradigm shift here is not one of actual accomplishments on the part of what President Bush refers to as "evil-doers," but rather the awareness on the part of society that it's happening.

The decade of security

All of the paradigm shifts discussed above combine into an ultimate conclusion: If for no other reason than the attacks of September 11th, the current decade will be remembered by most people in the IT field as the Decade of Security—just as the 1990s are likely to be remembered as the decade of productivity, and the 1980s as the decade of quality.

To some, this may seem like an exaggeration; after all, what if there are no more events like September 11th for the remainder of the decade? What if it turns out that the coordinated attacks on the Pentagon and the World Trade Center were the *only* clever things that the Al Qaeda terrorists had in mind? Or what if the subsequent attacks they had in mind were thwarted by the military campaign in Afghanistan, the law-enforcement crackdown throughout Europe and the United States, and the heightened awareness of the intelligence community?

---

30. As noted in Chapter 2, the threat of such activity was one of the major reasons the U.S. government pushed so hard for its "Clipper Chip" technology in the early 1990s, which would have mandated a "backdoor" in commercially available encryption products, so that the FBI, DEA, and CIA could decipher the messages sent by drug cartels, terrorist cells, and cyber-criminals. But aside from the privacy and civil-liberties issues that caused much of the controversy about this proposed legislation, it's virtually certain that the sophisticated drug-smugglers, cyber-criminals, and terrorists would have used widely-available *non*-Clipper encryption technology to keep their communications private. And they would have relied on the openness of the Internet to continue acquiring updated encryption tools in an attempt to stay at least one step ahead of law-enforcement agencies.

Such outcomes are possible; indeed, all of us presumably wish it to be the case. And one could argue that, after the horrific attack on the World Trade Center in January 1993, nearly nine years went by before the towers were attacked again; in the ensuing years after the attack, security was gradually relaxed. On the other hand, the 1993 attack was followed, at intervals of roughly a year, by an attack on an American military housing complex in Saudi Arabia, bombings of American embassies in Tanzania and Kenya, and a devastating attack on the U.S.S. Cole in Yemen. Thus, unless the initial "quick strike" efforts following September 11th were overwhelmingly successful, it's reasonable to assume that somewhere, sometime in the not-too-distant future, more attacks will occur. And those additional attacks will ratchet the security efforts up to maximum again.

Indeed, even without any more high-profile attacks, there is a significant chance that the American military/government complex will slip into a long-term Cold-War behavior similar to what we experienced from the late 1940s until the Soviet Union collapsed in the early 1990s. President Bush and many of his Cabinet secretaries have already made this comparison, and once they've launched a large-scale Cold War on terrorism (in addition to whatever "hot" wars pop up in countries like Afghanistan), it will be relatively difficult to stop. Conceivably, George Bush could be replaced in 2004 by a new President who abruptly shifts the national focus to something else; but it seems more likely that the momentum of George Bush's first-term anti-terrorism efforts will carry over into whatever administration is in power for the 2004-2008 time period, just as the Vietnam War dragged on through both Republican and Democratic administrations.

To a greater or lesser extent, whatever policies are established at the national level by the government and military will trickle down into the IT industry—particularly if, as we suggested in Chapter 2, it is reinforced by Congressional funding and legislation. For example, by mid-October of 2001, the Department of Transportation was evaluating recommendations for airline security that may require a complete overhaul of the airlines' legacy IT infrastructure—and this is entirely separate from the more highly-discussed measures for screening passengers and baggage for explosives.[31]

In the past, most airlines might never have considered such an overhaul of their legacy systems, because they have tended to view security and safety as a *constraint*, rather than something to be "optimized" or "maximized" like profits, productivity, and efficiency. In the aftermath of September 11th, many airlines have been criticized for this perspective, for it has led to low-paid, unmotivated airport security personnel with a high degree of turnover. But *every* publicly-traded company looks at the world through these rose-colored glasses; if they don't, Wall Street punishes them for not meeting their expected revenue and profit goals, and their stock prices sink like a stone, and the top executives find themselves out of a job.

But September 11th has changed the political climate; Wall Street may still be looking for healthy profits, but security has a much higher priority than before. As a result, IT investments that would have been justified by productivity improvements (which presumably lead to greater profits) are now being replaced by IT investments that augment security—including, as mentioned before, investments as grandiose as replacing entire legacy systems in order to support the kind of security techniques and strategies discussed earlier in the Techniques and Technologies section.[32]

Changes like this don't always come easily, particularly if a company was already suffering from the recession and/or

---

31. See "Air security may require IT overhaul: Mainframe systems would struggle to perform functions feds are considering," by Jennifer Disabatino, *Computerworld*, Oct. 22, 2001. The problem is that the government is contemplating asking airlines to be able to respond to "event-based" queries, such as a search for all passengers who bought a ticket within the last X days to travel to cities A, B, or C on airlines P, Q, or R. Such queries are relatively easy to program with modern relational databases, but today's airline reservation systems were developed nearly 40 years ago, using simpler database mechanisms optimized for high-speed processing of a single reservation request for a single passenger.
32. See "Attack May Slow Productivity," by Jed Graham, *Investor's Business Daily*, Oct. 10, 2001, which also makes the point that some of the "resiliency" strategies that we'll discuss in Chapter 6 (e.g., redundancy, elimination of just-in-time manufacturing strategies) could have a dramatic impact on profitability, if not productivity.

the aftermath of September 11th. As a passenger, one might be irate that airlines don't *immediately* begin spending what-ever amount of money is required to achieve a reasonable level of security. And perhaps they should; but when they're simultaneously coping with a 25% decline in pas-sengers and the resulting need to lay off as many as 10,000 employees, it's not surprising to see the airlines dragging their feet at spending the vast sums that might be required to placate the passengers.

Indeed, the situation is complicated by a number of psy-chological, economic, and political factors. If the airlines don't spend enough money to have a visible effect on air-line security, then passenger revenues might decline even further as travelers opt for trains, buses, cars, or staying home. If they impose rigid security measures before they have hired a vast number of additional security personnel, then airport delays might become even worse—thus frus-trating passengers, and again leading to a decline in reve-nues as travelers opt for alternatives. On the other hand, if they spend too lavishly, too quickly, they run the risk of incurring substantial losses (which Wall Street frowns upon), or—at least in the case of a few airlines—possible bankruptcy. Faced with so many complex alternatives, and such emotional debates associated with each alternative, the easiest thing for shell-shocked senior executives is to do nothing at all.

It's also important to remember what the typical corpo-rate culture is like when it comes to spending money for *anything*: Moneys have to be proposed to higher-level exec-utives, and since there are always more proposals than actual money available, each proposal has to be justified using such financial measures as "return-on-investment" (ROI) or "internal-rate-of-return" (IRR). Unfortunately, when it comes to security, ROI and IRR calculations are far from obvious; one can imagine airline executives, for exam-ple, speculating and hypothesizing about passenger reac-tions to different security strategies—but for now, the best that the executives can do is make an educated guess.

At least for the next few years, it's likely that security investments will be justified as a "business necessity,"[33] whether or not they are accompanied by a credible ROI or IRR calculation. Sometimes the decision to spend the money, or make the investment, will be simplified by virtue of new government laws and regulations *mandating* such investments,[34] and sometimes it will be simplified by an embarrassing breach of security by hackers or email viruses.[35] And sometimes it will be justified by surveys and polls that create a "herd instinct"; thus, in November 2001, a survey indicated that more than half of IT managers expect to devote a higher proportion of their IT budgets to security than they did in the previous year.[36] And since November was a month when year-2002 budgets were being debated and finalized in almost *every* IT department, one can imagine that there were many security advocates trying to justify their proposal by saying, "Look, everyone else is doing it—so we should be too!"

This last point may sound somewhat cynical, but it's not meant to be. After all, many of the investments and expenditures during the Decade of Productivity and the Decade of Quality were justified by fits of emotion ("we'll be run out of business by our Japanese competitors if we don't adopt a Six-Sigma Total Quality initiative!") and vendor-funded surveys indicating that everyone was doing "it," whatever "it" happened to be (e.g., upgrading to the latest version of a vendor's database management system, bringing in expensive consultants to implement a Business Pro-

---

33. See "Security ROI calculations pose challenges for users," by Jaikumar Vijayan, *Computerworld*, Nov. 5, 2001.
34. See "Terrorism taxes IT planning," by Patrick Thibodeau and Lucas Mearian, *Computerworld*, Nov. 5, 2001.
35. See "Record-breaking year for security incidents expected," by Dan Verton, *Computerworld*, Nov. 26, 2001, which cites a recent CERT Coordination Center study estimating that the number of reported computer-related security incidents in 2001 will exceed 40,000—more than twice the number reported in 2000.
36. See "Survey: More IT spending targeted for security," by Julia King, *Computerworld*, Nov. 13, 2001, which says that only 5% of the surveyed managers expect to spend *less* on IT security in 2002 than they have in 2001. Interestingly, the survey also says that IT organizations will be spending nearly 10% of their overall budget on security.

cess Reengineering initiative, switching from one
programming language to another, buying Computer-
Aided Software Engineering (CASE) tools for every member of the IT department, etc.) Sadly, many of these initiatives—including the ones that had a credible ROI
justification—didn't work as planned; and it should not surprise us, if we learn at the end of this decade, that many of
today's emotionally-charged IT security initiatives don't
work either.[37]

But whether they succeed or fail, they *will* be attempted;
and if we are unlucky enough to sustain additional high-
profile terrorist attacks, the emphasis on security will escalate even higher. Thus, for better or worse, the basic paradigm shift for the IT industry during this decade is likely to
be one of shifting away from investments in quality, productivity, and innovation per se, to investments in security.
Welcome, then, to the Decade of Security.

Strategic Implications

What does all of this mean? If this is indeed the Decade of
Security, what should you *do* about it? The answer, of
course, is: It depends. It depends on far more variables and
factors than I can possibly discuss in a book like this—e.g.,
it may depend on where you live (urban New York versus
rural Taos), what you do for a living, and (unfortunately)
where you were born, or even what religion you practice. It

---

37. See "Study: Constant security fixes overwhelming IT managers," by
Dan Verton, *Computerworld*, Nov. 30, 2001. The article notes that security
administrators at a typical company with only nine servers and eight
firewalls were confronted with 1,315 security patches and software
updates during the past 12 months—which works out to five updates
per business day. The article also illustrates the point made in an earlier
section of this chapter about the amount of data associated with logging
of user activities: A company of this average size would have to manage
more than 500,000 log entries, 150-200 firewall-generated "alerts" and
150-200 server-generated "alerts" each day. See also "Gartner: Most IT
security problems self-inflicted," by Juan Carlos Perez, *Computerworld*,
Oct. 9, 2001, which states that roughly 90% of security breaches occur
when attackers take advantage of software (such as Web servers) that IT
staffers have either failed to patch or have misconfigured.

also depends on future events that we cannot predict—e.g., additional terrorist attacks, the outbreak of war in the Middle East, or dramatic scientific innovations.

From an IT perspective, I can offer some constructive advice and suggestions to five categories of individuals:

- government and political leaders
- senior corporate executives
- mid-level IT managers
- technical IT professionals
- citizens

Government and political leaders

If you were ushered into the Oval Office, and given 10 minutes to offer advice and suggestions to President Bush on the subject of IT security, what would you say? It probably doesn't matter, since he has already heard every conceivable bit of advice from his high-level subordinates, most of whom are presumably channeling their advice through the newly appointed Secretary of Homeland Defense, Tom Ridge.

Nevertheless, it's an interesting question to contemplate, because at least some of the decisions being made at high levels of government are political in nature—which means that it's possible they might be influenced by a groundswell of support or criticism from the nation as a whole. Thus, for what it's worth, here's my list of recommendations for high-level government officials—not just President Bush, but also Cabinet secretaries, Senators, Congresspeople, governors, mayors, and anyone else whose policy decisions affect large numbers of people:

- *Balance the need for security with the right to privacy.* This recommendation is being made by politicians, pundits, philosophers, and experts far more eloquent than I, and I have no new insight or perspective to offer— with the possible exception of emphasizing that there is far more to be gained by following some of the subsequent recommendations in this list than by trampling on existing privacy rights in the process of enacting new security regulations.

- *Make your <u>existing</u> security mechanisms work effectively before launching a plethora of new mechanisms.* In early November 2001, a Congressional sub-committee issued a scathing report indicating that 16 Federal agencies had flunked a computer security review, and numerous others received a barely passing grade.[38] Meanwhile, initial reports in the aftermath of September 11th suggest that there is an almost overwhelming lack of coordination, cooperation, and sharing of data between Federal agencies who pick up tidbits, on their own, of relevant information about potential security threats. When it comes to security, it would be a good idea if the government learned to walk before it attempted to run, much less ride a jet-powered bicycle.

- *Monitor yourself at least as diligently as you monitor companies, groups, and individuals.* Some terrorists, criminals, and hackers are wandering about the country on their own, and some may have infiltrated companies in the guise of ordinary employees. But it's also possible that some may have infiltrated government agencies, and may have risen to high levels of trust and authority. There are already *lots* of people (and law-enforcement agencies) watching the IT-related activities of individual citizens and corporate employees. But who watches the watchers?

- *Remember that hardly anyone watches the programmers.* In both government and industry, it is a common practice for programmers to write their programs, and then compile them, test them, and place them into operational status *without anyone else ever seeing the code.* A formal, disciplined software development environment *does* include peer-group reviews or "inspections"; but these are often superficial in nature, and they are one of the first practices to be abandoned in the pressure of the "death-march" projects that we'll discuss in Chapter 8.[39] In addition to a lack of walkthroughs and inspections, many IT organizations

---

38. See "16 U.S. agencies flunk computer security review," by Scarlett Pruitt, *Computerworld*, Nov. 9, 2001.

(both inside and outside of government) have little or
nothing in the way of source-code control or configuration management practices, or a rehearsed and well-
tested backup/recovery procedure; as a result, it is
incredibly easy for a disgruntled employee or a
hacker/criminal/terrorist programmer to wreak
havoc.

SEI[39] Level	Commercial/ inhouse	DOD/Federal contractor	Military/Federal Organizations
1	34.9%	21.2%	52.5%
2	38.2%	35.5%	28.8%
3	18.5%	33.9%	11.3%
4	5.5%	5.2%	6.3%
5	2.9%	2.4%	1.3%

- *Hire "white-hat" security experts and then <u>listen</u> to their
  advice.* A "white hat" is a friendly hacker, one whose
  job is to probe an organization's IT security for weaknesses and vulnerabilities. White hat teams have been
  assembled on several occasions in recent years by various military organizations and intelligence agencies;[40] and in far too many cases, their assessments
  and conclusions have been so devastating and embarrassing that the final reports have been buried without
  any further action. September 11th may have changed
  that mindset, but the bureaucratic instinct for survival
  and avoidance of embarrassment is a powerful one.
  It's extremely important for high-level, *open-minded*
  government officials to hire white-hat security teams

---

39. Software inspections are one of the required practices in order to reach
    level 3 on the Capability Maturity Model (CMM) created by the Soft-
    ware Engineering Institute (SEI). But an August 2000 SEI report entitled
    "Process Maturity Profiles for the Software Industry" indicated that
    only a minority of IT organizations inside or outside the government
    were at level 3 or above.
40. See, for example, the discussion of the "Black Ice" simulation discussed
    in Chapter 2, which explored various "contingencies" for the 2002 Win-
    ter Olympics.

and make sure that their reports and recommendations *don't* get buried.

- *Educate and inform the public.* As noted earlier in this
chapter, one of the paradigm shifts in the security field
is the presence of millions of powerful home computers with high-speed, always-on Internet connections.
Very, very few home computer users have the faintest
idea that their computers could be an unwitting
weapon, manipulated remotely by a teenage hacker in
Amsterdam, or a military programmer in a hostile
country. I believe that the government needs to initiate
a long-term, sustained, non-alarmist education campaign to help citizens establish their own firewalls and
security protection.

Senior corporate executives

- *Get the basics in place before you spend enormous sums of
money on fancy high-tech security gadgets.* The advice
here is similar to that offered above for government
officials. If your employees are oblivious to the basics
of security, or if the prevailing culture is "anti-secu-
rity," you need to tackle that problem before you start
investing in biometric ID cards and other such gadgets.

- *Get a periodic audit of your company's security status.* Your
CIO will tell you that everything is under control, and
your security manager will probably tell you that
everything *would* be under control if only you would
give him a few million dollars for the latest gadget he
saw in *Soldier of Fortune* magazine. But the only way to
have a realistic assessment of the situation is to hire a
reputable, experienced *outside* security consultant or
company (depending on the size of your company) and
let them do a "white-hat" attack, along with a more traditional assessment and audit. Chances are that the
results will surprise and disappoint you; chances are
that if you repeat the exercise a year from now, the
results will surprise and disappoint you again.

- *Obtain regular __external__ briefings of major IT security threats.* When your CIO and security manager tell you that everything is under control, they not only mean that they believe there are no major security "holes" at the present time, but also that they believe they are keeping up with the steady stream of patches and updates provided by vendors like IBM, Microsoft, Sun, and Oracle. But as noted earlier, even a small organization is faced with a blizzard of such updates; and both the information about the patch/update, and the actual implementation of the patch/update is typically handled by a relatively low-level programmer or system administrator. If the administrator is sick, drunk, on vacation, or simply in a bad mood,[41] some of those patches might be overlooked or implemented incorrectly. If it's a minor patch, there might not be any consequences; but if it's a major patch, then it could (by virtue of not being implemented correctly) expose your company to massive damage. Thus, while the CEO certainly doesn't want to see a full report of the 1,315 security patches that his lower-echelon security programmer was supposed to implement, he probably *should* be alerted to the five or ten that could bring his company to its knees.

- *Tell your mid-level managers that they need to look at security from a "business imperative" perspective, not just an ROI/IRR perspective.* The reasoning behind this point was discussed in earlier in the Decade of security section; but the message has to come from the top, or the mid-level managers are likely to continue rejecting security proposals because they don't appear to generate a profit.

- *Remember that nobody is watching your programmers.* The message here is the same one given to government officials above. If your IT organization has been formally assessed at SEI-CMM level 3, 4, or 5, then your

---

41. If you want to get a sense of just how grumpy these system administrators can be (and if you can tolerate a moderate amount of four-letter words and obscenities), take a look at the adminspotting Web page (www.adminspotting.com).

security risks have been reduced—because (at least on paper) your IT development teams are carrying out software inspections and configuration management practices in a consistent, disciplined fashion. But if your organization has not been assessed, or if it is at levels 1 or 2, then—in a very realistic sense—neither you nor your mid-level IT managers have any idea of how much "rogue code" is being inserted into your systems by programmers who are grumpy, dishonest, or downright malevolent.

- *Prepare for a substantial increase in the number of viruses, DoS attacks, and other forms of cyber-attacks.* As noted earlier in this chapter, the CERT Coordination Center at Carnegie Mellon University estimates that the number of such attacks in 2001 is roughly double the number that occurred in 2000. It's highly unlikely that the number will decrease in the next few years.

- *Prepare for a substantial increase in the amount of security-related legislation from local, state, and Federal government agencies.* It doesn't take a rocket scientist to make such a prediction; but the point is that your organization needs to have at least one individual, if not an entire team, monitoring such legislation while it is still in its early phases. In the best case (from your company's perspective), you may be able to exert some form of lobbying influence to modify the legislation to make it tolerable for your organization; in the worst case, you need as much advance warning as possible in order to implement the new regulations and policies when they are enacted.

Mid-level IT managers

- *Make your own assessment of your company's security status.* As noted above, I believe that senior management should engage an outside firm to assess the company's IT security. But while you're waiting for that to happen, you can make your own informal assessment. Take a look at the written security policies (if you can find anything in writing); take a look at how those policies are being implemented. Wander through some end-user departments to see whether people are using passwords properly. Observe the security personnel (if there are any) to see if they are doing an effective job of enforcing security mechanisms and monitoring potential vulnerabilities. If all of these observations and assessment confirm that your company is doing a good job, then you can breathe a sigh of relief. But if it's doing a bad job (which is likely to be the case), then you need to make a choice: Lead, follow, or get out of the way. In the best case, perhaps you can become the in-house advocate/champion for better IT security; in the worst case, you may decide that it's better to seek greener pastures before a gaping security problem—which nobody wants to admit or confront—blows up in everyone's face.

- *Remember that __you__ are probably the one who will have to impose configuration management practices, and monitor the code written by programmers who report to you.* As mentioned earlier, an IT organization operating at SEI-CMM level 3 or above will have formal, well-defined, consistently-implemented processes in place for configuration management and software inspections. But if you work in an SEI-CMM level 1 or 2 organization (which represents the majority of IT organizations around the world today), then such practices either don't exist, or are ignored, or are practiced only when the programmers are in the mood to do so. If you tell your programmers to start following such processes, they'll give you a blank look, mutter something rude under their breath, and simply ignore you—after all, programmers know that *managers don't read code*, which means that nobody really knows what they are doing. The only way to change this situation is to (a) start reading the code yourself, which is probably an overwhelming task, or (b) *mandate* a formal review process, and force the programmers to participate in it. We'll discuss the practicality of such an approach in more detail in Chapter 8.

- *In a software development project, make sure that security issues are properly aligned with the appropriate life-cycle activity.* Some security issues are matters of law or company policy, and must be implemented regardless of the design or programming approach used by the development team; thus, they need to be identified during the systems analysis (or "requirements-gathering") stage of the project, and confirmed by the relevant users and stakeholders in the project. Other security issues are associated with the architecture and design of the system—e.g., most of today's well-known email viruses have to be handled very carefully in a Microsoft Windows environment, but are absolutely irrelevant in a Macintosh environment. Still other security issues are associated with coding techniques (most of the "buffer-overflow" vulnerabilities exploited by hackers fall into this category). Unfortunately, a typical software development project tends to jumble all of these issues together—so that end-users are asked to make decisions about matters of programming, and programmers end up making policy decisions that should have been left to the end-users.

Technical IT professionals

- *Perform your own security assessment.* The advice given to mid-level IT managers above is relevant for programmers, database specialists, network designers, and other categories of geeks, grunts, and techies.
- *Consider specializing in security as a new career.* Computer security has been a respected subset of the IT industry for many years; but for obvious reasons, the demand for security professionals has increased dramatically, and is likely to remain high for the foreseeable future. Thus, just as some COBOL programmers saw new career opportunities when Visual Basic became popular, and some user-interface specialists saw new career opportunities when HTML and the Web became popular, some of today's IT professionals may see a new career in security. You can't become a security expert overnight, and you're likely to be

sneered at by the veteran security professionals—but
it's not an insurmountable obstacle.

- *Be prepared to be watched more closely in the future.* This
  advice is relevant only if your manager, and the senior
  executives, and the government officials heed the
  advice given in the sections above. It won't happen
  overnight, and it won't happen in every IT organization; and it won't happen on projects where security is
  a non-issue. But in more and more companies, and in
  more and more projects where security *is* an issue,
  you're going to see increasing degrees of rigor and discipline when it comes to software inspections, source-
  code control, and configuration management.

- *Be prepared for increased security to slow down your work.*
  One of the most common explanations (or "excuses,"
  depending on your perspective) for avoiding rigorous
  peer-group code reviews is that it slows things
  down.[42] More broadly, inspections and configuration
  management and many other security-related procedures are viewed as productivity-killers; the perception, if not the reality, is that all of this slows down the
  development work, which (as we'll see in Chapter 8) is
  often taking place under enormous pressure, because
  of aggressive deadlines that have been imposed upon
  the project team. Thus, *if* tighter security is introduced
  within software development organizations, and *if* the
  perception of security-related bureaucracy is at least
  partially correct, then work will slow down and productivity will drop. This means something has to give:
  Either deadlines have to be extended, or more
  resources (people) have to be added to the project, or
  less functionality has to be promised to the end-users,
  or some kind of productivity-enhancing tools or processes has to be introduced. Unfortunately, all of these
  decisions are made by people *above* the level of the

---

42. Actually, it slows down the programming process but speeds up the
testing and debugging process, because most of the bugs are eliminated
before traditional testing begins. But not everyone agrees with this
point, even though it has been confirmed by study after study during
the past 20 years.

software developer; and the chances are that—at least in the short term—they'll attempt to ignore the problem, in the hope that it will go away. But as we'll see in Chapter 8, the problem already existed *before* the introduction of additional security measures; and a more general strategy needs to be formulated.

Citizens

- *Examine your philosophical attitude about the trend toward more security and less privacy.* You can complain about it, or you can follow Sun Microsystems' Scott McNealy's advice to "get over it." You can write nasty letters to your Congressperson, you can join with your neighbors to march on City Hall to protest your loss of privacy. You can resist every inappropriate effort by a company or government agency to gain access to your Social Security number; you can reject every cookie that a Web server sends to your machine. You can threaten to leave the country if a mandatory national ID card is legislated; indeed, you can make good on your threat, and move to whatever part of the world provides an acceptable balance between security and privacy. This is clearly an area where each of us must decide whether to lead, follow, or get out of the way. The sad thing is that most citizens won't think seriously about any of these issues, and will simply wake up one morning to find that they are living in a world they are completely unprepared for. Whatever choice you make in this area should be a conscious, informed choice; one way to accomplish that is to read the newsletters and Web sites of organizations like ACLU and EPRI.

- *Examine the <u>practical</u> impact of increased security and decreased privacy on your life.* In addition to our philosophical thoughts about rights and obligations in society, all of us have to muddle through our day-to-day lives—with our job and our family and our friends and our hobbies. Some of us have lifestyles that society clearly disapproves of, but has not rendered illegal; as long as the social norm is "don't ask, don't tell," we can continue to maintain that lifestyle. But if increased security measures make your medical history, your sexual preferences, your political affiliations, and other such details blindingly obvious to employers, government officials, and even neighbors, then your lifestyle may well be disrupted. *Now* is the time to think about such matters, not two or three years from now, when you suddenly find that you can't get a job, or can't buy a house in a particular neighborhood, or can't take a particular book out of the library.[43]

- *Make your <u>own</u> computing devices more secure.* If you have a home computer with a high-speed, always-on Internet connection, put this book down *right now* and install a firewall and an effective anti-virus security program on your machine. I won't recommend any particular vendors or products, because they change from one year to the next, and because the proper choice depends on the kind of hardware/software/network/email configuration that you're using. But if you have no idea what to do, talk to a computer-savvy friend, or visit a local bookstore to find an appropriate "Security for Novices" (or dummies, or complete idiots, depending on your self-image) book for your particular computer configuration. While you're at it, check the security vulnerabilities of your cell phone, Palm Pilot and other "smart" devices. In short: Recognize that your computing behavior has been roughly analogous to living in a house with the doors and win-

---

43. This topic could occupy a full chapter, if not an entire book. Fortunately, such books have already been written. If you only have time for one such book, read *Database Nation: The Death of Privacy in the 21st Century* by Simson Garfinkel (O'Reilly, Jan. 2000). If you want a sobering, perhaps even chilling, explanation of the inexorable government forces being brought to bear on Internet-related privacy issues, read *Code, and Other Laws of Cyberspace* by Lawrence Lessig (Basic Books, 1999). Another thought-provoking book is *The Hundredth Window: Protecting Your Privacy and Security in the Age of the Internet*, by Charles Jenning, Lori Fena, and Esther Dyson (Free Press, 2000). For a broader discussion about security, as well as privacy, see *Defending Your Digital Assets Against Hackers, Crackers, Spies, and Thieves*, by Randall K. Nichols, Daniel J. Ryan, Julie J. C. H. Ryan, and William E., Jr. Baugh (McGraw-Hill,1999) and *Cybershock: Surviving Hackers, Phreakers, Identity Thieves, Internet Terrorists and Weapons of Mass Destruction*, by Winn Schwartau (Thunder's Mouth Press, 2000).

dows wide open, 24 hours a day. It was a pleasant way to live, if you were in a small town in the 1950s. But you're living in the metaphorical equivalent of a big city now, and there are gang wars and drive-by shootings taking place all around you. It's time to close the windows, lock the doors, and practice what most big-city residents refer to as "street smarts."[44]

---

44. If you don't believe that you *might* have a security problem, visit the Gibson research site ShieldsUp page to find out exactly how vulnerable your computer is. Chances are you'll be shocked by the results.

RISK MANAGEMENT 4

Progress always involves risk; you can't steal second
base and keep your foot on first base.   ■

—Fredrick Wilcox

Basic Concepts _____

Risk management is a familiar concept to most managers,
and to IT professionals: If there are risks serious enough to
threaten the success of a project, and/or the smooth functioning of some business endeavor, then they need to be
identified and managed. In the aftermath of September
11th, we've also learned that *personal* risk management can
be important: An attack on one's employer can threaten
one's personal safety and survival, in addition to threatening damage or bankruptcy to the organization as a whole.
Related concepts include *contingency* planning and *disaster-
recovery* planning; for simplicity, I'll discuss all of these concepts under the heading of "risk management."

Risk management is an entire topic unto itself, and IT-
related risk management is also a substantive field. Entire
books have been written on the subject,[1] and they are rec-

ommended for the organizations that have been forced to acknowledge that, in the innocent days before September 11th, they ignored the area altogether. But as with the other topics in this book, my primary objective is to summarize the current concepts and techniques, and to focus on the paradigm shifts that have occurred in recent years. The real question, then, is not "what is risk management all about?" but "how is risk management *different* now?"

Of course, risks existed before September 11th, and in some cases they were considerable; indeed, *everything* in our lives involves some degree of risk, however minor. But in a simpler, safer world, risk management was a formality, something to be performed once a year, or once at the beginning of an IT development project—much like the visit to one's family doctor for an annual checkup. But in more troublesome times, an organization has to be prepared for entirely new risks—things that nobody anticipated— which can emerge at a moment's notice. The situation is further compounded by the fact that today's "lean and mean" business environment provides very little "slack," in terms of additional time, money, and people to cope with unexpected risks.

Thus, in today's world, risk management needs to be an oversight process that's applied on a continuous basis. For an IT project manager who guides a development project through the familiar phases of analysis, design, coding, and testing, risk management should no longer be thought of as a bureaucratic process to be done once at the beginning of the project (see Figure 4.1). As I suggested in a recent book,[2] it needs to be done *throughout* the project, on a continuous basis.

---

1. See, for example, Elaine M. Hall, *Managing Risk: Methods for Software Systems Development* (Addison-Wesley, 1998); Capers Jones, *Assessment and Control of Software Risks* (Prentice Hall, 1994); H. Petroski, *To Engineer is Human: The Role of Failure in Successful Design* (Vintage Books, 1992); Peter G. Neumann; *Computer-Related Risks* (Addison-Wesley, 1995); Barry Boehm, *Tutorial: Software Risk Management*. (IEEE Computer Society Press, 1989); Robert N. Charette, *Application Strategies for Risk Analysis* (McGraw-Hill, 1990); and Robert N. Charette, *Software Engineering Risk Analysis and Management*, (McGraw-Hill, 1989..
2. *Managing High-Intensity Internet Projects* (Prentice Hall, 2001).

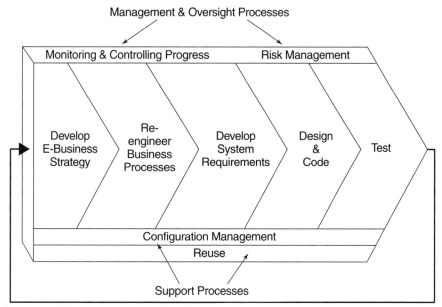

FIGURE 4.1 Risk management in the context of overall project management.

While it's important to be familiar with the standard, traditional risk management practices in the literature, it's also important to avoid having the "risk management police" overwhelm an organization with forms, reports, and other aspects of bureaucracy. Because of the limited amount of time in today's busy world, managers in some organizations follow a very simple process of having their subordinates identify and monitor the *top ten* risks in the project; these can be printed on a one-page form, and their status can be quickly reviewed on a weekly basis. A simple risk-management form—summarizing the risks associated with a systems development project—is shown in Table 4.1; it can be adjusted to suit the needs and preferences of a specific organization and the activities it undertakes.

Obviously, other approaches can work just as well; but the key is to ensure that it's one that will be understood, accepted, and followed by everyone involved—for as we'll discuss in more detail later in the Techniques and Technologies section, it's usually the employees at the bottom of the hierarchy who are usually the first to see the emergence of new risks. In a world where risks can take the form of hijacked airplanes flying at 500 mph, we don't have time to let the information trickle up to the top of the management hierarchy by memos and committee meetings; the risks have to be pounced on and attacked by the organization in order to prevent them from getting out of control.

TABLE 4.1 A sample risk-management form.

ID	Person Responsible	Description	Last Week	This Week	Next Week (estimated)
6	Susan	System crashes with Netscape 4.75	♠	♦	♣
8	Rocco	Slow response to order inquiry	♦	♦	♣
11	Joshua	Vendor may be late on delivering unit X	♠	♦	♦
17	Mary Jane	MJ exhausted and burned out, wants to quit	♠	♦	♣
19	Billy Bob	BB wants starring role in *Tomb Raider* sequel	♦	♦	♦
23	Rocco	System won't work with new version of Oracle	♠	♠	♣
24	Josh	User *hates* Josh's new user interface	♠	♦	♣
25	Everyone	Competitor has pre-announced "killer" app	♠	♦	♣
33	Susan	HumDinger code crashes system	♠	♠	♦
47	Billy Bob	System violates new gov't privacy regs	♠	♦	♣
♠ = high risk ♦ = medium risk ♣ = low risk					

The word "control" is crucial here, for management needs to distinguish between risk *assessment*, risk *control*, and risk *avoidance*. In the worst case, the organization reacts to risks *after* they occur—e.g., by assigning extra guards after the corporate offices have been burglarized. This kind of "fix on failure" approach, where the risks are addressed *after* they have surfaced, often leads to a crisis-mode form of "fire fighting" that can lead to utter collapse of a project or organization. Risk *prevention* is usually far better, and it means that the organization follows a formal process of assessment and control in order to preclude potential risks from occurring.

An even more proactive form of risk management seeks to eliminate the root causes of failures and risk; this is often the focus of quality-management initiatives within an organization. It tends to expand the scope of risk assessment to a broader horizon, in order to allow *anticipation* of risks; and it can lead to a very aggressive managing culture, which incorporates a "risk-taking" ethic by *engineering* the degree of risk that the organization can tolerate.

As risk-management guru Rob Charette observes, the major causes of "local failures" often exist in the overall organizational environment, or in the external business environment. Thus, as Figure 4.2 illustrates, an IT project manager might be focusing on the risks associated with his team's development processes and the code they're writing; but there are likely to be greater risks associated with the organizational environment and business environment — which are almost always outside the project manager's jurisdiction and political control. In addition, the project manager often doesn't know about those "external" risks until they come crashing into his project.

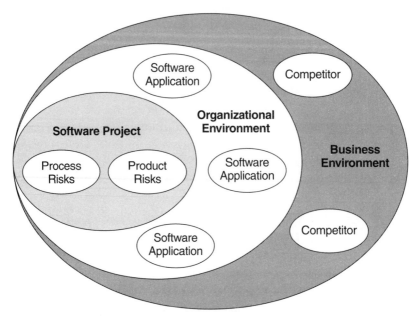

FIGURE 4.2 The scope of project risks

Of course, the converse can be true also: The software project creates risks that can affect the organization and the external business environment. But everyone knows that! Indeed, the project manager can expect to be reminded *ad nauseam* that the entire organization—if not the universe, and all of civilization!—is imperiled by any delays or risk of failure associated with his project. That's why it's important to have a risk management process that can assess project risks from several different organization perspectives and balance them appropriately; after all, what the software developers sees as a risk might be seen as an opportunity by the marketing department.[3]

Risk *assessment* is usually performed by evaluating the complexity of the system being developed or operated,[4] as well as evaluating the client environment and the project

---

3. A classic example of this situation is the risk associated with releasing a new system to the marketplace before the software developers are finished with their testing activities. The marketing department may see an opportunity associated with being "first to market" with the new system; that has to be balanced against the development team's concern that there may still be serious "show-stopper" bugs lurking in the code.

team environment. Product complexity can be assessed in terms of size (e.g., lines of code, number of people required to operate the system), performance constraints, technical complexity, etc. Risks associated with the client environment are often a factor of the number of user constituencies involved, the level of user knowledge, the perceived importance of the system within the user's business area, the likelihood that when/if the new system is installed it will lead to a reorganization or downsizing activity, etc. And the risks associated with the team environment include the capabilities, experience, morale, and physical/emotional health of the project team.

Typically, there are a hundred or more risk factors that could be included in a comprehensive risk model; as noted earlier, some project teams will consciously narrow their focus to just the top ten risks. Some of the risks can be quantified in an objective fashion—e.g., the response-time performance requirements, or the size of the system in function points. But other factors—e.g., the degree of user cooperation or hostility—may have to be assessed on a qualitative basis. As a practical management approach, it's usually appropriate to categorize such risks as "high," "low," or "medium" and to focus on getting a consensus on the state, or level, of the risk, on the part of everyone involved.

Once the risks have been identified and assessed, the manager and his or her subordinates can sometimes identify appropriate strategies to minimize or eliminate as many as possible. This is common sense, of course, but it's important to remember that in many cases, they *cannot* be eliminated through simple actions. On the other hand, if the risks are extraordinary, sometimes the solutions are too: While a manager might never have dared to ask the CEO or Senior Vice President to eliminate an "ordinary" risk by spending an extraordinary sum of money or eliminating a severe bureaucratic constraint, it's not unreasonable to ask for such things

---

4. Many IT managers focus on the risks associated with *developing* a system, but then ignore the many risks associated with *operating* the system—e.g., risks associated with security, system crashes, poor performance, obsolescence of the system's hardware/software components, etc.

when a severe risk presents itself unexpectedly. And if you don't ask—which will often require going around the chain of command, and circumventing several levels of brain-dead middle managers—then you'll never know whether you could have acquired the solution to your problems.

In any case, if there are high-risk factors that cannot be summarily eliminated, then they should be documented with a "risk memorandum" that identifies the risk impact, the possible higher-level actions, the contingency plans that need to be set in place, etc. This is not just a "cover your ass" political act, for if the risks do materialize, and if they cause a project to fail or significant injuries or business losses, there will usually be dire consequences for everyone involved. However, *denying* reality is also a common phenomenon in a typical political environment; it's common for both the bottom-level workers who first see the risk, and for the various levels of managers above them to put on their blindfolds and steadfastly ignore the existence of serious risks. It's not unreasonable to expect a manager and his or her team members to focus on "internal" risks with extreme diligence; but as noted earlier, the "external" risks often can't be controlled by the team members, because they're associated with organizational or business issues beyond their jurisdiction. Thus, a risk memorandum is an important *practical* activity, in order to force higher level managers to acknowledge what they would prefer to overlook and ignore.

Techniques and Technologies

There are many techniques and strategies associated with risk management; I've highlighted what I believe to be the four most important ones below:

- Establishing a risk-aware culture
- Realistic assessment of risks
- Ensuring that risks are *shared* between stakeholders
- Developing *processes* for risks

Establishing a risk-aware culture

It's impossible to manage the risks in an organization if the prevailing culture prefers to deny their existence. Thus, the explicit and/or implicit message from senior management in some organizations is "real men (and women) don't have risks"—the implication that every employee and manager throughout the organization should be able to cope with any problems that come their way, without whining and complaining and "passing the buck" to higher level managers, who are presumed to be very, very busy doing Important Things.

Another common corporate culture is the "don't worry, be happy" attitude of forced optimism. This is sometimes based on a statistical assessment of risks; and while it can be a useful strategy for preventing hysterical over-reaction, it can also create an environment in which anyone suggesting the possibility of a risk is labeled an "alarmist." Thus, in the aftermath of September 11th, some managers belittled their subordinates' concerns about air travel: "Hey, what are you worried about? The odds of being hijacked were low to begin with, and now they're infinitesimally small! You're more likely to be injured in a traffic accident!" Such an assessment may be statistically true, but it's not helpful if it stifles all discussion and assessments of the risks that *do* exist with air-travel.

Yet another common culture is the one that says "they will take care of us," where "they" includes vendors, business partners, and government leaders. Indeed, we'll return to this theme in our discussion of emergent systems in Chapter 5: If "they" includes the higher-level managers who are responsible for the safety and well-being of employees, and if those higher-level managers are unable or unwilling to carry out their responsibilities, then lower-level employees are left to cobble together ad hoc risk-management strategies of their own. Similarly, one might hope that IBM or Microsoft or HP won't let us down; one might want to believe that a trusted business partner will prevent his risks from disrupting our activities; and one might desperately want to believe the promises of government leaders that they will prevent biological, chemical, and nuclear threats from disrupting our lives. Unfortunately, such beliefs are not always realistic; but if the prevailing culture is, "We *will* trust our elected leaders to take care of us, because it would be unpatriotic not to do so," then it prevents any meaningful discussion of the risks that are staring one in the face, here and now.

In rare cases, the contradiction between promises and reality may be a sign of corruption, gross incompetence, or outright lies; but that's not the most common situation. When a vendor or business partner allows a serious risk to escalate beyond his control and disrupt our activities, despite his repeated promises that it would never happen, it's more likely to be a manifestation of the same risk-denial culture that we've already discussed—i.e., *his* organizational culture is typified by the attitude of "real men don't have risks," or "don't worry, be happy", or by placing too much trust in *his* vendors and suppliers.

It's also common to see situations where severe risks require someone to allocate scarce resources. It's hard enough to do that on our own, but when the decision moves beyond our control—to vendors, business partners, or government leaders—it can be dangerous to adopt the Pollyanna attitude of "they'll take care of us." Imagine, for example, that IBM or Microsoft discovers a severe security vulnerability in one of their products, and has to devote time, people, and money to help their customers fix the problem. Even a huge company like IBM has finite resources; how will those resources be allocated? Similarly, if a massive biological attack is unleashed upon the country, how will the limited resources of the nation's public-health system be allocated?

The appropriate response to such situations might or might not be self-sufficiency; in some cases, it may simply not be practical. One might be able to acquire enough technical proficiency to be completely independent of IBM, Microsoft, and all of one's IT suppliers; but that's probably not a practical option for small companies.[5] Similarly, an individual city or state might attempt to become self-sufficient in terms of biological and chemical threats, in order to eliminate its dependence on Federal assistance. But again, that's not always practical; at the time this book was being written, for example, there simply were not enough units of smallpox vaccine to inoculate everyone in New York or California, let alone the entire country; and in any case, the stockpile of vaccine was under Federal control.

Quandaries like these are enormously frustrating and troublesome; and for just that reason, the common tendency is to bury them and pretend they don't exist. And particularly when external vendors, partners, or government leaders are involved, the easiest way of doing that is simply to say, "They'll take care of us." It's a convenient simplification, but it doesn't make the risk go away; and it's a travesty to say that one is performing comprehensive risk management when one refuses to confront such risks.

As noted in Chapter 2, management guru Michael Hammer argues, in his new book, *The Agenda*, that the people who are first to spot an incipient risk are likely to be the front-line employees who have direct, day-to-day contact with customers, competitors, suppliers, vendors, and partners. Thus, one of the most important elements of creating a risk-aware culture is that of encouraging front-line employees to identify and report risks—without worrying that they will be accused of being disloyal, unpatriotic, alarmists, or whistle-blowers.

Realistic assessment of risks

A corollary to the idea of establishing a risk-aware culture is that of *realistic* assessment of risks—rather than trivializing them, or exaggerating them to the point where people are either paranoid or paralyzed. Among other things, this requires us to distinguish between the *probability* of a risk occurring, versus the *consequences* of the risk, if it does

---

5. An alternative, though, is the "open-source" movement, which allows small companies (and individuals) to acquire well-tested software at a nominal cost. A good example is the Linux operating system; there are also open-source versions of spreadsheets, word processors, database management systems, and many other basic applications.

occur. Thus, we might assess the probability of a serious auto accident as being very low; but since the consequences could be fatal, the appropriate risk-mitigation strategy is to wear a seat-belt. On the other hand, the risk of mosquito bites in the summer time is relatively high; but the consequences are very low, so our risk-management strategy can be minimal in nature.

This aspect of "realism" is fairly obvious and straightforward, though it often leads to emotional debates between those who focus exclusively on probabilities, versus those who focus exclusively on consequences. A balanced combination of the two factors is usually referred to, by mathematicians and insurance professionals, as "expected value": Thus, the expected value of a risk whose probability of occurrence is 10%, and whose consequences are $1,000, is $100. The same expected value is associated with a risk whose probability of occurrence is 1%, but whose consequences are $10,000.

Another important dimension of realism involves the *timeliness* and the *credibility* of the information with which we assess both the probability and the consequences of a risk. Last week's weather report isn't much use to us today; and the prediction of next summer's weather from the *Farmer's Almanac* may not be very credible. Again, this is an obvious point; but what we often forget is that events sometimes change so rapidly that "official sources" (whether they come from CNN, government spokespeople, or an Internet discussion forum) may not have the most credible, up-to-the-moment information about a particular risk.[6]

Thus, like old-fashioned journalists and detectives, it's a good idea to maintain a healthy degree of skepticism about *all* information pertaining to a risk. And it's a good idea to develop multiple *independent* sources of information about risks—so that they can be confirmed and verified before any action is taken. This, too, is obvious; but there is an unfortunate tendency in today's society to put implicit trust in

---

6. Indeed, the worst-case scenario happens more often than we'd like to admit: stonewalling, denials, half-truths, and disinformation ("I did *not* have sex with 'that woman'").

whatever one finds on the Internet, or whatever one reads or sees on television or newspapers.

Ensuring that risks are *shared* between stakeholders

Within any group, or any collection of organizations, there is a tendency to treat risks like a "hot potato": Nobody wants to hold onto them, and everyone wants to toss them on to someone else. Even within teams and collaborative partnerships, there is a tendency to assign "responsibility" for certain risks—which is a polite way of saying, "You're stuck with it, and I don't want to have anything to do with it."

Sometimes this is reasonable: If it's a self-contained risk, and if a particular individual (or organization) clearly has the resources, power, and authority to deal with it, then that individual (or organization) *should* be stuck with the hot potato. Unfortunately, the political climate surrounding such a commitment often makes it impossible for the responsible person to confess that the risk has gotten out of control—until it's *really* out of control, to such an extent that even the collective efforts of the other stakeholders are no longer sufficient to contain it. This is particularly common in contractual relationships that were negotiated in a somewhat hostile, confrontational environment; admitting that a risk exists might be viewed as an invitation to litigate, so both parties do their best to hide their risks.

All of this is familiar to anyone who has worked in a business environment; it's true of IT organizations, and it's even true in personal relationships. The only hopeful note we can offer is that when all of the stakeholders recognize that the risks are sufficiently serious to threaten *everyone's* well-being, there is a somewhat greater chance (though no guarantee!) that the risks will be shared.

Developing *processes* for risk management

A very important aspect of risk management involves the development of formal, documented, consistently-practiced *processes* of risk assessment, risk reporting, and risk mitigation. As opposed to a static approach, where risks are identified as part of a bureaucratic process and then ignored, a risk-savvy organization will create a process that supports ongoing, continuous risk identification. The "top-ten" risk-list mentioned above is a simple example of such a process.

An important part of such a process is to identify the risks early rather than late, so that the risk-mitigation strategy can be proactive rather than reactive. Even though many of us never handled needle or thread as children, we've all heard the proverb that "a stitch in time saves nine"—and in general, it's a familiar truism that it's usually cheaper and easier to prevent risks from occurring in the first place than practicing a "fix-on-failure" approach to deal with risks after they have occurred.

A fascinating aspect of this early-warning approach is discussed by Charles Perrow in a recent book, *Ordinary Accidents*.[7] Perrow notes that most serious disasters (which could be regarded as the manifestation of a serious risk) require the simultaneous occurrence of several "variables" or "parameters"—e.g., the September 11th attack on the World Trade Center succeeded because the airport security personnel failed to prevent the terrorists from boarding the flight, *and* because the weather was good, *and* because (unlike United Flight 93) the passengers did not overpower the hijackers, etc. But Perrow goes on to suggest that most such serious disasters were preceded by one or more "near misses," in which all but one of those necessary parameters were in place.

What's most important about Perrow's observation is that the near-misses are visible to all of the relevant parties, and that they're recognized as such. But the reaction to the near-miss is typically, "Whew! We sure were lucky, weren't we!?!", *and then everyone returns to business as usual.* Whether or not that proves to be the case with the September 11th attack remains to be seen; but it's worth noting that (a) the 1993 attack on the World Trade center almost succeeded, and (b) a single-engine plane, flown by a drug-addled pilot,

---

7. See *Ordinary Accidents: Living with High-Risk Technologies,* by Charles Perrow (Princeton University Press, 1999).

crashed on the White House lawn during the Clinton administration, and came perilously close to hitting the White House itself.

Thus, a crucial process for risk management today is the recognition of near misses for what they really are: a harbinger of a follow-on event, sooner or later, that *will* succeed in causing a serious disruption. If the near-miss is made the subject of nervous jokes, or simply buried by embarrassed managers and politicians, then the opportunity for proactive risk management disappears.

Paradigm Shifts in Risk Management

Risk has been a part of the IT world forever, and world-class IT organizations have long understood the need to manage their risks. So what has changed since September 11th?

Perhaps the most significant change is that the preponderance of less-than-world-class IT organizations have been forced to realize that risk management is no longer an abstraction, or a "Boy Scout" virtue like loyalty, patriotism, and thrift. It's real, and it's serious, and it needs to be a conscious part of the day-to-day activities of people developing and operating IT systems.

Beyond that, I believe there are four other paradigm shifts that even the world-class IT organizations need to factor into their plans:

- Low-tech threats
- Kamikaze players
- The rise of the "stateless" power
- Rapid changes

High tech can be threatened by low tech

By now, everyone is familiar with the fact that the September 11th terrorists used box-cutters to attack the airline crews and take control of high-technology airplanes. While the planning and organization of their attack apparently did use high-technology devices like flight simulators and the

Internet, the terrorists were able to circumvent the routine airport security procedures that were looking for high-tech weapons like guns and bombs.

This is not a new phenomenon, but it's one that high-tech IT professionals tend to forget when they're focusing on viruses and worms, firewalls and sniffers. One of the apocryphal stories that circulated among computer security professionals in the late 1960s involved a bank that had installed a high-technology night-depository box for its commercial customers. One evening, a bank robber appeared outside the bank wearing a guard's uniform; he hung a sign on the night-depository box that said "Out of Order," and then he stood beside it with a large canvas bag. Customers approached the night-depository box with their bags of cash and checks, looked carefully at the sign, and then dropped their cash into the pseudo-guard's bag. At the end of the evening, he disappeared, and was never seen again.

Thus, it's important for IT professionals and risk-management professionals to remember that attacks on their systems may involve techniques more like the *MacGyver* television show than the James Bond movies. Though the MacGyver show was, in its own way, just as fanciful and unrealistic as the razzle-dazzle James Bond movie, it did make the point that one could improvise a solution (or an attack) with ordinary odds-and-ends that one could find lying around the typical home or office. The show's character, played by Richard Dean Anderson, had an encyclopedic knowledge of chemistry, physics, electrical engineering, and the workings of engines of all kinds; and while it may be unrealistic to assume that any one individual in the "real world" would have all of this knowledge, it's *not* unrealistic to imagine that a group of dedicated criminals or terrorists might organize and assemble such knowledge. After all, they can find it on the Internet.

Kamikaze players

Another obvious lesson from September 11th was that some people are willing to die for whatever cause they're pursuing. Again, this is obviously not a new phenomenon; the kamikaze pilots of World War II are only one of the many examples from past history. But the risk-management and security strategies of many companies have been predicated on the notion that individuals and organizations behave in a "rational" way; thus, if we make it more dangerous and unpleasant to attack our systems than *we* would be willing to tolerate, we assume that it will also be too dangerous and unpleasant for anyone else.

Keep in mind that this discussion goes far beyond the direct concerns of security; we're talking about the broader issues of risk management. Thus, the owners and operators of the World Trade Center investigated the kind of guards and fences and barricades that could prevent someone from repeating the bombing attack of 1993; but they *also* had to consider the risk-management issues associated with evacuating people if an attack *did* occur, as well as the risk-management issues associated with insuring the buildings against attack. Such plans may or may not have acknowledged the possibility of suicide attacks; hopefully any such risk-management plans in the post-9/11 world *will* acknowledge such a possibility.

The rise of the "stateless" power

One aspect of risk management involves identifying the *source* of the risk. Man-made risks are usually associated with an individual, or with an easy-to-identify organization: a company, a government agency, a nation. But in more and more cases, we find ourselves facing risks caused by loosely-organized, difficult-to-identify groups like the drug cartels from South America and Asia; the terrorist groups of Hamaz and Al Qaeda; the new-generation spinoffs from the Mafia and Cosa Nostra; and ephemeral hacker groups that communicate and collaborate with one another on the Internet.[8] Just as the American government

---

8. Indeed, it's not just hackers who communicate on the Internet; disgruntled customers seek out one another, and seek out IhateXYZcorp.com Web sites. If a company introduces a new product, or even a new television commercial, that thoroughly offends some segment of the marketplace, those individuals can form an effective "guerrilla army" almost instantaneously.

finds it difficult to decide who to declare war against, and who to drop bombs on, many organizations have a difficult time identifying whom they should "attack" in order to eliminate their risks.

One of the consequences of this situation is that an organization's risk management strategy becomes more reactive than proactive—after all, if you don't know where your risks are coming from, how can you take proactive steps to confront them? On the other hand, what *can* be done proactively, as we discussed earlier in the Techniques and Technologies section, is intelligence-gathering in order to identify potential risks as earlier as possible. One reason this is particularly important with the "stateless" powers is that they often operate in a secretive fashion until they are ready to unleash their attacks. Thus, unlike an incipient risk from an approaching hurricane, an organization may have little or no advance warning of a risk that will be exploited by a group of hackers, terrorists, or criminals.

The rapid pace of change

It's always amusing to see television weather forecasters earnestly telling their viewers to prepare for an approaching rainstorm, when the viewers can open their window, look outside, and determine that it's *already* raining. Similarly, computer viruses often spread throughout portions of the Internet for several hours before the security-monitoring organizations become aware of them and sound the alarm. In today's fast-moving, globally connected world, risks emerge and propagate so quickly that the "official" sources don't always know the current situation, and can't always report on risks in a credible, accurate fashion. The anthrax attacks in New York, Washington, and Florida during the fall of 2001 were a good example: Postal employees, government workers, and ordinary citizens received information and guidelines that were often confusing, contradictory, ambiguous, and too late to do any good.

One could argue that this is not a paradigm shift at all, and that we were faced with a similar situation throughout the 1990s, and perhaps even the 80s and 70s as well. To some extent, it's a matter of degree: Whereas we might have had days to prepare for the arrival of a risk in the 1970s and 1980s, we often had only hours in the 1990s; and now it's down to minutes. In such a fast-paced environment, neither individuals nor organizations are likely to have time to *create* a risk-mitigation strategy between the time the first warning is received and the time the risk actually materializes. Thus, for risks that are "ordinary" and repeatable, individuals and organizations need to have pre-organized risk-management strategies that can be invoked on a moment's notice. To illustrate, consider the risk-management strategies one would expect for hurricanes versus tornadoes; in the former case, there is usually an advance warning of several days, whereas in the latter case, the warning may occur only moments before the tornado hits. Thus, the person dealing with hurricanes can wait until the weather forecasters confirm that the risk is "real"; but the person dealing with tornadoes has to have the storm shelter, and other plans and preparations, already in place.

What about the risks that are *not* ordinary, and are not repeatable? Whether such risks repeat themselves in the future is not the issue here; if they've never occurred before, and if it requires "thinking the unthinkable" to anticipate them, how can we devise a risk management approach? Again, the time-frame is crucial: If someone warned us that a massive comet was going to hit the Earth a year from now (i.e., the main plot of the 1998 Hollywood movie, *Deep Impact*), then we would have time to create a new, unique risk-management approach from scratch. But if you were unlucky enough to be looking out of your office window in the World Trade Center at 8:48 AM on the morning of September 11th, and you saw a plane approaching at 500 mph, there wouldn't be time to form a committee or call a meeting of the risk-management committee. A quick look at the company's official risk-management book might or might not provide specific instructions. Previously-designed and previously-practiced evacuation plans might help, but probably wouldn't indicate what to do if stairwells were blocked and elevator doors refused to open. What's needed in situations like this is a form of *emergent systems*, which we'll discuss in Chapter 5.

Strategic Implications

The strategic implications of the new, post-9/11 world of risk management will be unfolding for years to come. To the extent that we *all* face risks associated with massive biological, chemical, or nuclear attacks, some of the comments and suggestions in this chapter should have universal applicability. But as usual, there are different responsibilities, problems, and opportunities for different groups of people. I've summarized my suggestions for government officials, senior corporate executives, mid-level IT managers, IT professionals, and ordinary citizens below:

Government officials

- *Withhold information if you must, but don't lie to the public*—at the top levels of national leadership, there may be awareness of risks so awful that publicizing them might incite panic, or might provide deadly opportunities to terrorists, hackers, and unfriendly governments. It's not even clear that detailed risk-related information can be provided to the nation's 18,000 law-enforcement units without having it leaked; it certainly can't be broadcast to 275 million American citizens without having it simultaneously broadcast to the other 6 billion inhabitants of the planet. Nevertheless, there's a fundamental difference between prudent silence, and deceptive lies or half-truths. To the extent that the public becomes convinced that it has been misled—and that a particular set of threats (whether it involves anthrax, smallpox, bombs, or hurricanes) is either significantly greater *or* less than that articulated by the government, it will begin ignoring subsequent warnings.
- *Provide a central source of information about risks and threats*—a good example of this is the Federal Govern-

ment's *firstgov* Web site, which was created in 2000 as a centralized "starting point" for searching and navigating through the hundreds of government Web sites. At the time this book was written, the very top level section of the firstgov Web page provided a cogent summary of the key issues that most citizens were likely to worry about regarding the terrorist threat; but the top-level pages of the various state-government Web sites (all of which are accessible from the second-level page of firstgov.gov) were more likely to display pictures of the governor and lists of winning lotto numbers than information about risks and threats.

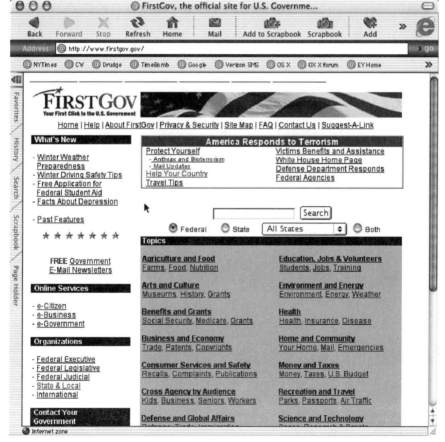

- *Provide opportunities for citizens to report risks*—as mentioned earlier in this chapter, front-line employees are

often the first ones to spot incipient risks to a corporation; by analogy, ordinary citizens are a valuable
source of localized information about threats of all
kinds. Interestingly, the firstgov.gov Web site does not
have an easily-recognizable mechanism for citizens to
report threats (or "tips"); by contrast, the *FBI Web site*
does have such a mechanism, as illustrated below:

- *Recognize that risks may change too quickly to be <u>controlled</u>*
  in a top-down fashion; endorse emergent systems—this
  might seem like a futile suggestion, since it is the
  nature of government bureaucracies to control whatever they can get their hands on. But during the planning and preparation for the Y2K problem,
  government officials at the federal and state level
  openly acknowledged that if widespread disruptions
  in the critical infrastructure did occur, they might be
  unable to provide rescue and relief resources to everyone, everywhere.[9] The same kind of realistic acknowl-

edgment of limited resources, and limited ability to control the situation, needs to be kept in mind in the event of various other risks and threats—e.g., severe environmental threats, biological/chemical terrorist attacks, etc. In circumstances like these, the concept of emergent systems will be vital; we'll discuss it further in Chapter 5.

Senior corporate executives

The recommendations for senior corporate executives are essentially the same as for government officials. One significant difference, though, is that employees can leave their jobs a lot more easily than citizens can leave their country.

Mid-level IT managers

Much of the advice offered to government officials and senior corporate executives is applicable at lower levels of management, too. Don't lie about risks; do provide access to such information; do provide a mechanism for your subordinates to report risks without falling victim to the "shoot the messenger" syndrome.

In many IT organizations, it's the mid-level managers who have to make the critical decision about whether they have the resources, the skill, and the authority to mitigate and control a risk, or whether they should pass it upward to senior management. Responsible mid-level managers obvi-

---

9. At a town meeting in February 1999, the mayor of Taos, New Mexico addressed a gathering of a few hundred citizens and calmly told them, "If the entire area has power failures and other disruptions on January 1, 2000, don't think that you'll all be able to come down to an emergency shelter in the school gymnasium, and be served filet mignon steaks for dinner. If *your* power is out, *ours* will be too. It's important for each neighborhood to make sure they're prepared, and to make sure that at least one home has candles and water and supplies. It's important that we all help each other out if there are problems." Most of the attendees nodded in agreement, but there were a few who were clearly shocked at the idea that the local government was effectively saying, "You're on your own. We aren't going to take care of you." (It should also be emphasized that the Mayor was firmly convinced that there would *not* be any problems, and that he was more concerned about forest fires during the summer of 1999 than the possibility of Y2K disruptions in the winter.)

ously want to "handle" any problems they can, in order to make a good impression on their superiors, and also to avoid bothering them needlessly. But in my work as an IT management consultant, I've often see middle managers misjudge the situation; for good reasons and bad, they avoid telling their superiors about risks that are clearly serious and beyond their ability to control. It's a judgment call that every mid-level manager has to make for himself or herself; but my advice is that whenever you're unsure of the situation, it's better to "share" the risk with your boss.

IT professionals

The advice offered to mid-level IT managers also applies to technical professionals, though the circumstances are often quite different. IT professionals typically feel that they're responsible for "handling" any technical problem that's within their area of competence; and they also believe that they're responsible for fulfilling any commitment they've made about finishing an assignment within the deadline they've promised. Though their intentions are usually quite honorable, the reality is that some technical problems—including such straightforward problems as finding a bug in one's code—are simply beyond the ability of an individual to solve on his or her own. And some commitments, made with the best of intentions, turn out to be unachievable.

Particularly when it comes to programming, design, and other aspects of systems development, it's often possible for the IT professional to hide this fact from his or her manager until the final deadline arrives. At that point, of course, it's almost impossible for the manager to rectify the situation; all that can be done is to invoke a "reactive" form of risk management. Thus, it's almost always better to report the risk—i.e., ask for help—as soon as it becomes evident that it exists.

Finally, recall the earlier comment that front-line employees are often the first ones to spot the existence of an "external" risk associated with suppliers, vendors, business partners, customers, etc. This situation occurs quite often with IT professionals: While their managers are busy attending meetings, it's the programmers and system engineers who are working side-by-side with vendor representatives, end-users, marketing people, and other external people. Thus, they're the first ones to hear the rumor and the gossip about business problems, technical problems, lawsuits, mergers, bankruptcies, and other serious risks.

Unfortunately, some IT professionals find themselves working in a corporate culture where nobody wants to hear this information. The prevailing message from the surrounding political culture is, "Shut up and do your job. We don't want to hear about rumors and gossip; and if there are any problems, the managers will take care of it." After a while, a jaded IT professional tends to shrug his shoulders and give up; why create a fuss if no one is going to pay attention?

In today's environment, though, the risks are sometimes serious enough that one *must* make a fuss, regardless of whether anyone wants to listen. Obviously, this needs to be done responsibly, and with a sense of proportion; but if a system administrator discovers that the corporate Web server has a gaping security hole that could cause all of the company's confidential information to be stolen or deleted, then he or she needs to make a huge fuss, even if it means waking up the CEO in the middle of the night.

Citizens

Finally, what about ordinary citizens? Like the IT professionals discussed above, they too are sometimes the first to become aware of a serious potential risk. But to whom does the citizen report such a risk? Depending on the circumstances, it may be a local law-enforcement officer, fire department, emergency-services organization, or public-health official; in other cases, it might be the FBI or even the Secret Service. Thus, as a starting point, it would be a good idea for all of us—as responsible citizens—to ensure that we've got the relevant phone numbers, fax numbers, email addresses, and/or Web sites of the organizations to which we might reasonably expect to report suspicious occurrences or dangerous risks.

In some cases, government officials have been much more receptive to such information than ever before. But it's inevitable that there will be cases where the government official we contact is disinterested, disbelieving, rude, unresponsive, or worse. Unfortunately, the same is sometimes true of one's neighbors, friends, and even family members—particularly if one is labeled a "Chicken Little" or a "doomer" or an "alarmist." As noted in the advice for IT professionals, any such warnings or risk-advisories must be made responsibly and with a sense of proportion; but ultimately, each citizen must decide for himself or herself how aggressive and persistent to be in the reporting of risks.

Finally, it's worth repeating the advice given earlier about "healthy skepticism": Because today's risks can occur and then change so quickly, and because they may involve completely unfamiliar situations (such as the anthrax attacks of October 2001), the "official" information about risk-status and risk-mitigation may be obsolete, misleading, ambiguous, or downright wrong. When given information about potentially serious risks, it's extremely important to look for alternate, independent sources of information— e.g., from news media in other countries—before reaching a conclusion about what to do.

EMERGENT SYSTEMS

Adaptability is not imitation. It means power of
resistance and assimilation.

—*Mahatma Gandhi*

Basic Concepts

When given a task to accomplish, how do we organize a
strategy for accomplishing it? If the task is simple enough—
e.g., moving a pencil from the left side of our desk to the
right side—the question is moot: We simply *do* it. But if the
task is sufficiently complex that it can't be performed
instinctively, or overwhelmed by brute force, then we typically have a choice of several strategies. If told to clean up
all of the clutter of papers and files on a messy desk, most of
us would pause for a moment or two, to determine how
best to accomplish the task.

With a single-person task, we typically have the luxury
of devising our own strategies. The way you clean up your
desk is not necessarily the same as the way I clean up my
desk. But when the task is large enough to require the
efforts of several individuals—e.g., members of a team,

155

employees in a company, or citizens within a country—then there are several obvious questions. Do the efforts of the individuals have to be coordinated and synchronized? Do the individuals have to communicate with each other during the performance of their activities? And perhaps most important: Does there have to be an organized "plan" for attacking the problem, and should that plan be articulated by a top-level "boss" and communicated through a hierarchy of mid-level bosses to the individuals at the bottom who are actually performing the work?

The latter approach is, of course, the one we are most familiar with. It is exemplified by military organizations, where generals and colonels devise the strategy, captains and sergeants devise the tactics supporting that strategy, and grunt-level privates march hither and thither in response to the orders they are given. A basic tenet of this approach is that, within a prescribed set of constraints defining allowable military conduct, privates are trained to obey the orders they are given, and are not expected to (or allowed to) initiate strategies on their own.

Admittedly, this is a simplistic and imperfect description of a military organization; but the overall strategy of hierarchical, top-down control applies broadly to the behavior of governments, corporations, and professional sports teams. In one form or another, it has been practiced since the Pharaohs organized legions of slaves to build the pyramids, and since the Romans organized armies to conquer most of the then-civilized world. It continues to be practiced today, for one fundamental reason: It works. Government, military, and corporate leaders speak proudly of their "chain of command," of the "discipline" of their mid-level managers, and of the unquestioning obedience that their bottom-level peons display to the rules they have been given.

But there are also circumstances where the top-down, hierarchically-managed approach doesn't work so well; and in the aftermath of September 11, we're beginning to recognize that there are situations where it doesn't work at all. Indeed, it appears that there are more and more situations where an ad hoc, bottom-up, grass roots *emergent* strategy is not only the best strategy, but the only one that works. As my colleague Jim Highsmith puts it, in an important new book about software development,[1] *"Emergence, characterized as arrival of the fittest, is significantly more important than survival of the fittest."* In an emergent organization, bottom-level individuals continually adapt their behavior (and the strategies that guide that behavior) to meet current circumstances, and the organization as a whole evolves as a result.

This, too, is somewhat of an oversimplification: Real-world organizations do not operate in a completely top-down *or* bottom-up fashion. Assembly-line workers in a manufacturing plant may not have any discretion about the way they perform their jobs, but more and more companies are organizing their workers into teams that *do* have a certain degree of flexibility about who, when, and how the individual tasks will be performed. Similarly, players on a sports team and soldiers on the battlefield may be operating under a strict set of hierarchically-imposed rules; but since *they* are the ones performing the tasks (while the coach stands on the sidelines, and the generals view the battle from afar), inevitably they have a certain degree of latitude.

The practical question is this: How *much* of a degree of latitude do the bottom-level participants have? And even more important: Is the organization's long-term goal to increase that latitude, or decrease it? If you ask the leaders to describe their vision of the ideal organization, would they describe one in which *all* of the planning, strategizing, and rule-making was performed by the managers, while all of the people at the bottom are unquestioning, highly efficient robots? Or would they describe one in which they, they managers, essentially had nothing to do, because the bottom-level workers took *all* the initiative? Of course, both extremes are unrealistic; still, it's important to understand which extreme they are pushing the organization towards.

The leader's decision to push the organization toward one extreme or the other may be based on a deep-seated personal belief that one extreme is intrinsically "right," or in

---

1. Jim Highsmith, *Adaptive Software Development: A Collaborative Approach to Managing Complex Systems* (Dorset House, 2000).

any case, far better than the other extreme. But most leaders are also pragmatists, so they'll push their organization in the direction that they sincerely believe will yield better results—more profits for a corporation, more victories over an opposing team, or a more effective national defense against terrorism. And as we'll discuss in the next section, the strategy that may have worked a generation ago, or even a decade ago, may not be the optimal one for the first decade of the 21st century.

Benefits of emergent systems and emergent organizations

A top-down, hierarchically-imposed management strategy can work well in a stable, deterministic world in which there are a limited number of strategies with known outcomes. It works well in a game of tic-tac-toe, and as noted earlier, it can work well in some assembly-line manufacturing environments, if one can make the optimistic assumption that there will be no unexpected perturbations or problems.

But it doesn't work well in situations where there are an overwhelmingly large number of possible strategies. One can formulate general guidelines for the game of chess, for example, but even those guidelines can be ignored; in a classic game, Bobby Fisher demonstrated that it's okay to sacrifice your queen if the local circumstances are right. And because of the globally-interconnected, computer-augmented world in which we live, most competitive situations (for businesses, sports teams, and entire countries) have become unbelievably complex. No one can predict, with absolute certainty and precision, how the stock market will behave or how a nation's economy will behave. And because our opponents also have access to a staggering amount of information (which may or may not be the same as, or better than, the information *we* have), game theory tells us that we cannot predict the strategy or the behavior of those opponents with absolute certainty and precision. Given a particular scenario, who really knows how the opposing football team, or the corporate competitor, or the hostile nation, will behave?

Even if a complete set of rules *could* be formulated for such complex situations, it would typically require enormous expertise, and years of study, to assimilate those rules. There are only a handful of people in the world who can play chess at the level of Bobby Fisher and Gary Kasparov—and they were obviously not grand masters when they first began. For everyone else, a limited set of general guidelines is all we have time for, and all that we can understand; while improvement can be achieved by memorizing ever more detailed textbook descriptions of strategies, most of us improve only because we *adapt* to whatever successful strategies *emerge* in the observed outcomes of ourselves and our competitors.

When using chess as an illustration, all of this may seem rather abstract. In the "real world" of business, sports, or government, many of us spend anywhere from 12 to 20 years acquiring a high-school, undergraduate, or graduate college degree that supposedly provides a rich body of detailed rules, algorithms, and strategies for success; this is reinforced by homework, practice, and periodic tests to ensure that we've absorbed it all. Arguably, this kind of "preparation for life" was successful throughout most of the 19th and 20th centuries; but as we've approached the end of the 20th century and the beginning of the 21st century, several things have rendered the traditional approach untenable.

First of all, the environment in which we apply our rules and strategies is changing so quickly that we don't have time to go through the thoughtful, analytical process by which we decide what to do. Watch a championship chess game between two grand masters, and observe how long they spend agonizing over each move; then watch a game of speed-chess, where the entire contest is conducted within the space of a minute or two. Many "serious" chess players adamantly refuse to play speed-chess; but in the real world, many of us don't have that option. The game is underway, whether we like it or not; and the clock is running much faster than it did in the past. Whether or not there was a deterministic strategy that guaranteed a successful outcome in the old world, the inescapable reality is that we don't have time to work out the details of such a strategy in today's world.

Even if the changes were occurring at a rapid pace, we might be able to cope with them if they were incremental in nature—simply by making an incremental change in our old, familiar strategy. Thus, in the good old days, a hacker might have unleashed a new virus upon the world every two or three months; now he's got the tools and the Internet connectivity to deploy a new one every two or three days. But if each new virus is only a minor variation on the previous one, the computer-security professionals might be able to keep up with it. Or, to use a less threatening example, imagine a competitor who used to cut the price of his products once a year but who has now begun instituting monthly price-cuts. As long as the price cuts are only one or two percent, we can probably keep responding—by squeezing out enough of a productivity/efficiency improvement to justify a similar price cut in our own products

What makes the situation untenable—in terms of maintaining control via a top-down, hierarchically-controlled management scheme—is *disruptive* change, where the new circumstances differ from the old circumstances by an order of magnitude. If our competitor used to offer his product for $10, we can figure out how to respond to a new price of $9.90—but what if he suddenly lowers the price to $1, and we're forced to make a quick response? If we had an advance warning of six months or a year, then senior management might be able to convene a task force, launch a crash R&D project, and try to achieve a similar breakthrough improvement. But what if the advance warning consists of a phone call from our best customer, who tells us that he's going to switch his business to our competitor unless we can respond to the price cut *now*?

Indeed, sometimes the rapidly-changing conditions are not only disruptive, they break the "rules of engagement" that we've taken for granted. What if our competitor goes beyond just cutting the price of his product by an order of magnitude, but gives it away free, or actually offers to pay the customer for the privilege of using his products? Why would anyone do such a crazy thing?[2] How can we be expected to respond to such an upside-down set of circumstances? There are dozens of examples like this in the competitive world of business; and as September 11th reminded us, there are also numerous opportunities for terrorists to break the rules, and find unorthodox ways to launch an attack on vulnerable parts of or our critical infrastructure.

In response to these rapidly-occurring, disruptive, rule-breaking changes, the response from senior management is often epitomized, as my colleague Jim Highsmith puts it, by the saying, "Anything worth doing is worth overdoing." If the ten rules that we used to formulate strategy in the old world are no longer sufficient, then we'll develop a hundred rules to handle the new, more complex situation. And if a hundred rules aren't sufficient, then we'll devise a thousand even newer ones.

To the extent that the massive quantity of new rules actually work, and to the extent that they can be automated and made available to every employee at the touch of a finger, perhaps it can work. To some extent, such an approach describes the strategy that allows pilots to fly supersonic military jets that are intrinsically unstable, and the strategy that allows stock, bond, and currency specialists to execute trades that are far too complex for the human mind to grasp within the short time that's allowed. But someone has to formulate the complex set of rules, and then test them to ensure that they work; in all too many cases, they turn out *not* to be fool-

---

2. It was only a few years ago that Netscape shocked the IT industry in just such a fashion, by giving away its "Navigator" Web browser. AOL had been practicing a similar low-tech strategy by mailing out millions of floppy disks to entice people to sign up for their service; but even the most naïve customer understood that it was only a minor variation of the Book-of-the-Month club marketing schemes that offer three or four popular books for a dollar. What intrigued people about Netscape was that the browser was *always* free to use; no consumer ever had to send a penny to the company. And what intrigued technology observers was that, by using the Internet as its distribution channel, Netscape had substantially reduced the cost of its marketing efforts. As for the marketing effort itself: It turned out to be a reversal of the old adage, "give away the razors and charge for the razor blades." In this case, millions of people suddenly had free "razor blades" (Web browsers), and that created a need for expensive, high-profit "razors" (Web servers), which Netscape was happy to sell to ISPs and e-commerce organizations.

proof rules with a deterministic outcome, but very clever heuristics with a better-than-average likelihood of success. IBM's Big Blue computer, for example, plays an awesome game of chess; but you can't *guarantee* that it will win, and if the International Chess Federation were ever to do something outrageous like changing the rules governing how a knight is allowed to move, it would be utterly helpless.

In many cases, senior management documents its "overkill" approach with a massive, multi-volume "rule book" that not only explains each required activity in excruciating detail, but also stipulates the approval process required for exceptions to the standard rules. The bureaucracy thus created simply can't keep up with the rapid pace of change, but there is an even deeper problem: Inevitably, the rule book is a "one size fits all" prescription that is supposed to applied to *all* tasks—large and small, domestic and foreign, trivial and life-threatening. Sometimes management makes a noble effort to provide several different alternatives to cover the obvious difference between large tasks and small tasks, trivial tasks and life-threatening tasks, etc. But in more and more cases, our world has as many variations as a game of chess; we can describe broad strategies, but only the grass-roots participants can truly see how to customize and adapt "generic" approaches to their situation.

There's one last point to emphasize: Even if management *could* articulate a foolproof strategy with deterministic results, people don't like being turned into robots. Yes, there are some situations where employees and citizens are willing to blindly follow a set of rules—because they know that the situation is too complex to figure out on their own, or because they're too lazy to figure it out on their own. But there are also a number of situations—at least within the American culture—where people in the trenches resent having rules imposed upon them from "on high," *even if those rules are effective.* Even as adults, we're not that different from the stubborn child who spurns offers of help and says, through clenched teeth, "I'd rather do it myself!" Whether this is a good thing (i.e., an effective way of learning something, through personal experience) or a bad thing is a matter of opinion and debate; the point here is simply that it's a deeply entrenched part of our culture, and one that the top-down hierarchy ignores at its peril.

This is particularly true of the post-modernist generation born in the 1970s and 1980s—often referred to as Generation X. They watched their parents "play by the rules" for most of their working lives, and then suddenly find themselves abruptly thrown out of work because of a corporate downsizing initiative; they've watched political scandals, environmental disasters, and one crisis after another where it was evident that the solemn promises and reassurances from high-level leaders were vacuous, misguided, or blatantly dishonest. As Peter Sacks observes in his thought-provoking book, *Generation X Goes to College*,[3] they've reacted to all of this by adopting the motto from the television show *The X-Files:* "Trust no one."

Characteristics of the emergent organization

I've characterized organizations that encourage emergent-systems behavior as "grass-roots" and "bottom-up" in nature; but that doesn't mean that they allow unbridled anarchy. In his book, *Emergence,* eminent scientist John Holland restricts the allowable behavior of emergent systems by saying, "I'll not call a phenomenon *emergent* unless it is recognizable and recurring." Thus, the game of chess has a handful of relatively simple rules, and they lead to recurring behavior in the sense that the same thing happens every time you castle your king; but as Holland observes, "The rules or laws *generate* the complexity, and the ever-changing flux of patterns that follows leads to *perpetual novelty*, and emergence."[4]

---

3. Peter Sacks, *Generation X Goes to College: An Eye-Opening Account of Teaching in Postmodern America.* (Open Court Publishing, 1996). Sacks suggests that the slogan of the modernist age is the *New York Times* masthead, "All the News That's Fit to Print," while the slogan of the postmodernist age is "Here we are now/Entertain us" (from the musical group Nirvana).
4. John H. Holland, *Emergence: from Chaos to Order* (Perseus Books, 1998). The quotations cited here are from Chapter 1, page 4 of the text.

So emergent systems (and emergent organizations) do have rules; but they tend to be relatively simple rules that can be articulated easily, communicated verbally, and remembered without effort. As an illustration, consider the breathtakingly intricate behavior of a flock of starlings as they fly in formation and turn sharply and quickly; researcher Craig Reynolds was able to simulate their behavior in a computer program in which each simulated bird followed three simple rules:

- Maintain minimal separation from other birds.
- Align velocities with other nearby birds.
- Move toward the center of mass of nearby birds in order to cohere with them.[5]

While emergent systems are thus characterized by simple rules, they are also characterized by complex relationships. The reason grand masters spend so much time staring at a chess board before making a move is not because they are desperately trying to remember the rules for moving a pawn, but rather because of the complexity associated with the relationship between all of their pieces, in their present positions, as well as the relationship with the opponent's pieces.

In organizational terms, this typically translates into a considerable emphasis on teamwork, and peer-to-peer collaboration. As such, it's the opposite of the old-fashioned assembly-line approach, where the implicit (and sometimes explicit!) message to each worker was, "Shut up, and just do *your* job!" Watch the behavior of a championship basketball team, and you'll almost believe that each player has a "sixth sense" about his other teammates and what they are about to do. If you're lucky enough to have a front-row seat at such a game, you're also likely to hear a constant stream of chatter between the teammates as they collaborate on their overall strategy of getting the ball into the basket.

---

5.   See M. Mitchell Waldrop, *Complexity: The Emerging Science at the Edge of Order and Chaos* (Simon & Schuster, 1992). The important thing to recognize here is that Reynolds' program did not contain any rules for behavior of the overall flock; there were only rules for the individual birds. Yet the group behavior that *emerges* from these rules is complex, graceful, and astonishing to watch.

As mentioned earlier, emergent organizations do not tolerate anarchy; nor do they operate completely without higher-level management supervision. A flock of birds may not have a "CEO bird," but a basketball team does have a coach, as well as a "back office" of managers and owners. The important thing, though, is that the coach is on the floor of the basketball court, yelling instructions and warnings and advice on a continuous basis; if the situation calls for it, he can make an instant decision to call for a "time-out" in order to get the team huddled together to review their strategy. The same is true of football teams, of course, with the high-tech addition of microphones in the players' helmets, so they can better hear the coach's instructions from the sidelines.

The point here is that emergent-systems organizations tend to favor "lean" decision-making; the manager who has the authority and responsibility to make decisions on behalf of a team or an individual is immediately at hand, aware of the local circumstances, and empowered to make decisions in "real time." This is in stark contrast to the behavior of some organizations, where relatively trivial decisions are communicated by smoke signals to a manager located on the other side of the country, who may not even be in his office at the moment the decision needs to be made. By the time the decision is relayed back to the team, the ability to exploit an opportunity is gone, and/or the problem has escalated beyond control.

It's also interesting to consider the longer-term consequences of this kind of organizational behavior. At the very least, the response time of the organization is sluggish; and while that may have been acceptable in a stable, slow-moving business environment, it has obvious risks in today's chaotic, fast-moving environment. And since it's the front-line employees (e.g., the players on the basketball court, or the marketing representatives facing a customer in the field) who suffer the immediate consequences of this slow response time, they are likely to respond in one of two ways: Either they'll stop reporting problems and opportunities to their higher-level executives (because they know they won't get an answer soon enough to matter), or they'll take matters into their own hands, and suffer the consequences (e.g., reprimands from the boss) later.

Fans of *Dilbert* cartoons might interpret remarks like these as an implicit statement that bottom-level employees are martyrs, if not geniuses; and that managers are obstructionist idiots. But I'll leave those characterizations to Scott Adams; the point here is simply that the bottom-level employees *are* the ones who first receive the relevant information about rapidly-occurring, disruptive changes in the environment. If the managers are basing their strategy upon obsolete, inaccurate information, then their decisions are likely to be flawed; and if they take too long to make their decision, then it won't matter what they say. Thus, whenever possible, the emergent organization allows the bottom-level players to make their own decisions and carry them out in real time, through the mechanism of simple rules and complex relationships. And when a managerial decision is needed, it's made, whenever possible, by a "coach" in the field (or on the basketball floor), rather than an uninvolved manager in a remote office.

Again, this is not meant to imply that bottom-level employees are perfect, or that managers are incompetent. In complex, fast-moving situations, anyone can make a mistake—players and coaches alike. And that suggests yet another characteristic of the emergent organization: They are *adaptable*, and their adaptability is enhanced through learning, analysis, and postmortems. Once again, consider a basketball or football team: Each game is videotaped, and the players and coach review the videotape as soon after the game as possible, in order to learn what they did well, and what they can improve. There would be no point waiting until the end of the season to review all of their games en masse; not only would it be difficult to remember the details of an early-season game, but it would be too late to adjust their behavior in a meaningful way.

There are, of course, many techniques and technologies for enhancing and augmenting the learning/review process; we'll discuss a few of them later in the Techniques and Technologies section. The main point here, though, involves the nature of the corporate culture. In some organizations, bureaucracy and politics turn the reviews and postmortems into useless charades; and in some organizations, a defensive, hostile attitude culture discourages both workers and managers from questioning recent decisions in order to find opportunities for improvement. In the extreme case, an anti-intellectual attitude discourages anyone from suggesting that "models" can be created in order to explore problems and opportunities in a more organized fashion.[6]

The most extreme form of adaptation involves the mission and goals of the organization; rather than articulating a rigid set of objectives and then having a high-level manager decree that "It shall be so!", the emergent organization *speculates* what its mission and goals are—and gives itself the freedom to adapt those goals in the face of rapidly-changing, disruptive changes in the environment.

This may sound unacceptable, especially for those who believe strongly in principles, morals, and ethical behavior. But if we regard those principles as "rules" that require us to act in a certain way, under certain conditions, that still leaves us free to adapt our goals and objectives to circumstances that we might not have been able to anticipate when we first stated them. Whatever else we do as members of a team, a company, or a country, most of us are pretty strongly committed to principles of honesty, integrity, and the Golden Rule; beyond that, we should give ourselves the flexibility of modifying what we mean by "winning."

Thus, if you ask most corporate executives what their mission is, they'll usually spout some homilies about "serving the customer"; after a little more discussion, they'll usually acknowledge that their *real* mission is to "maximize

---

6. Models can be simple or complex; they can be formal or informal. While researchers like John H. Holland tend to emphasize mathematical models in *Emergence: from Chaos to Order*, and while computer professionals create models in the form of computer programs (e.g., the bird-simulating program created by Craig Reynolds), a model can also take the form of a map, a chart, a spreadsheet, a computer prototype, or a diagram. Consider, for example, the popular vision of a football coach explaining the strategy he wants his team to carry out on the next play: The model consists of "X"s and "O"s and arrows drawn on a blackboard with chalk.

profits," which usually gets translated into "grow to become bigger and bigger, and also become more productive and efficient, so that we make more and more money." A large organization has the luxury of spending a lot of time and money crafting a vision statement; thus, IBM's Web site says that "we strive to lead in the creation, development and manufacture of the industry's most advanced information technologies, including computer systems, software, networking systems, storage devices and microelectronics." If, because of unexpected competition or technological innovation, it should turn out that "networking systems" are an unprofitable and uninteresting business activity, one hopes that the senior executives at IBM won't commit hara kiri.

This sounds like common sense, but it's amazing to see how fanatical and rigid some teams, some organizations, some countries, and even some individuals, become about their stated mission and goals. Persistent determination can be a laudable character trait; but it makes far more sense when practiced in a stable environment that changes only slowly and incrementally. A mission that may have seemed attainable in today's world—albeit with extremely hard work and dedication—may be completely beyond reach in tomorrow's world, because the required "parameters" of success may have changed by an order of magnitude. Emergent-system organizations understand this; old-fashioned top-down, hierarchically-managed organizations often do not.

Techniques and Technologies_____

There is no "universal" set of techniques and technologies for creating emergent organizations; indeed, one can imagine the kind of mystique and hype associated with the concept—accompanied with consultants, textbooks, and seminars—that we've seen in the past with other management buzzwords like reengineering, e-business, and "total quality management."

But IT professionals will be pleased to know that their high-tech tools and gadgets can help support an organization whose culture is shifting towards emergent behavior. Some of the more useful kinds of tools are discussed below

Peer-to-peer communication mechanisms

Obviously, every organization has telephones, and almost all organizations have email for their employees; some of them also provide cell phones, pagers, and wireless PDA devices. Undoubtedly, there will be more of these in the future, and it's reasonable to assume that they will be cheaper, faster, smarter, and even more sophisticated.

But it's important to look at these devices to see whether they support emergent behavior, or whether they reinforce a hierarchical, authoritative, top-down management approach. At the same time, it's important to examine them in terms of *resiliency*, which we'll discuss in more detail in Chapter 6.

For example, in the aftermath of September 11th, companies attempting to call into, or out of, the metropolitan New York area found that both cell-phone and traditional voice circuits were overloaded; closer to Ground Zero, several companies lost switching centers, email servers, and other "centralized" communication mechanisms. Obviously, the same thing can happen with severe computer-virus attacks, hurricanes, fires, floods, and other environment disasters.

Those scenarios involve the issue of resilience. Above and beyond that, more and more organizations are installing firewalls and rigid controls on their Web servers, email servers, and Internet gateways. Some of these controls are necessitated by the security issues we discussed in Chapter 4; but some of them are based on management's determination to prevent employees from visiting pornographic Web sites, sending inappropriate jokes via email, and generally "wasting" valuable corporate resources.[7] I'm often surprised by the nervous response that I get from business colleagues who work in such environments: If I send them an innocent non-business-related message like "What did you think of the Yankees game last night?", the response is, "Please don't send personal messages to my office email address; I've been told that I'll be fired if I'm found to be responsible for allowing spam email inside the corporate firewall. From now on, please send non-essential, non-work-related messages to JoeShmoe@home.com".

Paradoxically, such an onerous set of constraints can actually help to create an "emergent" environment. After all, I don't want Joe Shmoe's boss to read my email (especially if he's a Boston Red Sox fan!), and the first time I get such a message from Joe, I send *all* subsequent email communications to his home.com address. In a similar vein, several companies strongly encouraged their key employees to acquire personal email addresses in the months preceding the Y2K rollover, and to share those email addresses with their peers with whom they might need to communicate in an emergency.

As I've suggested throughout this chapter, adaptive emergence and pre-planned, rigidly enforced hierarchies do not represent a simple either-or choice; they mark out the end points on a continuous spectrum. Thus, it's quite understandable that an organization dealing with sensitive, confidential materials (e.g., a law firm, or an investment banking firm) might want to have strict controls over the manner in which its employees access the Internet via email and the Web. But to encourage and support emergence—which, as we've suggested above, is more and more necessary for coping with rapid, disruptive change—we can *also* ensure that employees have AOL Instant Messenger, MSN Messenger, SMS text messaging on their cell phones, and other similar technologies.

---

7. The same mindset prevailed with telephone usage when I first entered the workforce in the mid-1960s. Even in a high-tech computer company, ordinary employees could not make long-distance calls from their office phone; they had to schedule the call with the company's telephone receptionist. When direct-dial long-distance became prevalent in the 1970s, it was common for cost-conscious managers to scrutinize the monthly phone bill with a fine-tooth comb, to see whether any employee had "wasted" the expensive telephone resource by making a long-distance call to his parents in a neighboring city. There may be some companies who still engage in this practice; but most companies have concluded that telephone service is cheap enough and plentiful enough that it's just not cost-effective to control it so rigidly.

An organization that doesn't feel so strongly about controlling its employees' behavior can integrate many of these peer-to-peer communication tools into the normal computing environment. As noted in Chapter 2, many employees and ordinary citizens took advantage of such arrangements on September 11th: On the day of the attack, America Online recorded 700 million messages from non-AOL subscribers on its free AOL Instant Messenger (AIM) service, plus another 500 million AIM messages generated by AOL subscribers.[8]

An organization that *does* feel strongly about controlling the behavior of its employees might still want to provide some assistance for such peer-to-peer tools to be used outside the office environment; the advantage (from a "control" perspective) is that it's more likely to have some potentially useful information about where people are, and how to contact them. But if the organization stubbornly refuses to do so, the employees always have the option of doing it themselves: After all, the technology is relatively inexpensive (and sometimes, like AOL Instant Messenger, absolutely free) and widely available. Thus, my friend Joe Shmoe can not only communicate with me by email—in an environment completely free from management control—but he can also communicate with me via cell-phone, land-line phone, and wireless pager.

One last point: peer-to-peer communications sometimes involves more than just text messages. Napster was a rude shock to the top-down hierarchical world of record producers, and it obviously involved sharing of MP3 music files; paradoxically, Napster's architecture was itself hierarchically-structured (with a central server and a directory of participants), so it was relatively easy to shut down once the record producers prevailed in court. Follow-on technologies like Gnutella really *are* peer-to-peer networks, and we can expect them to be used for transmitting music, video, graphic images, and various other file formats. Indeed, even AOL Instant Messenger supports file transfers between "buddies."

---

8. See "Internet messaging keeps businesses, employees in touch," by Jennifer Disabatino, *Computerworld*, Sept. 17, 2001.

Tools for collaboration

While text-message interactions between individuals is obviously important, many of the complex tasks and problems faced by today's organizations require *collaboration* between multiple individuals. To some extent, this can be supported by "group" emails, teleconference calls, video-conferencing, and old-fashioned face-to-face meetings. But more and more high-technology tools are appearing in the marketplace, and because collaboration also involves people outside the corporate boundary (e.g., vendors, suppliers, partners, customers), some of the most interesting collaboration tools are peer-to-peer in nature.

Internet chat rooms and discussion forums are one example of such collaboration tools; "closed" collaborative meetings can be organized with such services as egroups.com and eproject.com. Microsoft's Netmeeting is another tool for peer-to-peer multi-person collaborations; and another interesting tool is Groove, created by Ray Ozzie, the inventor of Lotus Notes.[9]

At the time this book was being written, one of the most significant limitations in such collaboration tools is adequate bandwidth—i.e., low-cost, universally-available, high-speed bandwidth that will support full-screen, real-time, interactive video. But if bandwidth technology continues to improve and proliferate at the same rapid pace that it has for the past several years, then truly effective collaboration tools should begin appearing within a few years.[10]

Modeling and simulation tools

As noted earlier, *models* are an important tool for studying and understanding emergent systems;[11] or to put it another way, models are a mechanism by which the members of an organization can better understand the emergent-system

---

9. Though it is a bit dated at this point, and though the book's title is (in my opinion) somewhat misleading, Michael Schrage's *No More Teams! Mastering the Dynamics of Creative Collaboration* (Doubleday-Dell Publishing Company, 1995) provides an excellent discussion of the technologies *and* the organizational processes associated with effective collaboration.

environment in which they work. And models can take a wide variety of forms, from low-tech to high-tech; low-tech models (e.g., paper-and-pencil drawings) are still the easiest, quickest, most flexible approach in some cases, and emergent-systems IT professionals should keep this in mind; it's all too easy to be seduced by the glamour of high-tech modeling tools.[12]

With that caveat, it's worth noting that steadily improving hardware technology, advanced programming languages, and multi-media integration have given us tools that are both inexpensive and awesomely powerful. While I'm personally happy to use everything from spreadsheets to prototyping tools when the occasion calls for it, I'm a particular fan of *systems dynamics* tools such as iThink (from High Performance Systems, Inc.), because they encourage the model-builder to explore and understand the time-delays between one part of a system and another, as well as the feedback loops between different parts of a system.[13]

While modeling tools help individuals and groups explore the behavior of an emergent system (which may

---

10. Futurist George Gilder argues that such advances are indeed likely. In *Telecosm: How Infinite Bandwidth Will Revolutionize Our World,* (Free Press, 2000), Gilder says, "In the new millennium, all the defining abundances of the microcosm are becoming relatively scarce and expensive. This reversal is forcing a massive and drastic reorientation of the entire structure of the information economy … Measured by the expansion of Internet traffic, the price of bandwidth is decreasing and its availability is increasing by a factor dwarfing Moore's law. Bandwidth is demonstrably advancing at a doubling rate of at least four times the 18-month pace of the microcosm."

11. For more discussion of this point, see Holland's *Emergence: from Chaos to Order,* cited earlier, as well his earlier book, *Hidden Order: How Adaptation Builds Complexity* (Perseus Books, 1995). For an alternative, and quite entertaining look at adaptive, emergent systems, see *Turtles, Termites, and Traffic Jams: Explorations in Massively Parallel Microworlds,* by Mitchel Resnick (MIT Press, 1994).

12. For an interesting discussion of modeling and simulation, see *Serious Play: How the World's Best Companies Simulate to Innovate,* by Michael Schrage and Tom Peters (Harvard Business School Press, Dec. 1999).

13. A famous example of a feedback loop in software development projects is "Brooks' Law," first described in Fred Brooks' 1975 classic, *The Mythical Man-Month* (20th anniversary edition, Addison-Wesley, 1995); it says "adding more people to a late software project just makes it later." In some cases, a feedback loop can create what's often known as a "vicious circle," leading to chaotic results.

consist of their own organization, or a particular business process within the organization, or the marketplace as a whole), they also serve another purpose: creating a *shared understanding* among the individuals who have to collaborate and work together in the execution of their common task. In a landmark book, *The Fifth Discipline*,[14] Peter Senge coined the phrase "mental model" to describe what's involved here: an internal "vision" of the way things work, which we need to articulate and communicate to our colleagues and co-workers.

Anyone who has gone through this process (and that includes just about everyone!) knows how frustrating it can be to communicate one's mental model with arm-waving and disjointed words and sentences. Charts, diagrams, and pictures are enormously helpful—particularly if they can be understood without first having to attend a three-day class to learn the nuances of the notation and terminology.

And because we are accomplishing tasks, solving problems, and building systems within an environment where things *do* change rapidly and disruptively, it's also helpful to have models that illustrate the *dynamics* of the underlying task/problem/system, rather than just a static description. When we look at a spreadsheet that shows a company's revenues and profits over, say, a 12-month period, we can attempt to mentally visualize the dynamic behaviors that are involved in increasing January's revenues by 10% to achieve February's results. But if the spreadsheet shows that revenues double or triple between January and February, it's much more difficult to visualize the chaotic dynamics that must be involved. Did we double the number of sales representatives to achieve these results? Was the order-processing system swamped, and were there backlogs in the shipping department? Was the manufacturing department working overtime to produce twice as many widgets as they did last month—and did the overtime

---

14. Peter M. Senge, *The Fifth Discipline: The Art and Practice of the Learning Organization.* (Doubleday, 1990). See also his subsequent book, coauthored with Charlotte Roberts, Richard B. Ross, Bryan J. Smith, and Art Kleiner: *The Fifth Discipline Fieldbook: Strategies and Tools for Building a Learning Organization* (Doubleday, 1994).

wages lead to disproportionately greater costs, and lower profits? All of this information can be gleaned from a static, lifeless spreadsheet; but if a collaborative team of sales, order-entry, and production managers are discussing the situation, it would be more useful to have an animated, dynamic model in order to achieve an effective shared mental model.

Paradigm Shifts

Emergent systems have existed since life began on this planet, and they have been the subject of intense study since the 1980s, if not earlier. Corporations have faced global competition and disruptive changes for the last several decades, and governments have faced terrorist threats for centuries, not just decades. So, what's new and different in today's world? Where's the paradigm shift?

The answer, I believe, is a matter of degree and awareness. Yes, the world has been changing for quite a long time, but the pace of change continues to increase, and the degree of disruptiveness has also been increasing. Technology change is often expressed in terms of Moore's Law, which says that computer power—measured in terms of price, speed, storage capacity, etc.—doubles every 18 months. Even a single such change would be a shock in many of today's industries; imagine being told, for example, that within 18 months you would be able to purchase twice as much "automobile-power" (in terms of speed, fuel efficiency, passenger space, etc.) for the same amount of money! But when it comes to computers, cell phones, televisions, and various other computer-augmented electronic devices, we've become rather blasé about the improvements that we see from one year to the next.

Occasionally, though, it occurs to us that the accumulated effect of these year-after-year changes is not just a quantitative change, but a *qualitative* change. The Concorde only flies about twice the speed of an ordinary jet-liner, but for those who can afford the extra cost, it literally changes the way they do business—and if the price differential was eliminated, it would change the way *all* international business travelers do business. In the case of computer technology, improving the price-performance by an order of magnitude (a factor of ten) roughly every six years has also allowed us to change the way we do business—as exemplified by the transitions from mainframe to minicomputers, then from minis to PCs, and now from PCs to handheld wireless machines.

Roughly speaking, then, we could argue that business, government, and society have experienced a paradigm shift at least once each decade from the 1970s through the current time. It often appears that life is moving at 10 times the speed that we experienced in the early 1990s, the changes from one "state" or "scenario" to the next occur 10 times faster; and the degree of the change is 10 times greater. And correspondingly, the need for an emergent-systems approach is 10 times greater, while the ability of a traditional top-down, hierarchically-managed organization to cope with the situation is 10 times less than before.

The other aspect of the paradigm shift is *awareness*. Emergent systems and disruptive changes have existed for a long time, but a substantial part of American society was oblivious to this fact until they turned on their televisions on the morning of September 11th. Disruptive change is no longer just an abstraction that involves the refugees in Bosnia or the victims of terrorism in Israel and Palestine; it's no longer something safely confined to the other side of our twin, protective oceans. Now it's *here*, and it involves *us*.

Amazingly, there are still people in the United States (usually located far from New York, Washington, and other cities who are now visibly alert to the risk of terrorist attacks) who think to themselves, "Well, I don't have to pay attention to any of this, because nobody would bother attacking our little village—and besides, 'they' will take care us." But as we've suggested already in this chapter, things are often changing so quickly that 'they' (the hierarchy) don't even know what the current situation *is*, and thus may not be able to inform its subordinates in a timely, accurate fashion. Furthermore, the disruptive changes may take the form of threats against the hierarchy itself; thus, the workers in the trenches may have no recourse but to devise their own rules, their own procedures, and their own strategies for survival.

Thus, the message that is slowly sinking into American government, business, and society is: It's a new world out there. It's a world that changes abruptly, unexpectedly, without warning, and in ways that are sometimes dangerous and threatening. And we have to be prepared for the possibility that 'they' won't be able to control the situation, and might not even know what the situation is. We have to be prepared to take matters into our own hands and cope with the changes by ourselves, or with our immediate family, friends, and co-workers.

And *that*, I believe, is a legitimate paradigm shift.

Strategic Implications

What do we *do* about all of this? Well, since the first instinct of any organism is survival, there's a good chance that government leaders and senior corporate executives will respond by saying, "Nothing!" Conversely, the IT professionals, corporate workers, and ordinary citizens at the bottom of the hierarchy may be the ones crying out, "Yes! Yes! Let's ignore the hierarchy and control our own destinies!"

As I've suggested throughout this chapter, the distinction between a top-down, hierarchical, pre-planned organization and a bottom-up, grass-roots, adaptive, ad hoc organization is not an all-or-nothing distinction. Nor do the circumstances in today's world necessarily call for the wholesale replacement of one form with another. While some aspects of today's life *are* chaotic and fast-changing, there are others that are predictable and slow to change—if not downright stagnant. If a hierarchically-structured organization is successfully managing a relatively stable situation—e.g., the processing of marriage licenses at City Hall, or the processing of paychecks in a corporate payroll system—then the status quo will probably continue (if for no other reason than the survival-instinct efforts of the hierarchy to maintain the status quo).

It's the situations that *don't* work where it makes sense to talk about the strategic implications of an emergent-systems approach. Unfortunately, even this area is problematic because (a) not everyone agrees that a particular strategy or management approach or organizational culture has stopped working, (b) the inadequacy of the existing hierarchical structure may be associated with an impending crisis that has not yet occurred, and (c) even if the hierarchical structure *knows* that it can't cope, it may stubbornly cling to power.

Thus, consider the example of airport security—which is controlled by a hierarchy consisting of the federal Department of Transportation, the FAA, and various management hierarchies within the airlines and airports. Does it "work," as currently constituted and with the changes legislated by Congress in November 2001? Or would we better off augmenting that system—or possibly replacing it—with an emergent-systems approach involving pilots, passengers and others directly involved with flight?

Despite the widespread chorus of criticisms of airport security, it's important to note that, at the time this book was written, there was *not* an overwhelming consensus that the current system is broken. While a substantial majority of American citizens do support the various proposals for increased security, a Gallup report indicated that two separate surveys found that only 49 to 57% of Americans blamed inadequate security at airports for allowing the September 11th attacks to take place:

> "A mid-September Gallup poll found 49% of Americans assigning a "great deal" of blame for the attacks to airport security, compared to just 22% who blamed the CIA and 18% the FBI. A Newsweek poll around the same time confirmed this result, with 57% of Americans blaming "inadequate security at airports" for allowing the attacks to happen, compared to just 30% blaming the FBI and CIA for failing to identify and stop the terrorist plots from being carried out."[15]

And while the existing system may indeed be broken, the existing managerial hierarchy can continue to deny that fact (even to itself, apparently) as long as the ongoing security breaches—of which there have been several—are relatively minor compared to the tragedy of September 11th. Indeed, it's quite possible that every responsible official, all the way up to the top of the chain of command, is fully aware that the system is broken; but the existing bureaucracy of security contractors, airport managers, FAA officials, and Transportation Department civil-service employees, may be so deeply entrenched and so unwilling to relinquish power, that nothing changes.

In any case, as we noted in Chapter 2, it took the House and Senate *ten weeks* after the September 11th attack to pass legislation that merely shifted the somewhat decentralized airport-controlled hierarchies to a more massive, centralized hierarchy within the Transportation Department. And even though the legislation mandated that within *one year*, the 28,000-person airport security staff would be federalized and reorganized into a workforce consisting of American citizens with at least a high-school diploma, the education requirement was emasculated within a month with a revision that read:

(a) No certificate holder shall use any person to perform any screening function, unless that person has:

(1) A high school diploma, a General Equivalency Diploma, *or a combination of education and experience which the certificate holder has determined to have equipped the person to perform the duties of the position;*[16] [emphasis added]

Indeed, the only aspect of the airport-security system that *has* been transformed into an emergent-systems approach is the onboard behavior of the passengers. Prior to

15. See "Americans Want Tighter Airport Security at Any Cost: Majority supports every major proposal," by Lydia Saad, *Gallup News Service,* Oct. 31, 2001.
16. See [Code of Federal Regulations], [Title 14, Volume 2] [Revised as of January 1, 2001];TITLE 14--AERONAUTICS AND SPACE; CHAPTER I--FEDERAL AVIATION ADMINISTRATION, DEPARTMENT OF TRANSPORTATION;PART 108--AIRPLANE OPERATOR SECURITY--Sec. 108.31 Employment standards for screening personnel.

September 11th, most airline passengers (including me!) assumed that the FAA and airport security organizations really *were* in control of the situation; and they tended to remain in their seats, like docile lambs, no matter what she-nanigans were going on all around them. But the passengers on the doomed United Flight 93 demonstrated that (a) individuals *can* use peer-to-peer communications (cell-phones) to get an accurate, up-to-the-minute assessment of the situation, (b) work collaboratively, under pressure, with utter strangers with whom they happen to find themselves facing a crisis, and (c) adapt their strategy, in real-time, to the changing circumstances.

So the advice and guidelines that follow make the optimistic, and probably unrealistic, assumption that government leaders and senior corporate executives understand that, in many cases, their existing hierarchical control structures are broken, and that they have the vision, courage, and persistence to allow at least a modest degree of bottom-up, grass-roots, adaptive, emergent behavior to flourish. But the advice and guidelines are also aimed at the IT professionals and ordinary citizens at the bottom of the hierarchy, where the lesson from September 11th is that, if necessary, bottom-level individuals can take matters into their own hands and implement an emergent-systems strategy.

Government leaders

- *Publicly acknowledge those parts of the hierarchical control system that are broken*—this will require some courage, and will almost certainly expose the whistle-blower to varying degrees of criticism and accusations of partisanship, if not worse. And there is an obvious reluctance to highlight broken management-control mechanisms that might create opportunities for terrorism, theft, hacking, mischief, or even military attack. Obviously, government leaders (and citizens) need to act in a responsible manner; but there's a desperate need, in many cases, for someone in government to stand up and shout, "The Emperor has no clothes!" Chances are that most of the capable criminals, hackers, and terrorists already know about the vulnerabilities, and may already be exploiting them (as was the case with the September 11th attacks and the subsequent December 22, 2001 "shoe bomber" affair). Sooner or later, everyone else will become aware of the broken systems, and will see the systems as something to be circumvented and flouted, rather than something to respect and cooperate with.

• *Encourage bottom-level citizens, individuals, and groups to devise their own emergent-systems approaches*—as noted earlier in this chapter, local government officials often encouraged citizens to form grass-roots collaborative groups in preparation for the Y2K problem, because of their concern that the extent of Y2K disruptions might overwhelm their limited resources. Similarly, local government officials in various parts of the country encourage such grass-roots groups for dealing with crime, hurricanes, floods, earthquakes, and forest fires. Advice and encouragement of this kind has generally *not* been forthcoming from state and federal-level officials, perhaps because it was felt that there were no state-level or nationwide threats for which an emergent-systems approach would be appropriate—or, as suggested earlier, because no government official wanted to admit the awful truth that the existing hierarchical structure would be wholly inadequate for dealing with such a crisis. At the time this book was being written, for example, there was ample evidence to suggest that the country was utterly defenseless and vulnerable to a massive smallpox attack; the present public-health system is, from this perspective, "broken" until sometime in late 2002 when 300 million units of vaccine will hopefully be stockpiled. Meanwhile, the Centers for Disease Control (CDC) is continuing to augment and embellish the top-down approach to the problem; a check of the CDC Web site's "Interim Smallpox Response Plan and Guidelines" in mid-January 2002 provided *no* advice, guidelines, or encouragement for neighborhood-level, adaptive, grass-roots efforts to cope with any smallpox emergency that might occur. Similarly, the Federal Emergency Management Agency (FEMA) devotes a section of its Web site to "Family and Community Preparedness," but nothing in that section provides any advice for individuals, families, or neighborhoods to deal with anthrax or smallpox attacks. Even the Red Cross, while obviously not a government agency, was sadly lacking: Its Web site seems devoted mostly to self-congratulatory articles of its many fine deeds, and has no advice whatsoever to help individuals or families cope with the all-too-real threat of a bio/chemical/nuclear attack that might completely overwhelm the "official" government and public-health hierarchies.

- *Eliminate obstacles to peer-to-peer communication and collaboration mechanisms*—When faced with an unresponsive or unhelpful top-down management hierarchy, some (though, unfortunately, not all) employees and citizens at the bottom of the hierarchy will take matters into their own hands, and improvise the beginnings of an adaptive, emergent system on their own—unless they are completely prevented from doing so by onerous laws, ordinances, and regulations. In some cases, the laws are intended to "manage" a scarce resource, and to prevent hoarding by unscrupulous citizens; such laws might or might not make sense when dealing with old-fashioned resources like gasoline or food; unfortunately, it now includes new-age resources like access to cell-phone channels.[17] In the worst case, the top-down, hierarchically-controlled mechanisms are a thinly-disguised Ponzi scheme, wealth-redistribution, or social-engineering scheme camouflaged by flowery language that effectively says to the citizen, "We know better; and therefore we're going to impose this system upon you, whether you like it or not." Two obvious examples of such "systems" are the nation's public-school systems, and the infamous Social Security system.[18]

---

17. See "White House seeking priority wireless access for military, emergency crews," by Bob Brewin, *Computerworld*, Oct. 12, 2001.

Senior corporate executives

In general, my advice to senior managers is the same as for government leaders above: acknowledge those parts of your corporate hierarchy that are broken; encourage employees and groups to device their own emergent-systems approaches; and eliminate obstacles to peer-to-peer collaboration mechanisms.

In addition, I strongly suggest that senior executives develop a set of policies, procedures, rules, and strategies that corresponds to the Defense Department's strategy for military personnel who are incommunicado and stranded in enemy territory. Such policy documents effectively say, "If you can't communicate with Galactic Headquarters for more than X hours, here is how you should operate on your own." Note, by the way, that the creation of this document is an interesting opportunity to choose between a top-down, hierarchically controlled approach, versus a bottom-up, grass-roots, emergent-systems approach.

Mid-level IT managers

To the extent that mid-level IT managers have any real control over the events affecting their day-to-day work activities, then the advice offered to senior corporate managers and government officials is still valid. Of course, by the time you descend to the level of a first-level or second-level manager, more and more of the hierarchy is above you, not below you; and thus, your freedom to initiate and encourage grass-roots, ad hoc, adaptive, emergent behavior is ever more limited.

---

18. The public-school system, and Social Security, are also good examples of situations where citizens will take matters into their own hands, and develop their own grass-roots, adaptive, emergent approach—even if the top-down hierarchy penalizes them by forcing them to "contribute" their taxes to the official system. In the former case, the grass-roots approach is known as home schooling (or, in a milder form, private schools); in the latter case, it's a combination of IRAs, SEPs, 401-Ks, and old-fashioned savings accounts. Meanwhile, government authorities continue to display a maniacal determination to continue enforcing their existing systems, no matter how visibly broken they are.

On the other hand, some flexibility may be possible in the very area that IT managers are responsible for: the design, development, and implementation of IT systems. In this area, there is an exciting, energetic, and refreshing debate underway between the two "worlds" that we've discussed throughout this chapter. If any of the philosophical concepts in this chapter appear relevant and possibly applicable to the world of systems development, then the various books of the "extreme programming" (XP) community are strongly recommended, as well as the book mentioned earlier in the chapter by Jim Highsmith.[19] In addition, the Manifesto for Agile Software Development is highly recommended reading for mid-level IT managers, as well as the related articles, conference presentations, and Internet discussion groups spawned by that document.

IT professionals

IT professionals are typically at, or near, the bottom of the corporate hierarchy in terms of the issues and concepts discussed in this chapter. However, because they themselves operate in a world of rapid, chaotic change (i.e., the world of technology), the management-control hierarchy may have abandoned any effort to impose a great deal of control over their day-to-day lives. Indeed, many programmers, software engineers, testing professionals, and other members of the IT community effectively operate in a world of anarchy—simply because management doesn't understand what they are doing, and/or finds itself unable to keep up with the pace of change.

In other cases, management attempts to impose a control structure based on technological approaches of the 1970s or 1980s—e.g., a sequential "waterfall" systems development

---

19. See, for example, Kent Beck, *eXtreme Programming eXplained: Embrace Change* (Addison-Wesley, 2000); Kent Beck, Martin Fowler, and Jennifer Kohnke, *Planning eXtreme Programming* (Addison-Wesley, 2000); Ron Jeffries, Ann Anderson, and Jennifer Kohnke, *eXtreme Programming Installed* (Addison-Wesley, 2000); *Refactoring: Improving the Design of Existing Code*, by Martin Fowler, with Kent Beck and John Brant (Addison-Wesley, 1999); and Jim Highsmith, *Adaptive Software Development: A Collaborative Approach to Managing Complex Systems* (Dorset House, 2000).

approach that ignores the modern concept of prototyping, iterative development, and collaborative strategies such as the "dual programming" method advocated by the XP community. If a rigid control structure is mandated and enforced ruthlessly, then the IT professional needs to ask himself whether it works; as mentioned several times in this chapter, there are situations where a grass-roots, emergent, collaborative approach (such as the XP dual-programming approach, and iterative prototyping) can be combined with the top-down, preplanned approach (such as configuration management and risk management). And there may be an opportunity to overtly or covertly begin introducing some of the emergent-systems concepts; thus, the XP books recommended above for managers are also excellent reading for technical professionals.

However, the most important advice for technical professionals is this: *begin building your own peer-to-peer networks for communication and collaboration,* so that you can "invoke" them in circumstances of chaotic disruption. In a static world, managers can make all the decisions, and workers become robots; in a changing but predictable world, management make most of the decisions, but workers need to exhibit a modest degree of intelligence to get their job done. But in a world of chaos and disruption—whether caused by events like September 11th, or a pandemic hacking attack, or an environmental disaster, or the overnight bankruptcy of one's critical technology vendor—management is likely to be running around in circles, shouting nonsensical orders based on obsolete, inaccurate information. The ability of the organization to survive is likely to depend, to a much larger degree than ever before, on the ability of the bottom-level workers to reach out to their networked peers, and cobble together an improvised solution to the crisis.

Citizens

The advice offered to IT professionals can be generalized for citizens: Take a look at the hierarchical control structures that govern your day-to-day activities, and ask yourself whether they really work. Does Social Security work for you? Do the public school systems work for your children, and does the public-health system of Medicare, Medicaid, and HMO insurance systems work for your extended family? Are you confident that the hierarchical control structure that provides your utilities (water, sewage, electricity, telephone), transportation, food, banking, and other "critical infrastructure" services can cope with the disruptive changes lying ahead? If so, then you may conclude that this entire chapter was written for someone else, and move happily on to the next chapter.

But if not, then your choices are similar to those of the IT professionals. See whether the control-hierarchy actually pays attention to what you're doing, and ask yourself whether you're willing to take the risks associated with circumventing the hierarchy to do what you believe is the right thing to do. Sometimes the risk translates into a straightforward cost calculation, which you can evaluate like any other financial choice; my wife and I decided, for example, to incur the cost of private-school education for our children, but it's understandable that not everyone is able to, or willing to, make such a choice.

The more extreme choices involve circumventing hierarchy-control mechanisms that have legal consequences. It's not something that I recommend, or that I practice on a personal basis, but it's obviously an area where every citizen has to make a personal choice. For example, I personally consider the mandatory Social Security system to be outrageously unfair, immoral, and irrevocably "broken"; but I make no attempt to circumvent it, because I'm not willing to take the risk of spending time in jail.

Ultimately, the most important advice that I can offer citizens is the same as that offered to IT professionals: Build your own peer-to-peer collaborative communications network, and be ready to call upon it if you find yourself in a disruptive crisis that overwhelms the resources and capabilities of the existing top-down, hierarchical control system. The details will differ from person to person, but the kinds of questions you should be asking yourself are:

- Do all of my family members and close friends have cell phones or pagers or AOL Instant Messenger accounts, or some mechanism (such as amateur radio,) that will allow me to contact them quickly if there is an emergency and the primary phone and email systems are down?

- Do I have the phone numbers, email addresses, and alternate contact information for all of the people I care about, *always with me, on my person at all times,* so that I can contact them if an emergency occurs when I am away from home and office?

- Do I have the names, phone numbers, and email addresses of my immediate neighbors? Do they have mine? If there is an emergency, are they willing and able to contact me, and can I depend on them for mutual assistance? Are any of my neighbors elderly, disabled, or in need of special care if there is an emergency?

- Do I have the names and phone numbers of neighborhood-level emergency-services, fire-department, police, hospital, and other services that I might need to call in an emergency?

- Do I have names and phone numbers of friends with basic medical expertise (assuming that I don't have it on my own), whom I could call in times of emergency, when the "official" sources of medical assistance were overloaded, unresponsive, or unavailable?

- Do I have a basic understanding of what I would do, to protect myself and my family, in the event of a major biological/chemical/nuclear attack in my local geographical area? If, for example, there were a major outbreak of smallpox in my city, and a combination of curfew and quarantine prevented me from taking my children to the hospital for treatment, do I have a layman's understanding of the basics of how best to deal with the situation?

- Do I have a battery-powered radio or television, or some other mechanism (e.g., shortwave radio, which could be particularly useful if a regional emergency knocked out all nearby broadcasting stations) that would enable me to get current, credible news information from more than one source?

- If the grocery stores and gas stations and banks were closed for a few days, and if the phones were out and the electricity was cut off for a few days, do I have a clear idea of what I would do to prevent my family and me from experiencing severe hardships? If the outages extended from a few days to a few weeks, do I have a fallback plan that would keep me going?

These are not pleasant questions, and they imply catastrophic scenarios that none of us enjoys contemplating. The easiest solution is to assume that they won't exist, or that 'they' will somehow have the resources and the managerial skill to deal with such a catastrophic situation. It's debatable whether government officials and corporate executives could do an effective job even in the situations where "crises" were predictable and orderly; but it's far more difficult to put one's faith in government and senior management when the crises are unpredictable, chaotic, and disruptive.

This does not suggest that we should abandon government altogether, or reject the many advantages and benefits that we've enjoyed from the top-down hierarchical management structures that we've built over the past thousand years. When and if government shows up in a timely fashion to help in a crisis, articulates a sensible policy, provides the resources and management skills to implement such policies in a timely and effective manner, most of us are so grateful that we'll accept the bureaucratic inconveniences with only minor complaints.

Unfortunately, we have to be prepared for the unpredictable, disruptive, chaotic crises of the future—in which government may not show up at all, may show up when it's too late to help, and may exacerbate the problem by imposing bureaucratic rules and regulations that do more harm than good. It's situations like this where the grass-roots, peer-to-peer collaborative networks will prove to be not just a convenience, but a life-saver.

RESILIENT SYSTEMS

6

One learns to itch where one can scratch. ■

—Ernest Bramah

Basic Concepts

In 1930, a British astronomer-turned-biologist wrote *The Genetical Theory of Natural Selection,* widely regarded as the best known book in evolutionary biology after Darwin's *Origin of Species.* In that book, new editions of which appeared in 1958 and 2000,[1] Sir Ronald Aylmer Fisher asserted what has come to be known as Fisher's Fundamental Theorem: "the rate of increase in fitness of any organism at any time is equal to its genetic variance in fitness at that time."

A simpler statement of this principle (which may or may not be acceptable to biologists and geneticists!) is, "The more highly adapted an organism is to a specific environ-

---

1. See, for example, *The Genetical Theory of Natural Selection,* by R. A. Fisher, J.H. Bennett (editor), and Henry Bennett (editor), Oxford University Press, 2000.

ment, the less able it is to adapt to a new and different environment." And if we broaden our view of an "organism" to include corporate organisms, governmental organisms, and social organisms, Fisher's principle has profound implications in today's post-9/11 world.

In many aspects of business and government, for example, there has been an intensive drive for efficiency and productivity during the past decade. But many of the strategies and systems—including many of the IT systems—for achieving substantial increases in efficiency/productivity depend upon the assumption of a stable, predictable environment. Whether it's an airline trying to predict the number of "no-shows" for a particular flight, or a manufacturing organization trying to plan its order of parts and materials to minimize inventory, there are common elements to the strategy: Steady increases or decreases in the external variables are okay, seasonal cycles are okay, and even random events can be tolerated if they can be modeled fairly accurately with mathematical formulas. Thus, manufacturing companies have "just-in-time" (JIT) delivery systems to support a "lean inventory" strategy; airlines have statistically-optimized algorithms for overbooking their flights in such a way that their flights will be as full as possible *without* an excess of passengers who show up at the gate, expecting to get on the plane. Shipping companies have elaborate algorithms to maximize the utilization of their trucks, trains, and ships within the partially-predictable constraints of weather delays, traffic congestion, and driver/pilot availability. Software development organizations devise life-cycle methodologies, based on the Software Engineering Institute's Capability Maturity Model, to maximize the statistical predictability and repeatability of finishing their projects on time and within budget. The list goes on and on...

Unfortunately, the "efficient" systems often turn out to be "brittle," in the sense that they are unable to withstand severe, unanticipated shocks to their normal operation. As we saw in the aftermath of the September 11th attacks, companies like Ford were unprepared for the possibility that the Canadian border would be closed for a week, halting the shipment of parts and materials between various manufacturing facilities located on either side of the border. Shipping firms, and companies of all kinds, were unprepared for the possibility that the entire air-transport industry would be closed down for a week. Software development organizations are usually capable of sustaining the loss of one or two programmers who quit in the middle of the project; but if two-thirds of the programmers quit en masse to protest some management decision, the "system" won't be able to handle it. Again, the list goes on and on...

When a severe, unanticipated disruption occurs, there's a natural tendency to dismiss it as a "once-in-a-lifetime" anomaly. This allows us to avoid taking responsibility and parceling out blame for the consequences of that anomaly; and it also allows us to avoid the expense and effort of preparing for a recurrence of that anomaly. This attitude permeates our culture; for example, at a meeting of the New York City Software Process Improvement Network (SPIN) in mid-October 2001, several Wall Street disaster-recovery specialists told me, in stunned disbelief, that their senior executives had refused to allocate additional funds for contingency planning and disaster recovery, arguing, "You don't seriously expect any more suicide-airplane attacks, do you?" And that very same attitude can be heard in the comments of business travelers across the nation, as they returned to airports a week after September 11th, expecting to resume their hassle-free, no-delay, curbside-baggage-checking mode of traveling.

A popular Hollywood movie entitled *The Perfect Storm* introduced a popular new phrase into the national vocabulary: "storm of the century." Variations on that phrase were employed by computer companies like Compaq to explain the extraordinary loss they announced for their September 30, 2001 fiscal quarter: They had suffered a "storm of the century" consisting of the recession, the September 11th terrorist attacks, and a typhoon in Taiwan.

I suspect that we'll see more declarations of a "storm of the century" in various parts of the business and corporate and social environment in the coming years. And it remains to be seen how long we'll retain the attitude of aggrieved innocence: If an event was so rare and so catastrophic that it occurs only once a century, why should we be expected to invest and time or money preparing for it? Why should we plan a system that can withstand the "storm of a century," as opposed to something that will cope with circumstances that can be foreseen over the next year or two?

The answer—which some will accept, and some will not—is that what we've regarded as the storm of a century is now occurring *more* than once a century. On a less cataclysmic scale, what we used to think of as "the storm of a decade" may be occurring every year or two in today's environment. Some of this is caused by the rapid changes in technology, and the increased rate at which information (including news, gossip, rumors) travels around the world. And some of it is caused by political factors; for all we know, we may be moving into a new era of terrorism that involves more frequently-repeated, large-scale attacks than anything we've experienced in a thousand years.

To the extent that we believe that the future will include more frequent, more unexpected, and more severe "storm of the century" disruptions than ever before, Fisher's Fundamental Theorem provides some useful advice. Massive dinosaurs ruled the earth millions of years ago, and their dominance suggests that they had adapted more successfully than other animal species to the warm, wet, vegetation-rich environment of the time. But when a sudden climactic change occurred—either because of the sudden onset of an Ice Age, or the sudden impact of an asteroid that darkened the skies and killed the vegetation—the dinosaurs were less able to adapt than the cockroach and other lowly species whose adaptation to the old environment was far from perfect.

The cockroach is resilient to change; the dinosaur was not. And in today's post-9/11 world, it is more and more important to build resilient systems and resilient organizations —so that when (or if) another severe shock occurs, we have a better chance of surviving and flourishing.

Techniques and Technologies_____

Familiar techniques

Many of the techniques and strategies for building resiliency into systems are straightforward and familiar; the biggest problem will not be figuring what to do, but rather convincing managers and the organizational culture that it's worth doing.

For example, one of the most obvious strategies is to incorporate some "buffers" or "slack" into systems that have heretofore been designed to run as close to 100% capacity as possible. Instead of a lean inventory system, a manufacturing company can adjust its inventory to assure that it can withstand disruptions of weeks or months, instead of just hours or days. An airline could adjust its reservation system to put passengers on a "stand-by" basis once their flights were, say, 90% full. On a more subtle level, companies could relax the pressure on their overworked employees, so that they too had some "slack" available for coping with unexpected disruptions.[2]

Another obvious strategy is to deliberately introduce some redundancy into the system. Depending on the situation, this might involve redundant hardware, redundant telecommunication networks, redundant suppliers, or redundant people. It's a strategy that many middle-aged people found necessary a generation ago, when our systems consisted of less-reliable components that could not be quickly or easily replaced. In today's environment, many of us are so accustomed to highly reliable components and quick-response repair/resupply mechanisms that we don't pay much attention to redundancy. A small example: When I drove a rental car across the Mojave Desert in the mid-1960s, I made certain that I had backup sparkplugs and fanbelt, as well as extra oil, water, and gasoline in case the car broke down in the middle of nowhere. When I drove a rental car across the same stretch in 2001, it didn't occur to

---

2. An eloquent argument in favor of this strategy can be found in Tom DeMarco's book, *Slack: getting past burnout, busywork, and the myth of total efficiency* (Broadway Books, 2001).

me to bring any backup supplies, nor did I even check to see if the car had a spare tire. My (unrealistic) assumption was that if something went wrong, I could simply call for help on my cell phone.

The obvious disadvantages with slack and redundancy is that they add costs to whatever system we're building or operating, and to whatever business activity we're carrying out. In today's highly competitive environment, we've driven cost out of every aspect of our systems—largely through the benefits of high-reliability components, fast-response repair systems, and sophisticated resupply algorithms that help us minimize the need for inventory, buffers, and spare parts. But as noted earlier, those strategies were devised on the basis of predictable, reasonably stable environments. In today's world, we may need to rethink those strategies.

Of course, this is easy to say but difficult to implement in a typical organization with slim profits, limited resources, and a recessionary economy. The typical objection that one will hear in a private-sector organization is, "Where is the return-on-investment (ROI)?" The rational answer has to be something along the lines of, "We believe that disruptions are X times more likely than before; and because the disruptions are so unpredictable and potentially so severe, the financial consequences will be Y times greater than before; thus, we feel it's prudent to have Z times as much slack and redundancy than we had before."

In the best of all worlds, a spreadsheet model can be constructed so that "what-if" simulations can be performed for different values of X and Y: if the disruptions are, say, twice as frequent as before, and if the financial consequences are three times greater than before, what is the proper value of Z? In a more sophisticated simulation, X and Y will not be represented by a simple, scalar variable, but rather by a probability distribution;[3] and one might then ask, "What is

3. For example, we might model Y as a "normal distribution," so that we could document our assumption that the expected mean (average) financial impact of a disruption is $1 million—but that there is a 10% chance that it could be as low as $100,000 and a 10% chance that it could be as high as $10 million.

the proper value of Z in order to reduce the 'expected value' of our losses from $100,000 to $1,000?" An even more sophisticated organization might use a "system dynamics" simulation of potential disruptions, because the real problem is not the initial manifestation of a disruption, but rather the "ripple-effect" and "vicious circle" consequences related to the feedback loops and time-delayed interactions between various components of the system.[4]

Slack and redundancy are common strategies for avoiding *any* interruption, shutdown, or disruption in a system. But another useful strategy (which can be used to augment the strategies discussed earlier) is based on the concept of "fail soft," or "graceful degradation." Again, this was a more familiar strategy a decade ago, when the expectation that many of the less-reliable components of a system *would* fail—but we didn't want them to fail so catastrophically that our system would be entirely unusable. The universally familiar example of a fail-soft design in today's world is the tire on a modern automobile. The reinforced, composite materials used for today's tire are intrinsically tougher and more durable than the tires of, say, the 1950s; thus, they are far more impervious to small chunks of glass in the road. But if one has the misfortune of driving over a 6-inch spike, chances are that the tire *will* fail; however, if we're driving at 75 mph on an Interstate highway (which we would not have been doing in the 1950s), we don't want the punctured tire to explode and shred. Ideally, we'd like to be able to continue driving with a so-called "run-flat" tire (albeit at a much slower speed) for another 10-20 miles until we reach a gas station; at the very least, we'd like it to deflate slowly and smoothly, so that we can bring the car to a safe halt.

That concept is broadly applicable to a wide range of situations in today's environment; again, we've tended to ignore the concept in many cases, because we've had the luxury of using very high-reliability components and systems. But in today's environment of unexpected, severe dis-

---

4. Systems dynamics modeling approaches were also discussed in Chapter 5.

ruptions, we need to re-examine and re-introduce strategies that were common up through the 1970s and 1980s:

- *Reduced functionality*—rather than shutting down an entire system, we can often arrange to continue using just *some* of its features and functions. Thus, if a portion of our computer system stops functioning, we might be able to enter orders, but not cancel them. If our telecommunications connection to credit-card systems stops functioning, we might allow our customers to make cash purchases, but not credit-card purchases. If the braking system on our car fails, we might avoid hills and drive cautiously on level ground, using the gearshift system to bring the car to a halt.

- *Lesser performance*—rather than shutting down an entire system, we may be able to operate it more slowly, and we may tolerate a slower "response time." We may expect our computer systems to provide sub-second response time under normal circumstances; but in a degraded mode of operation, we may tolerate a response time of 5-10 seconds until repairs can be made. If the air-courier service that we normally use for shipping orders to our customers stops functioning, we may be able to persuade our customers to accept shipments via rail, truck, or US Postal Service.

- *Reduced availability*—rather than shutting down an entire system completely, we may limit its availability to 9-to-5 business hours. Or we might limit its availability to certain high-priority users, or to a smaller subset of "ordinary" users.

- *Switch to a less sophisticated technology*—if our automated system breaks down, perhaps we can fall back to a manual system. If our car breaks down, perhaps we can switch to a bicycle until repairs can be made.

All of these examples are intended merely as illustrations; the details obviously depend on the specifics of a system, the tolerance and patience of the system users, and the importance of maintaining at least a subset of the full functionality, performance, and availability of the system. It's not trivial to devise practical fail-soft strategies for every conceivable kind of system failure—but there's nothing mysterious or magic about the concept.

Obviously, one of the biggest problems with a fail-soft strategy is the additional cost of planning and implementing the various forms of graceful degradation. From the perspective of the designers and developers of systems (whether it's a computer system, a business process, or an organizational system), it's a lot easier to assume that if something goes wrong, the entire system will be shut down, and then restarted (or replaced) when the problem is identified and fixed. Another problem is that users and customers may be impatient and annoyed by the inconveniences associated with a degraded mode of operation—especially if it requires them to learn an alternative set of procedures, or to become familiar with an alternate set of tools and technologies ("Bicycle?!? You want me to use a *bicycle* when the car is broken? But I don't even know how to ride a bicycle—and besides, it's undignified for a person of my stature to be seen riding down the street on a bicycle!")

Early warning systems

One of the reasons that today's unanticipated disruptions have such severe consequences is that we have little advance warning of their imminent occurrence. In Chapter 4, we implied that this might be a "fact of life" with which our risk management strategies would simply have to cope; thus, while we have advance warning of hurricanes, and can improvise a strategy in the hours or days before it arrives, we have little or no advance warning of tornadoes.

But our suggestion here is that we should not always accept the inevitability of a "surprise" disaster. Even tornadoes are less of a surprise than before; weather forecasters can't provide as much advance warning as they can for hurricanes, but the difference between a five-minute warning and a 30-minute warning can literally be the difference between life and death.

Sometimes this requires better technology—e.g., better weather-forecasting models, more powerful computers for doing the associated number-crunching of weather-related data. This, too, costs money and is thus likely to meet the same kind of resistance mentioned earlier. To the extent that there are more tornadoes than before, and/or to the extent that they have become more severe, it should be possible to formulate a return-on-investment justification for spending more money to improve the early warning system.

Sometimes, though, the problem is not the *creation* of the early warning, but the *communication* of that warning to affected parties. We like to think that communication is instantaneous in today's digital world; but we forget about the *human* communication that's required, not to mention the bureaucratic processes of analysis, review, and approvals. Thus, the weather forecaster in the field may spot the whirling funnel of an oncoming twister, and he may have a cell phone for relaying the information back to his office. But the call might be received by a secretary; who has to walk down the hall to communicate the message verbally to a supervisor; who then has to convene a committee to discuss how serious the tornado seems to be; which then has to get the approval of the department chief before declaring an emergency to the local police and news media; which then invokes another set of bureaucratic activities before the sirens are sounded and the warning messages appear on television screens.[5]

Tornadoes, of course, are a well-known phenomenon; thus, there is an established set of bureaucratic communications, analyses, and approvals to follow. If we discover that tornadoes are moving more quickly than ever before (which may or may not be a meteorological possibility), and if we conclude that the bureaucratic response time is too slow, then we can usually initiate a "business process redesign" to make the necessary improvements.

---

5. It's worth noting that *resilience* and *emergence* are often related, compatible concepts. For example, as my friend Steve Heller observed to me, many weather spotters are amateur radio operators who report their findings over the radio on an open frequency. Thus, anyone who is listening to the "weather net" can hear about the tornado the instant it is spotted—which means that no top-down, hierarchically-controlled bureaucracy intervenes between the information and the ultimate recipients of that information, which could be a matter of life and death.

But as we learned in the aftermath of September 11th and the ensuing anthrax attacks, sometimes the problem involves a lack of coordination between the various parties who need to communicate and collaborate about the appropriate early-warning signal for an unanticipated disruption. Thus, a weather forecaster who works in a balmy climate might recognize the tell-tale signs of a freak tornado, but might not know who to call—because no weather-related emergencies have occurred in the community for several decades.

The anthrax attacks of October 2001 illustrated another common problem with the effective implementation of an early-warning system: Sometimes the first people to spot the signs of an impending crisis are not trained, professional scientists or high-level, authoritative managers. Sometimes they're ordinary citizens who observe some puzzling information—a skin rash, or flu-like symptoms—but don't know what to do about it. In a business environment, the people who have access to the earliest of the early-warning signals are likely to be the front-line employees with direct, day-to-day contact with customers, competitors, suppliers, vendors, and partners. And as we noted in Chapter 2, management guru Michael Hammer argues, in his new book *The Agenda*, that these bottom-level workers are often discouraged from articulating their warnings and concerns.

Thus, in order to make our organizations and systems more resilient, we need to make it easier for front-line observers to communicate their warnings quickly and effectively, without worrying about being criticized as alarmists. In the emergent-systems culture that we discussed in Chapter 5, the first instinct of these front-line workers will be to communicate their warnings to their immediate family, friends, and co-workers. That can be enormously helpful for situations like the World Trade Center attack, but there also needs to be a mechanism to enable front-line workers to communicate their warnings to "Galactic Headquarters" so that appropriate top-management actions *can* be taken, if appropriate.

Some organizations understand this point at a very deep, cultural level—because they were already operating in a hostile, dangerous, fast-changing environment before September 11th. But for the majority of our business, government, and social organizations, this kind of emphasis on early-warning systems and procedures will require a large, expensive, contentious change. Some will do it, and will find that they *are* more resilient; and some will not, making their survival more tenuous than ever before.

Mechanisms for rapid change

Having an early warning system isn't much use if it takes an inordinate amount of time to respond to the disruptive event. But this can involve the very issues we discussed in the previous section: If the organization has no slack, and no redundancy, sometimes it's impossible to make a change. An individual, an organization, or even a country may recognize a threat, and may have enough time to cogitate on the fact that its very survival is threatened—but it may be simply incapable of making the required changes. As we discussed in Chapter 5, this is a particularly common event in a rigidly hierarchical top-down organization; in an organization where an emergent-systems culture is allowed to flourish, it's far more likely that an ad hoc response will, quite literally, *emerge*.

To the extent that a conventional organization *does* want to increase its ability to respond quickly to disruptive changes, it should develop appropriate business processes for doing so. This goes beyond the risk-management processes that we discussed in Chapter 4; the task here is to develop *processes for change*. Remember: We're not talking just about changing an organization in response to *one* disruptive event, but rather creating the "change-management" processes that will enable the organization to go through one change after another.

As Dorine Andrews and Susan Stalick discuss in an excellent business process reengineering book[6] from the mid-1990s, such changes affect several different areas of an

---

6. Dorine C. Andrews, and Susan K. Stalick. *Business Reengineering: The Survival Guide* (Prentice-Hall/Yourdon Press, 1994).

organization. The areas of impact are illustrated in Figure 6.1 below.

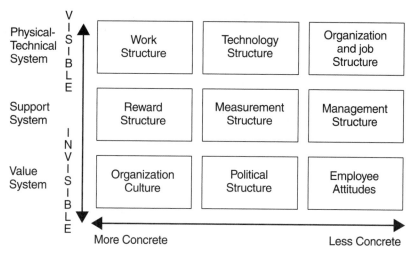

FIGURE 6.1 The organizational impact of a disruptive change.

The top row of Figure 6.1—the so-called "physical-technical system" is where we see the changes in the work structure, the technology structure, and the organizational/job structure.

- *Work structure*—This is where we ask such questions as, "What inputs and outputs are produced by this business process? What steps must be carried out, and how must they be done?"

- *Technology structure*—This is obviously where we see discussions and proposals about various Internet-related technologies, ranging from Web servers to wireless technology to whatever new gadgets the vendors are unveiling this season. A common temptation in this area is to become enamored of some new "silver bullet" technology before anyone has even figured out what the problem is; it's far better to look for appropriate technology structures *after* we have a good idea of the required work structure and modified work processes.

- *Organizational/job structure*—Changes in work structure and technology structure inevitably change job definitions and organizational structures. This is where we see changes to reporting hierarchies and work-group relationships It also changes the "accountability" of the work—i.e., who "owns" the process, and who is responsible for seeing that it is carried out properly? It's likely to change the job content, knowledge requirements, and the required skill levels. All of these issues are "visible," which is why we've put it at the top level of Figure 6.1; but it has an immediate impact on less visible areas of culture and employee attitudes, which we'll discuss below.

The middle level of Figure 6.1—the so-called "support system"—is where we see changes to the reward structure, the measurement structure, and the management structure. Or to put it another way: If you *don't* change the reward structure, the manner in which people's work is measured, and the manner in which they are supervised on a day-to-day basis, you're likely to find that all of the "visible" changes implemented in the top layer of Figure 6.1 have no impact.

- *Reward structure*—Rewards can motivate individuals and teams in a variety of ways—but changes to the reward structure are tricky, because they may lead to unanticipated consequences. In general terms, though, people do what they are paid to do and what they are recognized for—and they don't bother doing the things for which there is no apparent reward or benefit or recognition from their employer. Obviously, politics or culture may make it difficult to make radical changes in the reward structure to accompany radical changes in other parts of Figure 6.1; indeed, idealists may argue that it's impossible to develop a reward structure that will guarantee ideal process performance. But it's evident in many cases that *any* change in reward structure would be an improvement over an existing situation, which virtually guarantees dysfunctional behavior because of the way it penalizes people for doing more work, better work, or dramatically *different* work than what they are doing now.

- *Measurement structure*—Ideally, this involves measuring *outcomes* and results, rather than "Big Brother" measurements of how many bathroom breaks they take, and how many keystrokes per minute they type on their computer terminal. When focusing on this area, many organizations discover that one of their existing business processes is that nobody measured anything. In any case, failure to institute a measurement structure as part of the change-management often leads to disastrous results in new business processes.

- *Management structure*—the management structure involves such things as whether people are included in business decision-making, availability and support for personal growth and development, and how the workers are treated (orders vs. consensus). It can also include other changes that reinforce people's behavior on a day-to-day basis (can they use the new Internet-based system telecommute, and work from home? Are they still required to punch time cards to prove that they are "working"?)

Finally, the "value system" involves changes to the organization's culture, the political structure, and the employee attitudes.

- *Organizational culture*—the organizational culture involves the rituals, myths, symbols, and language of "how we do things around here." Tasks are carried out in a certain way because they have become rituals over time—e.g., it's common to hear remarks like "I learned how to do things this way before you whippersnappers were even born!" The older the culture, the more difficult it is to change.

- *Political structure*—an organization's political structure includes formal and informal organization leaders, including unions, special interest groups, etc.; it also informal relationships among key members who play golf together, or who congregate at the local bar after work each day. Political leaders promulgate and reinforce organizational values and beliefs; and as many change-management teams have learned, an entrenched political structure rarely cooperates in changes that cause it to lose its power.

- *Employee attitudes*—Aside from organizational culture and political structure, employees have their own "mental model" and beliefs that affect their attitude and behavior in the organization. This involves cultural characteristics like impatience, skepticism, openness, control, rigidity, or flexibility. Employee attitudes *can* be changed, and it's sometimes crucial that they be changed in order to cope with whatever new environment is created by the disruptive event. But it's usually a slow process, and it requires active leadership, "walking the talk" (i.e., demonstrable evidence that the organization's leaders are exhibiting new attitudes), etc. In some cases, it requires throwing out the "old guard," and bringing in a fresh new generation of employees.

This last comment—about throwing out the old guard—brings us to a final observation about speeding up the organization's ability to respond to disruptive events. Ideally, one would prefer *not* to have these processes invented by external consultants who don't really understand the organization; nor does one want them created, as a theoretical exercise, by people who have never been through it before. On the contrary, the people who are best equipped to identify what kind of changes will need to be made in the various areas summarized by Figure 6.1, and how to make those changes as quickly and effective as possible, *are the people who have been through it before.* Thus, the Executive Committee, or "task force," that guided the organization through the disruptive changes caused by a hostile merger, or a sudden deregulation within the industry, or other similar events, is likely to be the best-suited group for writing the "strategy book" for making subsequent changes in response to subsequent crises.

Unfortunately, the members of such groups are often so exhausted, and have accumulated so many enemies, by the end of their disruptive-change effort, that they retire, quit, or get transferred to some remote outpost of the organization. Thus, if an organization has the luxury of planning for disruptive changes *now*, during a peaceful lull between crises, it would be a good idea to track down those battle-scarred veterans from some previous crisis that everyone naively thought was a "once-in-a-lifetime" anomaly.

Paradigm Shifts

As with so many of the other concepts discussed in this book, resiliency is not a new idea. As we've suggested in this chapter, it was a commonly practiced concept in older times—because, even if the surrounding environment was not hostile, threatening or rapidly changing, the technology and the systems that we depended on were less reliable and trustworthy than they have been for the past decade or two.

But the *reason* for encouraging resiliency today is different than it was a generation ago. Our systems and our critical infrastructures are, for the most part, more reliable than before, but now they are exposed to attack by hostile terrorists, hostile competitors, or hostile governments. The disruptive shocks to our organizations are no longer accidental, benign, or acts of nature; now they are deliberate and malevolent.

Also, as we've mentioned elsewhere, the pace of business, technology, communication, and social change is much faster than it was a generation ago. It's easier to be resilient when you have time to fully assimilate one set of changes before the next one arrives. In today's environment, the "storm of a century" disruptions are occurring, one right after the other, so quickly that we're still reeling in shock from one disruption when the next one arrives.

Strategic Implications _____

As we have seen in this chapter, the most common strategies for achieving resiliency involve investments in redundancy and "slack" in the productive capacity of a system.
Thus, the strategic implications for management, at all levels, will largely revolve around the issue of investments:
quantifying them, justifying them, gaining financial
approval for them, and launching them. But there are additional suggestions and advice for management, as well as
some advice for the IT professionals and citizens who operate at the bottom of the management hierarchy.

Government officials

- *Identify those parts of the critical infrastructure that are not
  resilient.* As noted throughout this chapter, America
  (and several other "advanced" nations around the
  world) has built a society in which the critical infrastructure is, in general terms, highly productive, efficient, and reliable. But because of these admirable
  characteristics, we tend to overlook how *brittle* those
  infrastructures might be. An example of brittleness is
  the fractional reserve system of the nation's banks: less
  than 10% of the deposits owned by individuals and
  companies are actually held by the banks as cash.[7]
  This form of brittleness is well known, and strong
  political pressures will probably keep it from changing; but the brittleness of other parts of the infrastructure may not be so well-known.[8] Thus, one of
  government's first tasks—not just at the federal level,

---

7. As long as deposits and withdrawals occur in a steady, predictable
   fashion, the banks can continue to maintain the illusion that every
   depositor can withdraw his money whenever he wants. If a sudden disruption is anticipated far enough in advance, then the banks and the
   Fed can take appropriate steps to increase the money supply; that was
   done at the end of 1999, in anticipation that many people might withdraw large sums of cash because of Y2K concerns. But as the December
   2001 financial crisis in Argentina has demonstrated, events can sometimes get out of control: the brittleness of the Argentinean financial system became evident when the government was forced to close the
   banks and freeze depositors' accounts.

but also at the state, county, and municipal levels—
should be to identify the degree of resiliency in their
infrastructure systems, and then make a realistic
assessment of the changes that need to be made to
cope with a greater degree of disruptive shocks.

- *Invest in resiliency.* As already noted, it costs money to
  pay for redundancy and slack in the system; unless
  there is a substantial financial surplus, this means
  additional taxes and/or reductions in other services.
  In the political climate of the post-9/11 period, taxpay-
  ers are more likely to understand and accept this
  financial burden; but if we are lucky enough to experience long periods of tranquility and stability in the
  months and years ahead, there will gradually be pressure to cut back on those resiliency-oriented reserves.

- *Invest in early warning systems.* The federal government
  accomplishes this through agencies like the CIA and
  NSA, as well as economic forecasters, environmental
  forecasters, and so forth. But this kind of early-warning mechanism is often lacking at the state, county and
  municipal levels—primarily because of limited
  resources, but also because many of the localized
  regions have been lucky enough to enjoy good economic times, and an absence of crises. We may have a
  sufficient understanding of environmental trends to
  know, for example, that we don't need an early-warning system for hurricanes in Phoenix, Arizona; but the
  economic disruptions, terrorist disruptions, and critical-infrastructure disruptions could occur almost anywhere. Phoenix (and every other locale) *does* need to
  think about the possibility of disruptions to its electri-
  cal-power system, its telecommunications systems,
  and other parts of its critical infrastructure.

---

8. An example is the electric-power system in the state of California:
   Because of the assumptions that guided its energy-deregulation plans,
   the state's main utility companies were extremely vulnerable to sudden,
   sharp increases in the cost of electricity. However, it's also worth noting
   that the utilities had a carefully-engineered "fail-soft" system: If power
   reserves fell below certain thresholds, "rolling blackouts" were used to
   reduce the likelihood of a calamitous *total* shut-down of the system.

- *Encourage citizens to develop their own resiliency.* This has to be handled carefully and responsibly, in order to prevent panic and hoarding; but the American culture has a vocabulary for discussing it, even though it dates back to the Depression years. We talk about having a "nest egg" and "rainy day" funds to tide us through periods of unemployment caused by a sudden layoff. We understand the notion of investing a modest portion of our income in insurance, in case our house burns down or our car is damaged in a wreck. The Red Cross and FEMA advise us to make sure that we've got candles, batteries, and enough food and water to last for a few days—just in case. But during the "good times" of the 1980s and 1990s, the current generation of young adults gradually stopped listening to this kind of advice; in today's uncertain times, the government could invest a very modest amount of money to reinforce this basic message of self-sufficiency. It's a good investment, too: A nation of resilient individuals and families will require far less government support in an emergency than a nation of brittle individuals who have nothing to fall back on.

Senior corporate executives

The advice for senior corporate executives is essentially the same as that for government leaders: Assess the degree of brittleness in your existing systems; invest in additional resiliency; invest in early-warning systems; and encourage your employees to become *personally* resilient in terms of their day-to-day work.

Interestingly, most medium- and large-sized companies went through exactly this process in preparation for the Y2K rollover. And they learned that it was important to broaden their perspective beyond the boundaries of their own organization. It wasn't enough to have redundancy and additional "slack" in their own systems;[9] they had to investigate their "supply chain" of vendors, partners, suppliers, and even customers to ensure that they, too, were ready for Y2K. In some cases, business relationships with non-Y2K-compliant vendors were terminated; and in some cases, additional suppliers were sought, in order to provide slack and redundancy.

Because senior corporate executives typically have more power over the day-to-day activities of their employees than government leaders have over the day-to-day activities of their citizens, there is one more thing that can be done: Initiate "resiliency drills," and practice them on a regular basis. Essentially, this is a generalized version of the "fire drill" concept that we all learned as children; and again, most medium- and large-sized companies went through this process as part of their Y2K preparations. Ironically, those very drills played a significant role in the ability of thousands of workers to evacuate the World Trade Center on September 11th; hopefully, that lesson will be remembered in the years ahead.

Mid-level IT managers

To the extent that mid-level managers have some of the power and authority of their superiors in the executive suite, they can follow the same advice I've given above.

And since mid-level IT managers are likely to be much "closer" to the day-to-day operations of critical systems within the organization, they're in a better position to alert their superiors to the potentially dangerous "brittleness" of those systems. Chances are that many mid-level managers have attempted to do this in the past, but have been ignored—or have been told that there was no room in the budget for the money that would be required for the redun-

---

9. The "slack" typically took the form of stockpiled quantities of raw materials and parts, in case of a breakdown in transportation, communication, or banking systems. The nation's electric utilities used a combination of redundancy *and* slack to prepare for the Y2K rollover. The lower energy demands of a winter holiday weekend would normally have suggested shutting down some of the generating plants, and running the others at near-capacity levels. Instead, most of the utilities fired up *all* of their generating plans, and ran each of them at a lower-capacity level. Thus, if there were any Y2K-related computer problems (which were, in fact, reported at a handful of plants around the country, though all of them were said to be minor in nature), there was enough built-in resiliency to avoid a total blackout.

dancy and "slack" needed to achieve resiliency. The same budget problems are likely to exist in the recessionary economy that existed when this book was being written; but on the other hand, senior management may be more receptive to such proposals in the aftermath of September 11th.

It's also important to remember that brittleness in the organization can be associated with critically-important personnel. Because of retirements, resignations, transfers, and terminations, there may be only *one* person who knows how to operate the Frammis machine, or fix the Widget system when it breaks, or install upgrades and vendor patches to the ancient Gizmo system. A casual investigation may reveal that that employee has plastered his cubicle with caustically sardonic Dilbert cartoons, and has a countdown calendar on his desk showing the number of days remaining before he, too, can retire. As a visitor to many large companies around the country, I am often staggered by how obvious these situations are, and how studiously management ignores them... until, one day, the critical employee simply doesn't show up for work. In the spirit of building resilient organizations, this is a good time for mid-level managers to identify these situations, resolve the problem if possible, and alert senior management of the risk.

Finally, mid-level IT managers should ensure that resiliency is identified as one of the important "ilities"—along with maintainability, portability, flexibility, usability, etc.—when developing new systems. Again, recognize that this is an issue that involves *people* as well as redundancy and slack within the computer hardware and software. That is, the end-users of today's IT systems are often quite "brittle," in the sense that they *demand* that their systems work perfectly, 100% of the time, 24 hours a day, 7 days a week. Faced with even the slightest disruption or limitation in the functionality of their systems, they explode in rage and declare that the system is completely unusable. Systems analysts and IT project managers are familiar with the concept of "managing expectations" of the user community when they are developing a new system; in today's environment, they need to manage the users' expectations in terms of their own resiliency.

A good example is the telephone system. Most American citizens expect that their traditional land-line phones will work 100% of the time, with no exception; if they pick up their phone and fail to get a dial tone *instantly*, they go berserk. By contrast, nobody expects cell phones to work perfectly—except European visitors, whose expectations are influenced by their own experiences at home. But Americans are resilient when dealing with cell phones: Both they, and the party with whom they are speaking, realize that there may be noise and static on the line, and that the conversation may be cut off at any moment. Only in rare cases do they put themselves in a position where they depend, totally and completely, on the perfect functioning of their cell-phone infrastructure. We would all appreciate better cell-phone service, and we may someday have the same expectations of our cell phones as we do of our land-line phones. But in the meantime, there is something to be said for a "cell-phone mindset" with regard to *all* of the systems we use.

IT professionals

My advice here is similar to that for mid-level IT managers: advise your superiors of any significant brittleness in the systems you are involved in developing or maintaining. Programmers, network designers, database designers, and other such IT professionals are, of course, most likely to see the brittleness of the hardware/software environments with which they work. Indeed, they may have been instructed to *create* such brittleness in the past, by eliminating unnecessary redundancy and slack in their systems.

In many cases, IT professionals make their own decisions about such things, without a great deal of guidance from their managers, customers, or end-users. This is particularly true in small companies, and on small IT development projects where one or two programmers are working directly with the end-user who wants the system. Of course, the programmers may not have the discretion to purchase a complete backup of the PC hardware, database system, and other expensive components; but they *do* have the discretion to design their software so that a certain degree of "fail-soft" behavior is built into it. Whenever possible, it's advisable to raise this issue and discuss it openly with the end-user, customer, and stakeholders in the project; but there are many situations where the stakeholders are uninterested, or too preoccupied with their own problems to worry about such issues. They may also abdicate any responsibility for the decisions about resiliency, telling the programmers that they regard it as a "technical issue" that they expect the programmers to handle on their own.

Most IT development projects also require an examination and assessment of the "business processes" surrounding the computer system; indeed, one of the reasons for building a new computer system is to simplify or improve those business processes—e.g., by replacing time-consuming, expensive manual processes with faster, cheaper automated processes. In any case, it's an opportunity for the systems analyst (or, on a small one-person project, the programmer who is also writing the code) to advise the end-user about the brittleness of the business processes, in addition to whatever assessment needs to be made about incorporating resiliency into the hardware/software environment.

Imagine, for example, that a programmer is building a Web-based order-entry system for a business person. At an early stage in the project, the programmer might say, "Do you realize that, with the system you've asked me to build, *the only way* that customers will be able to transmit orders to us is via their Web browser? What if we have a serious computer virus attack, and have to shut down our connection to the Internet for a week? Wouldn't it make sense for us to tell our customers that they can also fax their orders to us?" Since it's up to the user to decide what business processes they're willing and able to carry out, the programmers/analysts typically won't be able to make such resiliency-related decisions on their own; but at least they can offer advice.

As we noted above, *people* are part of any system, and people with critical skills or business knowledge may represent part of the overall brittleness of the system. Again, it's the systems analysts or programmers who may be the ones to recognize this phenomenon, particularly if their development project involves interviewing lower-echelon adminis-trative/clerical personnel to ascertain the policies, business rules, and business processes that will have to be docu-mented and then transformed into software.

On the one hand, the act of transforming a manually-per-formed business process into computer software *increases* the resiliency of the system—because if the person who pre-viously performed that process manually should have the misfortune of being run over by a beer truck, the newly-cre-ated computer system will be able to continue performing the process. But on the other hand, one of the key decisions in a systems development project is the determination of the "automation boundary."[10] Because of politics, tradition, union rules, or an inability to articulate the business rules with sufficient precision to automate them,[11] the decision might be made to build the new system in such a way that certain business processes continue to be carried out by a person ... but, as suggested earlier, a combination of resig-nations, terminations, and retirement may have left the organization in a position where there is now only *one* clerk who knows how to carryout the process. That clerk may be bored, disgruntled, distracted by personal crises, or looking for a better job. And in any case, there is always the prover-bial beer truck to worry about—not to mention falling debris caused by airplanes crashing into buildings.

Finally, IT professionals should realize that, in some cases, *they* are the source of brittleness—for all of the rea-sons articulated above. Again, it's amazing to see how often such situations exist, and how oblivious and callous manag-ers are about it. The situation is exacerbated by the recession

---

10. Before we became sensitized to issues of sexism, we often used the phrase "man-machine boundary" to distinguish between those parts of a business system that would be carried out by human beings, and those parts that were intended to be automated.

11. This is a particularly common problem when building so-called "expert systems," which attempt to mimic the judgment and decision-making capability of a human. In some cases, the human's decisions are based on a few simple, deterministic rules that can be clearly articulated and easily programmed. But in other cases—e.g., evaluating a mortgage application, or determining when a chemical process "smells right"—the decisions may be based on a combination of ambiguous rules, hunches, and instinct.

that was underway while this book was being written, and by the cost-cutting, belt-tightening, "lean-and-mean"[12] attitude that companies exhibit in their increasingly competitive marketplaces. Thus, if a programmer happens to mention to his or her boss, "Y'know, I'm the only one around here who knows how to maintain the Whizmo system, and we've been getting so many enhancement/upgrade requests from our user that I'm working at 110% of my capacity," the boss is likely to launch into a tirade about the pressures the company is facing, and the need for dedication, loyalty, and patriotism. In the worst case, the boss knows full well that there are no other jobs out there, and that while the programmers might whine and complain about their situation, they won't quit.

This creates a dilemma that needs to be handled in a responsible, professional, and ethical fashion—but also one that is pragmatic and protective of one's own personal priorities. IT professionals sometimes find it tempting to play "stick-em-up" and demand an exorbitant raise; and they sometimes feel that, because they've been overworked and insulted by their managers, they're justified in quitting abruptly and leaving the organization in the lurch. At the same time, they may realize that it's foolish to quit in the midst of a recession; so they may bide their time and wait for the economy to improve before turning in their resignation. On the other hand, responsible, mature IT professionals can often sympathize with the pressures that their managers and their company are facing, and they often feel a debt of loyalty in return for many years of happy employment.

Obviously, each IT professional must decide on his or her own what to do. But the reason I've brought it up, at this point in the chapter, is that brittleness is a factor in the decision. Whether or not IT professionals feel they are being

---

12. As Tom DeMarco argues eloquently in *Slack: getting past burnout, busy-work, and the myth of total efficiency* "lean and mean" is just the opposite of how most of us would prefer to live our personal lives. Who, in his right mind, would want to live in a "mean" family, or participate in a "mean" relationship with husband or wife? And while none of us wants to be obese, who wants to be so "lean" that we exhibit signs of anorexia?

overworked and underpaid, whether or not they feel insulted by managers who show no sympathy for their situation, whether or not they feel that loyalty and professionalism require them to continue tolerating the situation, *there is always the proverbial beer truck.* Somehow, in as professional and non-threatening a way possible, IT professionals have to communicate to their managers, "Your system and your company are *not* resilient, because I'm the only one here with a particular set of skills and experience—and you won't be able to recover easily if I get run over by a beer truck, or die of cancer, or disappear for any other reason."

If an IT professional is certain that he has communicated this fact to his manager, and if he is certain that his manager understands the brittleness issue, and if he is further convinced that his manager (and the entire hierarchy of managers above him) is unable or unwilling to do anything about it, *then* he is free to make a responsible, ethical decision about staying or leaving.

Citizens

Perhaps the most important implication for individual citizens is to assess their own resilience, in terms of the systems and infrastructures they depend on to carry out their day-to-day lives. Obviously, each individual needs to decide for himself just how resilient he wants to be, or how "close to the bone" he wants to live. But that should be an "informed" decision, based on a realistic assessment of the *likelihood* of various kinds of disruptions, and the *consequences* of such disruptions.

Some people went through this exercise in the months leading up to the Y2K rollover. And while some may have overestimated the likelihood/consequences of Y2K-related disruptions, and while a few may have gone overboard in terms of their preparations and contingency plans, it was nevertheless an eye-opening experience for many. Americans, particularly those living in an urban environment, enjoy a lifestyle where everything works, all of the time. We turn on the water faucet in our kitchen and bathroom, and fresh, clean water magically appears—somehow, from somewhere. We pick up the phone, and we always get a dial tone. We turn on the light switch, and there is always electricity. We stroll down to the bank, and the ATM machines are always available; we can always see our bank balance and get access to our money.

Y2K forced many of us to ask ourselves: What if these things *didn't* work, at least not for a few days, or a few weeks, or even a few months? Merely asking the question shocked many of us into realizing that we had no reserves, no buffer, no slack, no redundancy. The average middle-class American family lives from paycheck to paycheck, with little or no savings—or with savings that take the form of high-tech stock options and illiquid equity in a home whose value can plummet overnight. The average family has no extra food in the pantry, no extra batteries or candles or bottled water, no extra cash, no more than a quarter-tank of gas in the car, and no "bug-out bag" that would facilitate a quick escape in the event of an environmental disaster or terrorist attack.

As we know, Y2K has come and gone. Some people feel foolish for having stockpiled Spam and rice in their pantry, while others feel grateful for changing their lifestyle and creating some reserves that will tide them through *any* kind of disruption. And it's this last point that's most important: Whether Y2K deserved the attention it got is a question that a few zealots continue to debate on Internet discussion forums. But for many, Y2K was an intangible, abstract problem involving computer technology that they didn't understand very well. By contrast, September 11th involved a very tangible, very real problem; any time we feel that we don't understand or remember what it's all about, all we need to do is turn on the VCR and re-play the video segment of the airplanes slamming into the side of the World Trade Center towers.

Whether each of us chooses to take action, and actually *do* something about it, remains to be seen. The concepts, as mentioned earlier in this chapter, are familiar: We all know about the concept of "insurance," and we all realize that one of the justifications for a savings account is to cope with unexpected unemployment, illness, or other forms of a "rainy day." We all understand the concept of redundant systems—whether it's in the form of a second car, or a spare set of house keys, or a photocopy of our birth certificate and marriage license. The question is whether we'll extend the concept to a broader range of basic needs and services (food, water, etc.), and to the critical infrastructures (tele-communications, banking, electric utilities), whose ubiquitous, reliable services we've taken for granted.

For those who do want to increase the resiliency of their personal lives, there are numerous books,[13] articles, and Internet sites[14] that provide detailed information and advice. Ironically, many of these came into existence, or were popularized, during the Y2K era; and while some have disappeared, others continue to flourish.

For those who are middle-aged parents, with children who grew up in the 1980s or 1990s, I have one final piece of advice: *Teach your children.* As noted throughout this chap-

---

13. See, for example, *Square Foot Gardening,* by Mel Bartholomew (Rodale Press, 1981); *Live off the Land in the City and Country,* by Ragnar Benson, with Devon Christensen (Paladin Press, 1982); *The NEW Passport To Survival:12 Steps to Self-Sufficient Living,* by Rita Bingham, James Talmage Stevens, Esther Dickey, Clair C. Bingham (Natural Meals Publishing, 1999); *Where There Is No Dentist,* by Murray Dickson (The Hesperian Foundation, 1983); *The Encyclopedia of Country Living* (9th Edition), by Carla Emery (Sasquatch Books, 1994); *Back to Basics: How to Learn and Enjoy Traditional American Skills* (Readers Digest, 1997); *Making the Best of Basics: Family Preparedness Handbook* (Tenth Edition), James Talmage Stevens (Gold Leaf Press, 1997); *Where There Is No Doctor: A Village Health Care Handbook* (Revised English Edition), by David Werner, with Carol Thuman and Jane Maxwell (The Hesperian Foundation, 1992).

14. See, for example, the "preps link" page at the *TimeBomb2K* Web site, which includes Kurt Saxon's site at *www.kurtsaxon.com/foods/contents.htm;* the Old Timer "How We Used To Do It" page at *http://walton-feed.com/old/index.html;* Sally's Kitchen, at; *www.sallyskitchen.com/;* Rocky Mountain Survival Group; *http://www.artrans.com/rmsg/toc.htm;* Epsilon Library at *www.ezonline.com/ditto/howto.html;* Frugal's Food/Garden Index at *www.netside.com/~lcoble/password/food.htm;* Survival Bible at *www.netside.com/~lcoble/bible/bible.html;* Preparedness Insights at *www.beprepared.com/Insight/informa.htm;* Holly's site at *www.millennium-ark.net/News_Files/Hollys.html;* Nursehealer at *www.nursehealer.com/Sitemap.htm;* The Greenspun archives containing Y2K prep information, at *http://hv.greenspun.com/bboard/q-an...0%20%28Y2000%29;* and the Wilderness Survival site at *www.wilderness-survival.net/* among many, *many* others.

ter, those of us who grew up in the 1950s or 1960s still remember an era when Things Didn't Work Very Well. And we were raised by Depression-Era parents who constantly reminded us that When Things Get Bad, You're On Your Own. Thus, as a trivial example, I was not allowed to drive the family car as a teenager until I could demonstrate my ability to change the oil, change the spark plugs, and replace a flat tire. We *did* have power failures from time to time, and everyone was expected to cope with the inconvenience; and we lived in a world where the banks were *not* open 24 hours a day ("Yes, Virginia, there was a time when ATM machines didn't exist; in fact, there was a time when credit cards and debit cards didn't exist.")

Middle-class children in today's advanced countries have obviously been raised in far different circumstances; and it is not intended as a criticism when I suggest that our children probably don't know how to change a flat tire, function effectively without access to ATM machines at 3 AM on a Saturday morning, or survive for a day or two without the convenience of their electric appliances ("Where's my MTV? Why doesn't my hair-dryer work?"). As noted earlier, they understand that today's cell-phone technology is imperfect, but they would be stunned if they turned on their television set and found nothing but "snow" on all the channels.

Of course, a similar phenomenon has occurred with each new generation, ever since the beginning of the Industrial Revolution. I would have great difficulty if a time-machine threw me back to the unpredictable, chaotic Depression-Era world that my parents were raised in; and they would have had similar difficulties if a time-machine had thrown them back to the turn-of-the-century world *their* parents grew up in. So we should not be surprised, let alone critical, if *our* children find it difficult to comprehend the implications and ramifications of a less-reliable and more-chaotic world like the one we inhabited in the 1950s and 1960s.

This is not meant to imply that civilization is collapsing, or that we are regressing back to the Stone Age. Some of what we are experiencing now is clearly associated with a political phenomenon that may disappear within a few years if governments around the world succeed in eradicating terrorism. But some of it is also the result of technological improvements and global interconnectedness—and that is more likely to increase, rather than decrease, for the foreseeable future. It remains to be seen whether our government leaders, economists, scientists, and business managers will eventually be able to analyze and control these rapidly-evolving systems to the point where we can once again enjoy a stable equilibrium. But if such a happy event does occur, it's likely to be several years from now. In the meantime, we have to be prepared for more unanticipated disruptions, which are likely to be more severe than whatever we've experienced in the past several years. And to cope with that, we need to become ever more resilient. For middle-age people, it is—at least to some extent—a return to what we once knew and practiced. But for our children, it will be a new concept, and it may be difficult for them to learn.

As Margaret Mead observed, in her classic study[15] of the "generation gap" that was causing debate and concern in the late 1960s, there are three common cultural states in a society: postfigurative, cofigurative, and prefigurative. Postfigurative cultures are associated with stable, or even stagnant times, where things have not changed for many generations (e.g., the Amish culture in the U.S., or the Samoan culture in which Mead did much of her formative work); in such societies, parents know everything worth knowing when their children enter the world, and everyone expects that children will learn from their parents. Cofigurative cultures are those that find themselves competing with another, dominating culture and losing influence and power (e.g., immigrant cultures and, arguably, the Islamic cultures of today's Middle Eastern countries); in such cultures, parents and children are forced to learn new things at the same time, and the parents often find it difficult to abandon their old ways. Finally, the prefigurative culture is one in which rapid change is the rule, rather than maintenance

---

15. See *Commitment and Culture: the new relationships between the generations in the 1970s,* by Margaret Mead (Columbia University Press, updated and revised edition, 1978).

of the older cultural status quo; in this case, children are almost always able to learn and assimilate the new ways more quickly—among other things, they have less "baggage" to leave behind.

Mead argued that in the post-World War II 1960s, we had entered a cofigurative period in the United States; and that that was the major explanation for the generation gap and the degree of hostility between the generations that exceeded the hostility between the generations of the earlier part of the 20th century. If Mead were still alive today, she would almost certainly agree that we now have prefigurative culture: the MTV generation finds it extraordinarily easy to assimilate cells phones, Tivo machines, and even multi-colored tomato ketchup, while the older generation fumbles with its cell phones, mis-programs its Tivo machines, and violently rejects the notion of green ketchup.

However, there is one anomaly in today's fast-moving, hip-hop, prefigurative world: It now includes, as we've discussed throughout this book, the possibility of chaotic disruptions that may render the New-Age technology temporarily (or, in the worst case, permanently) unusable. And at least in that one small area, we may have returned to a postfigurative world: we middle-aged parents actually know what do in a world of unpredictably unreliable critical-infrastructure services, and we have much to teach our children.

Whether our children choose to listen to us, and to learn whatever lessons we're capable of passing on, is a topic beyond the scope of this book. Indeed, it would be a worthy topic of exploration by the estimable Margaret Mead.

GOOD ENOUGH SYSTEMS

> Everything runs to excess; every good quality is
> noxious if unmixed.   ■
>
> —*Ralph Waldo Emerson*

I discussed the concept of good-enough software in a 1996 book entitled *Rise and Resurrection of the American Programmer*; and I touched on it again in a 1997 book entitled *Death March*. I'll summarize that material briefly in the next two sections; but if you've seen either of my two earlier books, you can skip ahead to the section called Paradigm Shifts. On the other hand, if you have no idea what I'm talking about, and want *much* more detail, feel free to pick up a copy of either or both of those earlier books.

Basic Concepts

"Le mieux est l'ennemi du bien," wrote the French philosopher Voltaire in his *Philosophical Dictionary* some 200 years ago.[1] "The best is the enemy of the good." Though most IT professionals are probably not familiar with the details of

Voltaire's philosophies, they can certainly understand the issues involved in this commentary on the negative characteristics of "best." And many would strongly disagree with it: There is a common tendency of IT professionals to focus on such attributes of technical quality as maintainability, flexibility, portability, performance, and—most of all—an absence of bugs.

Unfortunately, this seemingly noble quest for technical quality can detract from other aspects of "total quality" that customers, managers, users, and other stakeholders care strongly about, and it ignores the fact that many stakeholders simply aren't concerned about technical perfection anyway. The "good enough" approach, by contrast, requires IT professionals to work with the project stakeholders (especially users) to determine a pragmatic balance between cost, functionality, schedule, technical defects, and other "dimensions" of quality.

This is not a new concept,[2] nor is it an academic one; indeed, there are dozens of widely-observed examples throughout the computer industry. At the beginning of the 1990s, for example, Microsoft released the first of its "graphical user interface" operating systems, Windows 3.1 with some 5,000 known bugs—i.e., bugs that Microsoft knew about, but had not had the time or resources to remove before the product was shipped. Nevertheless, the marketplace decided that Windows 3.1 was "good enough," and millions of copies were sold over the next few years, before eventually being replaced by Windows 95 and a succession of subsequent operating systems.[3]

The presence or absence of bugs is one dimension of "good-enough," but not the only one. For example, the widespread criticisms of Microsoft Word 6.0 for the Macintosh (released in the 1995 time frame) suggests that functionality is another important aspect: If a software product,

---

1. *Philosophical Dictionary*, by Francois-Marie Arouet Voltaire, Theodore Besterman (editor), Viking Press, 1984.
2. It was already being debated in the IT industry by the mid-1990s. See, for example, "When Good Enough Is Best," by Ed Yourdon, *IEEE Software*, May 1995; and "The Challenge of 'Good Enough' Software," by James Bach, *Tester's Network*, Dec. 1996.

or an application program, is too big, too slow, too ugly, or too limited, it will be judged *not* good enough. At the time, Microsoft thought it was "good enough" to produce a new word processor with—as the company put it—ten times the functionality and three times the amount of code as the earlier version, with the expectation that it would run approximately as fast on the then-available Macintosh hardware configurations as the previous version (Word 5.1) ran on older Mac platforms. But it wasn't clear that the marketplace was prepared for the hundreds of new features, especially when a few critical features, including the all-important feature of booting up the word processor, were significantly slower; subsequently, many people (including me) abandoned Word 6.0 for the "good-enough" functionality of the older Word 5.1.

Functionality, quality, and schedule are the three most important elements of "good-enough" in most software today; they form a triangle, as illustrated in Figure 7.1. The key point, of course, is that all three dimensions are interconnected: If you change the schedule for a software project, the functionality and the quality are likely to change. There are additional dimensions of cost and staffing, too, but we'll leave them out of this discussion; the trade-off between people and time has already been discussed eloquently by Fred Brooks in *The Mythical Man-Month*[4].

---

3. Metrics guru Capers Jones gave a keynote presentation at the Fifth International Software Quality Conference, in which he said that (a) the number of "latent" defects in a typical software system could be estimated by raising the size of the system (as measured in function points) to the 1.2 power, and (b) that Windows 95 represents approximately 80,000 function points of software. If this estimate is correct, it would suggest that Windows 95 had approximately 1,345,434 latent bugs (i.e., bugs injected during the development process, and which had to be exorcised through inspections, code review, in-house testing, and beta testing). If all of these testing activities removed 99 percent of the defects, that would still leave 13,454 to be uncovered *after* the software was released. Meanwhile, of course, Microsoft has moved on to Windows NT, Windows 98, Windows Me, and Windows XP.
4. Fred Brooks, *The Mythical Man-Month*. (20th anniversary edition, Addison-Wesley, 1995).

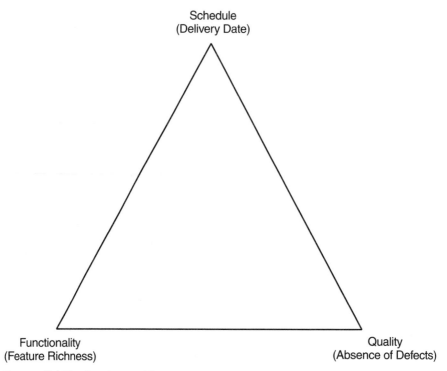

Schedule
(Delivery Date)

Functionality
(Feature Richness)

Quality
(Absence of Defects)

FIGURE 7.1 The "good-enough" triangle

The trade-offs between schedule, functionality (or "feature richness," as Microsoft likes to call it), and quality are never easy to calculate; Larry Putnam has explored the topic in his *Measures for Excellence* book,[5] and has demonstrated mathematically what we all know intuitively: It's not a linear relationship. If you double the number of required features for a software product, and hold the quality constant (as well as cost and manpower), then the schedule is likely to more than double.

There are a couple of key points to keep in mind about all of this:

- It's the *customer* who determines what combination of schedule, functionality, and quality they will tolerate—not the programmer, or the quality assurance

---

5. Larry Putnam and Ware Myers. *Measures for Excellence: Reliable Software on Time, Within Budget.* (Prentice Hall, 1992).

department obsessed with its ideal of "zero-defect" programming.

- The balance between schedule, functionality, and quality shifts dynamically during a project. It has to be reevaluated by the customer and the project manager, often on a daily basis, and the changes have an impact on the design and programming of the software, as well as testing strategies, risk management, and managerial assignment of staff resources to various programming tasks.

Most IT professionals do understand that for the typical application, it's not worth wasting time and effort within the project schedule to save a few microseconds and bytes of memory. But where we *really* have trouble is the idea that it's not worth spending more time in the project schedule to reduce the number of defects, or perhaps even eliminate them altogether.

Obviously, we don't want *any* bugs in the software for a pacemaker or a nuclear reactor or the air traffic control system for commercial airline flights. And in the best of all worlds, our users would like us to develop software instantly, at no cost, and with no defects. But that's just not possible in today's world; in more and more application domains, we've been forced to accept the fact that the reengineering slogan of "faster, cheaper, better" really means "fast enough, cheap enough, good enough." The surprisingly large numbers of defects that are publicly acknowledged in popular shrink-wrapped software products—e.g., word processors, spreadsheets, tax calculation programs, and PC operating systems from a variety of the best-known software companies—suggests that those products *are* good enough. And if a vendor offers the marketplace an alternative set of products with a different combination of functionality, quality, cost, and availability (i.e., the ability to buy it *now* rather than waiting an extra six months for it), it's not always obvious which one will succeed.

Software projects for nuclear reactors and pace-makers will probably continue focusing on zero-defect software, but the shrink-wrap software industry and the corporate IT application software industry are clearly shifting toward a paradigm that says, "It's okay to have bugs as long as you can give me the software *now* with the basic features that I need." As industry observer James Bach says, "It's okay to have bugs in the software you ship—but you should choose *which* bugs you ship."

What impact does all of this have on us when we plan and organize our software development efforts? In the past, we often negotiated critical project success parameters *once*, at the beginning of the project, and then attempted to optimize a few other parameters that the customer was often unaware of. For example, the functionality, schedule, budget, and staff resources were typically negotiated in terms of political constraints: We were told that our task was to deliver a software system with a certain amount of functionality (which was often ambiguous, misunderstood, and poorly documented) within a certain schedule and budget (which was based on hysterically optimistic estimates, or simply imposed by managerial fiat), and with a relatively fixed staff of developers. Within those constraints, the developers often attempted to optimize such features as maintainability, portability, reliability, and efficiency. Thus, the battle cry for many projects was: "We'll deliver high-quality, bug-free software on time, within budget!"

For an important class of software projects, that battle cry is still relevant—as previously noted, nobody wants to fly on an airplane whose guidance control software has as many bugs as our Web browsers and email software. Nobody wants their telephone system or their bank's ATM system to crash as often as their desktop operating system. But for another class of software projects—which is arguably far larger today than the class of "critical" software systems—rapid delivery of the software to the customer is sometimes more important than the number of defects it contains. In other situations, "feature richness" may be the dominant factor; in still others, cost might the only thing the user cares about.

Much of the shift that we're now experiencing is associated with the fact that information technology is now a consumer commodity: Unit costs are low, and everyone can have it. In the past, IT professionals typically worked on customized, proprietary, one-of-a-kind systems with schedules measured in years, and budgets measured in millions of dollars. Today, some software engineers are still employed by organizations who want customized systems—but the schedules and budgets have shrunk considerably. And the customers will often point out to us that they can achieve almost the same results by lashing together a jury-rigged combination of Microsoft Word, Excel, Access, and Excel, which they can obtain from a mail-order discount catalog. The shrink-wrap software may be clumsy and limited in its functionality for the user's application, but it's cheap—and it can be put into service tomorrow morning.

Thus, IT project manager must recognize that *each* of the project parameters—cost, schedule, staffing, functionality, and quality—is potentially critical today, and it is up to the customer to decide what the proper balance is. It's also crucial to remember that the balance between the parameters is a dynamic one, and may need to be re-adjusted on a daily basis. After all, the business environment is likely to change in a dramatic, unpredictable way—and this can easily change the customer's perception of the importance of schedule, cost, etc.

As a mental abstraction, any intelligent customer—especially one who has survived in today's tumultuous business times—is aware of the need to make trade-offs and balance priorities. But customers are often naive about the details; for example, it may not occur to them that defects (aka "bugs") are an aspect of the software that we have to consciously plan for, and for which we have to establish trade-offs in terms of other parameters. And, of course, they may not want to make cold-blooded, rational, calculated decisions about those tradeoffs: It's understandable (even though immensely frustrating) for a customer to demand a software system in half the time, and half the cost, with half the staff and twice the functionality, and half as many defects as the developers believe is technologically possible.[6]

What does this mean for the project manager? If we can assume for the moment that we're dealing with rational customers, and that a rational negotiation can determine the criteria for project success, then it is incumbent upon the manager to be as forthright and detailed as possible about *all* of the relevant success criteria. Thus, instead of just *assuming* that zero-defect quality is required, the project manager should be able to say something like, "Our standard approach for developing the software you've described will require X number of people, and Y units of time, with a cost of Z dollars; we'll deliver P units of functionality, with a defect level of Q bugs per function point."

Chances are that the proposed combination of X, Y, Z, P, and Q will *not* be acceptable to the customer; the likely response might be "You can't have Y units of time; we need to have the software in half that much time." A less rational response might be, "We want twice as much functionality as you proposed, but you can only have half as many people, half the time, and half the cost." This is possible, assuming (unrealistically, most likely) that the customer completely relaxes the constraint on the number of defects; after all, I can deliver an infinite amount of software, with an infinite amount of functionality, in zero time... if it doesn't have to work at all. The least rational response of all, from our customers, is one that constrains *all* of the project success parameters to some level that is demonstrably unachievable.

It *is* perfectly rational for our customers to challenge our proposal for X, Y, Z, P, and Q—particularly if we can get them to focus their attention on one parameter at a time. If the user wants the software in half the time originally proposed, then it's incumbent on us to provide a counter-proposal that shows the impact that such a change will have upon one or more of the other parameters. Back in the mid-1970s, Fred Brooks reminded us, in *The Mythical Man-Month*, that time and staff-resources are not interchangeable in a linear relationship; if we reduce the project schedule in half, it will *more* than double the required staff. Or we can

---

6. We'll discuss the frustrating politics associated with such negotiations in more detail in Chapter 8, which covers "death-march" projects.

cut the schedule in half, keep the staff constant, and increase the cost in a non-linear fashion (e.g., by having the constant-level staff work extraordinary levels of overtime).

The mathematics of the relationships between X, Y, Z, P, and Q are something we don't know enough about at our present level of software engineering. Larry Putnam and Ware Myers have explored this in their book, *Measures for Excellence*, but much more work is necessary. Similarly, some of the commercial estimating packages allow for some exploration of the tradeoffs between these parameters when establishing the initial project estimates and plans—but they rarely allow for dynamic renegotiations once the project has commenced. Renegotiation may not be all that important on a project that only takes three months; but in a project that extends over a year or two, it's almost inevitable in today's turbulent business environment.

It will be indeed difficult to say to our customers, "I'm going to deliver a system to you in six months that will have 5,000 bugs in it—and you're going to be *very* happy!" But that is likely to be the world many of us are likely to live in for the next several years. As James Bach argues,

> ...we have some idea what software quality is, but no certain idea. We have some methods to produce it and measure it, but no certain methods. Quality is inhibited by the complexity of the system, invisibility of the system, sensitivity to tiny mistakes, entropy due to development, interaction with external components, and interaction with the end user. In summary, creating products of the best possible quality is a very, very expensive proposition, while on the other hand, our clients may not even notice the difference between the best possible quality and pretty good quality.[7]

No respectable IT professional wants to build "shoddy" software; on the other hand, sometimes we become obsessed with building "perfect" software. What is it that prevents us from satisfying our customers by delivering what they regard as "good enough" software? I've already hinted at some of the reasons; here's a more complete list:

---

7. James Bach. "The Challenge of 'Good Enough' Software," *American Programmer*, October 1995.

- We have a tendency to define quality only in terms of defects—and we assume that fewer defects means better quality, and that "mo' better" quality is always preferred by user. At the 5th International Software Quality Conference, metrics guru Capers Jones showed the results of a survey of a survey of senior management opinions about quality. "Defects" typically ranked fourth or fifth in a list of ten items; issues like "time to market" and cost were typically among the top three priorities.

- We define quality (defect) requirements/objectives once, at the beginning of the project and keep it fixed. This makes sense in a stable environment, but nothing about today's development projects is likely to be stable—including the technology that we use, the vendors we rely on, and even the members of our project teams.

- We've been told for such a long time that processes are crucial, that we often forget that processes are "neutral." Processes don't build high-quality software; they merely provide a framework for good people, supported with good tools and technology, to do good work. But quality-oriented approaches such as ISO-9000 and the SEI-CMM don't help if you have incompetent people: A fool with a "process-tool" is still a fool. And the wrong process can be a disaster, too; as Abraham Maslow once observed, "If your only tool is a hammer, all your problems look like a nail."

- We pursue quality with a fixed process that we define once, at the beginning of the project—or, even worse, for all projects in the whole company. Many well-intentioned organizations apply process improvement principles at the end of a project, so that the next project will follow a better process—but they won't allow the project manager to modify the process (or in the extreme case, scrap it entirely) during a project. But common sense tells us that we might need to do just that, and a project manager needs to know that it's acceptable to change the game plan if necessary, without being visited by the process police.

- We underestimate the non-linear tradeoffs between such key parameters as staff size, schedule, budget, and defects—at the "macro" level of planning, which usually occurs in the early stages of the project, our users naively assume that the relationships are all linear. IT professionals intuitively understand the non-linearity, but typically don't have any quantitative alternatives they can show the user. There are several good, commercial estimating packages to assist in this kind of planning, but only a small percentage of projects use them.

- We ignore the dynamics of the processes: time-delays, feedback loops, etc. This usually happens at the "micro" level of planning, later in the project, when the project manager says, "If we decide now to drop function X from the development plan, it will save us 3.14159 work-days of effort..." —but there is almost always a "ripple effect" associated with these decisions, and most organizations lack a systems-dynamics modeling approach that would make it practical to study the consequences of those ripple effects.

- We ignore the "soft factors" associated with the software development process, such as morale, adequacy of office space, etc. It's very hard to build good-enough software if your project team members are demoralized, grumpy, and exhausted. This still comes as a surprise to some managers!

Techniques and Technologies for Developing Good-Enough Software

As noted above, some IT professionals feel who that the concept of "good-enough" software is heresy, and often describe it as a "flight from quality," or an acceptance of mediocrity on the part of an IT organization in its people, its products, and its processes. And indeed, there is a very real danger of falling into this kind of mind-set: Whether it's in software development or any other profession, we sometimes see people responding to projects and deadlines and customer requests by delivering the *least* amount of value they can get away, at the *last* possible moment. Under normal circumstances, most of us would prefer to think that we had delivered the *most* amount of value that we could manage with the limited resources available to us, and that we did so as *early* as possible in order to be proactive rather than reactive.

And "good-enough" software can be approached in this fashion: as a conscious, aggressive, proactive strategy to deliver the best possible combination of functionality, low-defects, and quick delivery—given that we have limited resources and a great deal of uncertainty about every aspect of software development. Software quality guru James Bach argues that there are five "key process ideas" involved in creating good-enough software:[8]

A utilitarian strategy

Bach describes this as the "art of qualitatively analyzing and maximizing net positive consequences in an ambiguous situation. It encompasses ideas from systems thinking, risk management, economics, decision theory, game theory, control theory, and fuzzy logic."

What does this mean in practical terms? Obviously, it means that the classic waterfall strategy for developing software should be tossed out; but more than that, it means that any fixed, rigid, authoritarian methodology, or life-cycle approach, for developing software should be tossed out the window. Some organizations follow a software development approach that allows the project team to customize the life-cycle and the overall development process at the beginning of the project; that's a good beginning, but as we'll see below, we even need to allow customization during the software project.

Some organizations follow a rapid-prototyping approach, or variations on the iterative, spiral, or evolutionary lifecycles that have described methodology gurus like Barry

---

8. See the previously cited article, "The Challenge of 'Good Enough' Software" (*American Programmer*, October 1995), for details.

Boehm over the years. A good summary of these methodologies can be found in Jim Highsmith's recent book, *Adaptive Software Development*,[9] which also discusses some of the emergent-systems concepts that we covered in Chapter 5.

An evolutionary strategy

Bach notes that "evolution is discussed [in the literature] mainly in regard to the project life cycle. What I'd also point out is that we can take an evolutionary view of our people, processes, and resources."

This kind of evolution *does* happen in the real world, whether or not we want to acknowledge it. A project might begin, for example, with a team of ten people and a set of resources consisting of workstations, offices, conference rooms, funds for research and training, etc. But as the project continues, we might find that some of the project team members leave, while others acquire more experience and skills. The resources will increase or decrease, depending on the economic fortunes of the enterprise. And the development processes used by the team can change in an evolutionary way, too, depending on the availability of technology, people, and resources.

Typical elements of an evolution strategy include the following:

- Build good-enough versions of the deliverable system in self-contained stages, using some form of a time-box approach. Among other things, this will give you and the customer an opportunity to see which combination of feature-richness, defect-elimination, and rapid delivery characterizes "good enough."

- Acknowledge at the beginning of the project that you won't be able to plan everything—i.e., that some aspects of the project are essentially unknowable until you've actually carried them out.

- Integrate early and often; Microsoft's "daily build" approach is a good one to emulate here—i.e., generate

9. James A. Highsmith, *Adaptive Software Development: A Collaborative Approach to Managing Complex Systems* (New York: Dorset House, 2000).

source code, compile it, install it, and build an operational, working prototype of your application every day.

- Reuse, purchase, or salvage existing software components wherever feasible.

- Record and review the experiences that occur during the project. This is another aspect of the dynamic, evolutionary approach: The few organizations that I've seen carrying out such evaluations refer to them as post-mortems, a term originally used to describe a medical examination of a dead body. A post-mortem of a completed project—whether or not it was a success—is typically nothing more than an exercise in recording vaguely-remembered bits and pieces of history. As Tom DeMarco points out in his book, *Why Does Software Cost So Much?*[10] the post-mortem has little or no effect on subsequent projects. "We really made a terrible mistake when we did X," the project team will write in their post-mortem report. "We should resolve never to do X again on any future project." But by then, everyone is already working on another project, and since nobody pays much attention to the details of a dead project, X has already been done again. But what about a post-mortem review *during* a project—i.e., at the end of each deliverable version? It doesn't have to be a protracted exercise; a half-day, or full-day meeting (preferably off-site, away from the office) gives the team a chance to review its recent activities while it still matters. Lessons learned can be applied to the next deliverable version; processes, tools, and even personnel assignments can be modified to increase the chances of success for the next milestone.

Heroic teams

Bach describes as heroic teams as "not... the Mighty Morphin Genius Programmers, ... [but]...ordinary, skillful people

10. Tom DeMarco, *Why Does Software Cost So Much? and other puzzles of the information age* (New York: Dorset House, 1995).

working in effective collaboration." One of the places where you'll see evidence of the "heroic teams" is the "shrink-wrap" PC-software-product companies; software is the very essence of the business, and its senior executives are frequently the ones who developed the company's initial software product. And given the demands for surviving—as a world-class competitor—in such a business, it's not surprising that the shrink-wrap software companies are the ones who have developed, articulated, and championed the concept of good-enough software. Other companies that are beginning to recognize the crucial value of software heroes are the multimedia companies, the software-game companies, the interactive-entertainment companies, the information service-providers, and... yes, even a few banks and insurance companies and stodgy old widget manufacturers.

The impact of all this on the IT profession is both subtle and profound, and it's particularly evident in the published literature. The situation could be compared to the art of warfare: There are far more books about waging war with conventional armies and navies than the relatively few books that have been written about strategies for commandos and guerrilla soldiers. In the IT field, *everyone* knows about the startup software companies that are clearly populated by heroes, and whose activities may be highly successful, but are also highly risky and uncertain. But while we sometimes do see books about these software "personalities" like Bill Gates or Steve Jobs, there is rarely any formal discussion about the process their company's product teams use for developing successful software products. Jim McCarthy's book about software development at Microsoft[11] is the closest thing that I've seen to an overt discussion of strategies for developing good-enough software.

What we *do* see in the software literature is an enormous amount of discussion about software processes as the key "driver" in developing world-class software; the SEI's capability maturity model (CMM) is a very visible and important example of that school of thought. There are some

---

11. See *Dynamics of Software Development*, by Jim McCarthy (Microsoft Press, 1995).

excellent concepts embodied in the SEI-CMM; but there are also some potentially serious weaknesses in such process-driven approaches, particularly in today's topsy-turvy business environment, for it creates an environment where people can abdicate personal responsibility by delegating everything to the process.

For example, consider the adage that says, "If there's a defect, don't blame the person; blame the process that led to the defect." Well, that's fine: it preserves the software professional's ego and sense of self-worth, and we can presumably modify the process so that we won't have the same problem on the next project (assuming that there *is* a next project). But meanwhile, what about *this* project? Whose job is it to recognize that the process failed on this project? Whose responsibility is it to forge ahead, solve the problem, and find a work-around to the faulty process? Whose job is it to *get the job done?* And as for the next project: How do we know that the modified process will work? After all, the environment is likely to have changed again, so that a different set of conditions will be encountered by the next project team.

James Bach observes another problem with conventional software processes, especially the ones that are developed and documented and enforced in large organizations:

> Orthodox methodologies don't fly with good-enough software companies for one reason more than any other: They're boring. Bored people don't work hard. They don't take initiative, and they avoid ambiguous problems instead of tackling them with gusto. Take care to create an exciting environment that fosters responsible heroism, and great software will follow.

This doesn't mean that we should abandon all processes and resort to complete anarchy or uncoordinated efforts by individual superheroes; a good-enough software team *does* have processes, but as noted above, those processes are dynamic, and they operate within an evolutionary framework. It's a question of degree: If you're fighting a war with an army of a million people with average talents, you use one set of tactics. If you're waging war with a guerrilla army of a few dozen or a couple hundred people, you need a different caliber of people and a different set of tactics. Good-enough software, combined with software heroes, is just such a combination.

Much of the exciting, successful software that we've seen in the IT industry in the past 30-40 years has indeed been developed by such guerrilla teams, typically involving less than a dozen people. On the other hand, the trend for most IT organizations (including, interestingly, some of the high-flying dot-com companies) was the creation of ever-larger software armies, sometimes leading to projects involving hundreds of people. Some of those projects did succeed, but many of them resulted in spectacular failures; such projects have been banned in many large enterprises, and they no longer represent the dominant trend in software development. Nor are they necessary in many cases today: The power of modern programming tools often makes it possible for a small team of five to accomplish the same results as a team of 500 people using an older generation of technology.

Dynamic infrastructure

Bach describes this as the antithesis of bureaucracy and power politics. An IT organization with a dynamic infrastructure is one in which upper management pays attention to projects, pays attention to the market, identifies and resolves conflicts between projects, allows the project to "win" when there are conflicts between projects and organizational bureaucracy, and one in which project experience is incorporated into the organizational memory.

What this basically means is that good-enough software development probably won't succeed in the highly political environment that we still find in many IT organizations today. If the organizational climate is characterized by back-stabbing, empire-building, and following rigid procedures because "that's the way we've always done things around here," then good-enough software can still be developed in isolated circumstances, but typically only when a fanatically devoted project team finds a way to sneak off and carry out a "skunk-works" project.

Dynamic processes

Bach describes dynamic processes as those that change with the situation—"processes that support work in an evolving, collaborative environment. Dynamic processes are ones you can always question because every dynamic process is part of an identifiable metaprocess."

He suggests that three key attributes of dynamic process are portability, scalability, and durability:

- *Portability*: How can the process be shared with others, applied to new problems, and carried into meetings for discussions with others?
- *Scalability:* Can the process be carried out manually by one person on a small project, as well as be carried out with automated support on a big project—so that it's applicable across a broad range of projects taking place within the organization?
- *Durability:* Can the process withstand misuse and neglect?

Paradigm Shifts _____

The concept of good-enough IT systems was a recognized, publicly-discussed concept throughout the 1990s; and it's based on a concept of engineering trade-offs that dates back to the ancient Romans and Egyptians, if not earlier. So what's new and different at this point?

The paradigm shift, at least in terms of the good-enough concept that we've practiced in the IT industry for the past decade, has two elements:

- Malevolent threats
- Life and death circumstances

Malevolent threats

Those building military systems obviously realize that their systems are likely to be probed and attacked by hostile individuals and groups. The same is true for banking systems:

People have *always* tried to steal money from banks, so it's second-nature for the IT professionals building such systems to assume the worst.

But for the vast majority of business organizations, the discussion about the tradeoffs and compromises of a good-enough system have assumed that the system would operate in a relatively benign environment. In particular, we've assumed that software defects would represent an inconvenience or disruption in the day-to-day activities of end-users *who were trying to use the system to carry out its intended purpose.* Not only that, we've assumed that whatever defects remain in a system, after we've accomplished a good-enough degree of testing, will be relatively obscure, and will probably be associated with features and situations that occur only rarely.

But in today's world of terrorists and hackers, we must assume that at least some of our users make a deliberate effort to *find* the defects—not to write a critical review in a computer trade magazine, but to exploit the defect to circumvent the systems security and protection mechanisms, or to cause a system crash, or to cause the destruction or corruption of the system's database. Thus, the determination of a good-enough balance between functionality, cost, speed of development, and defects must now take into account the likelihood that some of the users will deliberately and aggressively look for ways to *mis*-use the system.

This is not an abstract point; in particular, it has a profound impact, for example, on the testing strategies used by the project teams who are developing e-commerce systems (which is a far broader category than banking systems), Web browsers, operating systems, email systems, database management systems, and any other computer system that could be exploited for the purpose of creating a large-scale impact. For example, many of the successful attacks on Web sites during 2001 (including the Code Red worm) were accomplished by taking advantage of a "buffer-overflow" problem in Microsoft's IIS Web server[12]—i.e., by deliber-

---

12. See "IIS Vulnerability (Code Red worm)," by Cam Beasley, *University of Texas IT Security & Policy Office,* July 24, 2001.

ately sending messages of such an extravagant length that it would overflow the memory area that had been set aside for such messages. Hackers discovered a similar bug in AOL's free and widely-distributed Instant Messaging software in January 2002;[13] by exploiting a buffer-overflow bug, they could take complete control of someone's personal computer from a remote location.

One could argue that such defects should never have existed in the first place; after all, a basic principle of good software development is to make one's program as "idiot-proof" as possible. But the real problem is that most software testing departments have limited time and resources for conducting their testing. Exhaustive testing, in which every possible aspect of a system is tested, is completely impossible for all but the most trivial of systems; and even a reasonably thorough test—of the kind that we *would* expect to see for a military system or a banking system—is not practical, with the available time, people, and money. This is particularly true in so-called "death-march" projects, which we'll discuss in Chapter 8.

Given the limited resources available, testing professionals obviously have to prioritize; and in some cases they practice a more cold-blooded form of "triage," in which they effectively say, "We're not going to bother testing this portion of the system, because..." Until recently, the "because" involved the perceived importance of some features or functionality in the system (as perceived by the end-users or marketing department), and/or the perceived likelihood that the features would be used frequently. Thus, the testers might say, "We're not going to test functions X, Y, and Z because we think it's highly unlikely that anyone will actually use them—and if they don't work, nobody will care very much anyway."

Obviously, in today's world, the "we're not going to test this portion *because...*" has to be modified to include not only the possibility that a defect might have devastating

---

13. See "Messaging software has security bug: AOL program susceptible to misuse by hackers," by Elise Ackerman and Mary Anne Ostrom, *San Jose Mercury News*, Jan. 2, 2002.

consequences, but also the fact that it might be deliberately exploited to achieve those consequences.

Life and death circumstances

When the concept of good-enough systems was discussed throughout the 1990s, skeptics often introduced a "red herring" objection: "Would you want to fly on an airplane whose flight-control software was developed using a good-enough approach?"

The proper answer is "Of course I would! Now let's talk about our *definition* of 'good-enough' for safety-critical systems like air-traffic control, nuclear reactors, and medical instrumentation systems." As we discussed earlier in this chapter, the good-enough concept requires that we acknowledge the importance of all three of the "dimensions" of functionality, defect-related quality, and development schedule/cost. And in simplistic terms, what we began to realize throughout the 1990s was that there were several different "families" of systems, for which different strategies were required in order to produce different combinations of those three dimensions. Thus, there are safety-critical systems in which the schedule and budget typically have to be "relaxed" in order to meet stringent defect-related constraints and functionality constraints; and there are non-safety-critical business systems, consumer gadgets, and personal computer software systems in which the functionality and defect-related constraints have to be "relaxed" in order to meet aggressive development schedules and budgets.

All of this was fine until two things happened: first, we suddenly realized (as discussed in Chapters 2 and 3) that many of the systems that we had characterized as "non-safety-critical" really *are* critical, because they can impact the country's critical infrastructure. And second, the consciously malevolent activities of terrorists, hackers, and technology-savvy sociopaths has forced us to adjust the previously-accepted norms of functionality versus defects versus speed/cost.

Many of the potential threats being contemplated by American society in the aftermath of September 11th go far beyond the world of computing and IT; we worry now about biological, chemical, and nuclear attacks as well as the more traditional terrorist acts of bombing, shooting, and flying airplanes into buildings. But as we discussed in Chapter 2, IT plays a critical role in many of these areas: We need computer systems to organize and deploy vaccines and health-care teams in the event of a biological attack, and we need computer systems to monitor the purchase, shipments, and disposal of chemical and nuclear wastes that might become terrorist weapons. And if used to their maximum capabilities, such weapons could conceivably kill not just thousands, but millions of citizens. Thus, while the debates in the 1990s about good-enough systems sometimes touched on life-and-death issues, the scale of potential disaster was measured in terms of a single life, or the lives of a relatively small group of people. As part of the paradigm shift in today's world, the good-enough strategies of IT developers have to contemplate the possibility of much larger-scale disasters.

Strategic Implications

As President Clinton famously remarked in response to a lawyer's interrogatory about his relationship with Monica Lewinsky, "It depends on what the meaning of 'is' is." Similarly, the most important implication of this chapter is the need for all of the stakeholders in large, complex systems to discuss what *is* "good enough." Often with the best of intentions, consumers and end-users and managers demand perfection of those who build their systems, while simultaneously mandating aggressive schedules, budgets, and lists of functional requirements. And in today's new world, with the stakes having changed so quickly and so dramatically, that negotiating position will have to change. If the best is the enemy of the good, in Voltaire's words, then we may have to acknowledge that the good is the enemy of survival—at least in cases where we have *no* protection, no defenses, and no system in place to accomplish vital functions.

All of this will have different implications for different categories of people; here are some suggestions for the five categories we have discussed throughout this book:

Government leaders

- *Be candid and honest with the public about good-enough tradeoffs*—Obviously, nobody wants to hear about safety-critical systems whose technical defects might cause injury or death. In the best of all worlds, responsible leaders will ensure that such a system is not put into operation until it has been tested sufficiently thoroughly to remove those defects. But in a crisis situation where the system *must* be deployed, there is a political tendency to obfuscate and deny the existence of defects and problems. Such a strategy can work as long as people aren't paying attention, and as long as major disasters don't occur. But if media coverage increases the level of attention and awareness, and if serious crises do occur because of defects and shortcomings with these systems, then the government's credibility with the public can be shattered.

- *Recognize that that an effective strategy requires an overt discussion of quality.* This may sound obvious, but the issue of technical quality often gets buried in the negotiations of functionality versus schedule/budget. The unspoken assumption is that the system will have *no* defects, or that whatever defects slip through the test process will be so minor that they will have no impact on the use of the system. Suppose, for example, that a high-level government official—e.g., the FBI Director or the Attorney General or the President—launches a "crash project" initiative to build a new system that integrates and consolidates all existing government databases that might contain information about suspected criminals and terrorists; such a system might include arrest records, prison records, and court records at the local and state level, in addition to the dozens (perhaps hundreds) of databases at the federal level. If the responsible government official says, "This system *must* be implemented in X months," where X is substantially shorter than anyone has every built a comparable system, then it's crucial for someone to say, "Well, we'll try very hard to get it done—but is it okay if, say, 10% of the records in the database are incorrect, and those people get arrested and locked up as a result?" An answer of "yes" may be morally repugnant (and perhaps illegal), but at least it tells the project manager that the good-enough "dimensions" of his project have been clarified; and an answer of "no" is acceptable, because it forces another round of negotiations to take place, which will hopefully provide more time or more resources to build the system. But if the response is "I don't want to hear about problems like that," then the seeds of disaster have been planted.

- *Recognize the short-term/long-term tradeoffs.* One of the reasons the good-enough approach works in the private sector is that technology changes so quickly that a "buggy" IT-related product can be replaced within a year or two by a newer, cheaper, faster, *better* product; furthermore, consumers are likely to accept a good-enough product if it's cheap, fast, and innovative *and* if they believe that this year's version of the product will be replaced by a more stable and defect-free version next year. But in the government world, this kind of rapid turnover of products and technologies is less common; governments tend to build huge systems and then remain stuck with them for decades. This needs to be kept in mind when discussions and negotiations concerning good-enough trade-offs take place: the system behavior that might be judged "good enough" for this year and next year might be completely unacceptable five years from now, when the same system is still operating.

Senior corporate executives

Because the politics and bureaucracy of a large company are often similar to that of government, the suggestions made in the Government leaders section above are likely to apply to senior corporate executives, too. As noted earlier, private-sector companies often have the advantage of being able to replace old (and buggy) products with new (less buggy) versions more quickly than government; but like their government counterparts, senior corporate executives need to be candid and honest when discussing the risks of trading off time versus functionality versus technical quality. And they need to discuss technical quality overtly, rather than simply pretending that the programmers will somehow write bug-free code.

As noted earlier in this chapter, more and more companies are facing malevolent attacks that deliberately exploit the defects and weaknesses in a company's systems. But while this is an unpleasant and potentially scary situation, it doesn't always involve life-and-death consequences. And if lives are not at stake, then senior management should delegate as many of the good-enough decisions and strategies as possible *downward* in the hierarchy, as low as possible— because, as we discussed in Chapter 5, the world is changing too quickly for a hierarchical, top-down management approach to operate effectively. As discussed earlier in this chapter, the good-enough tradeoffs between functionality, schedule/cost, and technical quality may have to be reassessed on a daily basis; furthermore, what's good enough in the company's New York market may not be good enough in its London or Tokyo markets. Convening the company's senior vice-presidents on a daily basis to discuss these tradeoffs is usually not practical or appropriate, unless there are lives at stake or significant legal issues involved.

Mid-level IT managers

Mid-level IT managers are typically the ones who have to turn statements of policy and philosophy into action; in this case, they are the ones who have to take a negotiated tradeoff between functionality, schedule/cost, and technical quality and somehow direct their project team to actually build a system that meets those constraints. The discussion in the Techniques and Technologies section highlights some of the strategies used by IT managers to actually build a good-enough system; and numerous textbooks can provide additional guidance.

I believe that the largest problem of mid-level managers will be forcing their senior managers to articulate *specifically* what they mean by "good-enough" in today's troubled times. As noted earlier, this involves some difficult political issues—especially if the stakes are large, and if circumstances mandate that the system *must* be developed with aggressive constraints on schedule, budget, and resources. The natural political tendency of a high-level leader—whether in public-sector or private-sector organizations—is to leave unpleasant realities unspoken, and unpleasant expectations ambiguous.[14] Obviously, this makes it more difficult for the mid-level managers to make firm choices as they attempt to achieve a precarious balance between the good-enough dimensions.

This is one of the many areas where IT managers and IT professionals will need to reassess their own personal values and ethics in the years ahead. What should a mid-level project manager do if he is told to build a system with schedule, cost, and functionality constraints that virtually guarantee a bug-riddled result, *and* if his senior management won't acknowledge, discuss, negotiate, or accept responsibility for those defect-related consequences? In the past, some mid-level managers have essentially shrugged their shoulders and abdicated any ethical responsibility: "Even if the senior management won't acknowledge it, they're the ones who are creating this situation," the mid-level manager thinks to himself. "So it's not my problem, and frankly, I don't care how it turns out." In the good old days of the 1990s, one could ignore the pangs of conscience caused by this abdication; after all, it usually only led to mediocre products and disgruntled customers. But today,

---

14. In this context, it's interesting that in several speeches following September 11th, President Bush emphasized that lives would be lost in the American military response to the terrorist attacks, and that civilian casualties were likely, too. Unfortunately, the statements were so vague that they probably had little personal impact on anyone besides military families. Ordinary citizens are sobered by discussions of possible casualties; but as long as it doesn't involve themselves, their spouse, their siblings, or their children, it's still relatively abstract.

much more may be at stake; and it is the mid-level IT man-ager who will have to decide whether to lead, follow, or get out of the way.

IT professionals

Just as mid-level managers need to force their senior execu-tives to articulate clearly what is meant by "good enough," so the IT professionals on today's "critical" projects will have to force their project managers to do the same thing. Unfortunately, many mid-level IT managers will obfuscate and issue bland, ambiguous statements, just like their higher-level managers; and thus, by default, it ends up being the programmers, systems analysts, testing specialists and other IT professionals who make the critical decisions.

Of course, it should not be the programmer who makes the final decision about whether to curtail additional testing and leave a dozen undiscovered bugs in the system. In the first instance, it should be the project manager who makes the call; and ultimately, the decision should be made by senior management and/or the various stakeholders who approve and control the overall conduct of the project.

This involves a very basic philosophical aspect of the good-enough approach, which has been the subject of debate since the term was first popularized in the early 1990s. Quite understandably, some programmers and soft-ware engineers will say, "I'm a professional! I'm not willing to do low-quality work! I won't release this piece of code that I'm working on until I'm satisfied that it meets *my* stan-dard of quality!" It's a noble statement, but the reality is that the programmer is being paid by a customer to deliver a software-related product or service; and thus, in our free-enterprise system, it's the customer who has the privilege (and the responsibility) of choosing an acceptable balance between functionality, schedule/cost, and technical qual-ity.[15] If the programmer doesn't like the choice that has been made, then he should find himself a new customer to work for—a customer whose appreciation for technical quality matches his own.

For some IT professionals, the concept of good-enough software may be new and unfamiliar; indeed, the very first thing that may need to be done is to accept the basic concept and reassess their opinions about quality. But even the veterans who have lived through a decade of making good-enough tradeoffs on their computer projects may need to do some reassessments; as my colleague James Bach remarked recently, "Good enough isn't good enough any more!" In particular, the malevolent exploitation of system defects means that programmers and testing professionals and their managers need to re-examine their testing strategy as they decide how to apply their limited resources to identify and remove as many defects as possible.

Citizens

What role do citizens play in all of this? For the most part, they serve as a counter-part to the government officials discussed above. That is, citizens must acknowledge the concept of good-enough systems, and they must articulate their expectations and preferences as clearly as possible, so that government leaders (as well as senior corporate executives) can make informed decisions.

To some extent, citizens make their opinions known by surveys and polls; and to some extent, they vote with their feet, by shifting their loyalties and their purchases from one place to another. Thus, in the months following the September 11th attacks, airplane travel has dropped by roughly 25%—suggesting that, regardless of the rhetoric and legislation from the government, people still do not completely

---

15. The circumstances are different if the programmer is also an owner/shareholder in the enterprise that builds the software; the extreme case is the self-employed programmer who creates software products for his own entertainment, or to sell in the open marketplace. Just as Orson Wells popularized the phrase, "We will sell no wine before its time" in an old Paul Masson wine commercial, some programmers are determined that they will sell none of their software until "its time" has come. But in most high-tech startup companies where IT professionals have become (minor) shareholders via stock options, their attitude toward good-enough software changes dramatically. Yes, technical quality is important—but it's also important to ship the product out to the marketplace in time to generate some revenues!

believe that airport security is good enough. Interestingly, survey after survey has indicated that passengers are fully prepared to pay a few additional dollars per trip to pay for higher levels of security; what's less clear is the degree to which they'll tolerate delays and inconveniences associated with additional security measures.

Of course, different citizens will have different expectations about the good-enough tradeoffs. Business travelers have, to a large degree, simply shouldered the extra burdens associated with post-9/11 air travel—because, in their minds, they have no choice. But some vacationers and tourists are unwilling to make any compromises: They want the pre-9/11 combination of convenient plane schedules, competitive prices, and the perception (or perhaps the illusion) of adequate security. Obviously, the attack of September 11th made it clear that the security mechanisms were "buggier" than we thought; as citizens, we have the choice of accepting that lower standard of security, or demanding more security in return for higher prices and less convenience—or we can find an alternative form of travel whose good-enough tradeoffs are more acceptable.

When it comes to IT systems, citizens will find themselves faced with similar tradeoffs. The malevolent exploitation of software vulnerabilities has an obvious impact on a citizen's home computer, particularly if it's infected by a destructive virus. So, as time goes on, we citizens will have to reassess the situation, and then articulate our expectations to the Microsofts and AOLs and Amazons and eBays with whom we interact electronically. Whether or not citizens realize it, the good-enough concept has been well-established in the consumer-oriented PC world for years: you don't have to explain the need to tolerate buggy software to a typical consumer, because he has put up with it for years! But since the attacks are becoming ever more malevolent, the likelihood is that consumers will start demanding higher levels of quality, even if it means they have to pay more money, or wait longer for new products, or accept fewer "bells and whistles" in the functionality associated with their products.

It's one thing to talk about viruses in one's email, and bugs in one's word-processor or desktop operating system. The more serious debate will revolve around the good-enough characteristics of the "critical infrastructure" systems that depend on computers. This is an area about which citizens need to educate themselves, so that they can make intelligent choices and articulate realistic expectations to the government and major infrastructure providers. If there is another terrorist attack, for example, how much "quality" are we willing to sacrifice in our nationwide telecommunication system? Conversely, how much more would we be willing to pay *now*, on our monthly phone bills, in order to subsidize the development of a more robust telecommunications environment that could continue providing "full service" even in the midst of a major attack? How many errors—errors of both omission and commission—are we willing to tolerate in the nation's law-enforcement intelligence systems, in order to maintain the current combination of costs (in the form of taxes), and functionality (in the form of civil rights)?

Interestingly, this kind of discussion and assessment took place, to a limited degree, during the Y2K era—when citizens worried that a non-malevolent computer bug might disrupt the nation's computers. Unfortunately, only a small percentage of the population participated in that process, and the ensuing dialog with government and industry was limited at best. This time, the stakes are potentially much higher; and the threat is much more real and tangible than it was with the Y2K bug. We can only hope that a national dialog does begin, and that it takes on a coherent form so that responsible government officials can be guided by it.

DEATH-MARCH PROJECTS

I discussed death-march projects in a 1997 book by the same title; and I covered some related issues in a 2001 book entitled *Managing High-Intensity Internet Projects.* I'll summarize that material briefly in the Basic Concepts and Techniques and Technologies sections below; but if you've seen either of my two earlier books, you can skip ahead to the Paradigm Shifts section. On the other hand, if you have no idea what I'm talking about, and want *much* more detail, feel free to pick up a copy of either or both of those earlier books.

Basic Concepts

What is a death-march project?

For the last several years, I've found that the phrase "death-march project" requires no definition or explanation in the

IT field; the most common reaction is, "Oh, you mean *my* project!" What I didn't expect was the email messages that I began receiving shortly after the publication of my *Death March* book, from people in numerous industries outside of the computer field. Health-care professionals, insurance underwriters, aerospace engineers, and people from all walks of life wrote to me and said, "What makes you computer people think you have a monopoly on this kind of project?"

But every once in a while, I still meet someone who has no idea what I'm talking about. If you're one of those people, here's a loose definition: A death-march project is an ambitious, aggressive project that dramatically exceeds what would normally be expected in terms of schedule, resources, and cost. By "dramatically exceeds," I don't mean 5% or 10%; 50% or 100% is more likely to be the expectation. Especially in high-technology fields, you'll occasionally hear people talking about "order of magnitude" improvements over their normal expectations—i.e., attempting to accomplish some kind of project ten times faster or cheaper.

Sometimes the focus is on cost: You'll hear people talking about "shoestring budgets" or complaining "we ought to have a budget of $1 million to build this system properly, but they've told us we can only get $500,000." And sometimes the focus is on resources, which usually means people; thus, you'll hear about death-march projects being carried out with a staff of three, when any "reasonable" plan would have called for five or six or seven people. But the most common focus of all tends to be speed: Thus, the team that estimates they need a year to develop a system is told that they *must* be finished in six months.

As we'll see in the Techniques and Technologies section, there are various strategies for increasing the odds that a death-march project will succeed. But by far the most common, and most obvious, strategy is intense effort on the part of the project team, with substantial overtime over long periods of time. It is the protracted overtime effort—e.g., 70-hour weeks over a period of 6 months or longer—that creates the phrase "death march." It's not as brutal as the military death-marches that took place in World War II, or in the transfer of Native American tribes to their reservations in the 18th and 19th century; but they can be quite inhumane, and they can lead to divorces, nervous breakdowns, and other health problems.

Why do death-march projects exist?

From the brief description above, it sounds like death-march projects are unpleasant, if not downright uncivilized. After my *Death March* project was published, I received indignant email messages from people who asked, "Why are you condoning such projects? Why aren't these projects banned?"

It's naïve to imagine that an author could ban death-march projects by the stroke of his pen, but one *could* imagine a labor-union or a government regulation banning the intense overtime work typically associated with death-march projects. As for condoning death-march projects: I personally believe there are a few situations where they are justified, but most of the time, they occur simply because some manager decrees that they will occur—*and workers willingly accept that decree.* Prisoners of war embark upon a death-march at the point of a gun; but most workers in a free-enterprise society have a choice; thus, as we'll see below, the more important question is why any rational person would agree to participate in such a project.

As for management's rationale for creating such projects, the reasons are fairly straightforward. As I explained in my *Death March* book, the typical causes for death-march projects are as follows:

- *Politics*—when politics becomes a dominant force in a large, complex project, it's likely to degenerate into a death march. It may be a power struggle between two fast-track managers in your organization, or the project may have been set up to fail, as a form of revenge upon some manager who stepped on the wrong toes at the wrong time. The possibilities are endless.

- *Naive promises made by marketing, senior executives, project managers, and project team members*—unrealistic commitments are often made by people who have no idea how much time or effort will be required to build the system they want. Unfortunately, when it eventually becomes clear that the initial commitments *were* optimistic, a rational mid-course correction is not always possible. In the worst case, the person making the commitment knows full well what's going on— e.g., when the marketing manager confesses to the project manager over a beer after the celebrations accompanying a new contract from some gullible client, "Well, we wouldn't have gotten this contract if we told the client how long it will *really* take; after all, we knew that our competitors would be coming with some really aggressive proposals. And besides: you guys always pad your schedules and budgets anyway, don't you?"

- *Naive optimism of youth: "we can do it over the weekend"*—the technical staff on the project team is sometimes the source of the unrealistic estimates that lead to a death-march project. Often, the naively optimistic software engineers responsible for making the death-march estimate don't even know what they're doing. Unfortunately, when they do realize that they are in over their head, they often collapse, resulting in truly irrational behavior or paralysis. In most cases, they haven't dealt with anything before that was so big and complex that it couldn't be overwhelmed by sheer cleverness or brute force (e.g., 48 hours of non-stop coding over the weekend).

- *The "startup" mentality of fledgling, entrepreneurial companies*—the dot-com phenomenon was a typical example of this situation. Startup organizations are typically understaffed, underfinanced, and undermanaged; they also tend to suffer from the kind of naive optimism discussed earlier. Many startup companies are founded by technical hotshots convinced that their new technology will make them richer than Bill Gates; other such companies are founded by marketing wizards who are convinced they can sell Internet-enabled refrigerators to gullible Eskimos. As a result, a large percentage of the projects associated with startup companies are death-march projects. A large percentage of these projects will fail; a large percentage of the companies will fail with them. Nevertheless, this scenario is often one of the *positive* reasons for embarking upon a death-march project, as I'll discuss in more detail below.

- *The "Marine Corps" mentality: <u>real</u> programmers don't need sleep*—Startup companies are sometimes vulnerable to the "Marine Corps" syndrome, but it's also common in some consulting organizations. It may reflect the personality of the corporate founder(s), and it may reflect the corporate culture in its earlier days. In essence, you'll be told by the appropriate manager, "*Every* project is like this, because that's how we do things around here. It works, we're successful, and we're damn proud of it. If you can't handle it, then you don't belong here." The important thing is to realize that such an attitude is *deliberate*, not accidental. Sometimes there's an official rationale for such corporate behavior—e.g., "We compete in a tough marketplace, and all of our competitors are just as smart as we are. The only way we succeed is to work twice as hard." And sometimes the death-march projects are set up to weed out the younger (weaker) junior employees, so that only the survivors of the death-march projects will reach the exalted status of "partner" or "Vice President."

- *Intense competition caused by globalization of markets*—Organizations that might not have tolerated death-march projects in the past are sometimes being forced to do so in today's environment, simply because of the increased level of competition associated with the global marketplace. The secondary factors here are universal telecommunications (including the Internet) and governmental decisions to open previously-protected markets or eliminate tariffs and quotas. Such projects are often accompanied by dire predictions from senior management of the consequences of failure—e.g., layoffs or even corporate bankruptcy. And, as I'll discuss below, this may prove to be the primary justification for participating in such projects.

- *Intense competition caused by the appearance of new technologies*—The introduction of radically improved technology may cause a defensive response from a company that was reasonably happy with products built around an older technology; or it may lead to a proactive decision to utilize the new technology for competitive advantage. If the corporate response to the new-technology situation is essentially defensive in nature, then the death-march project may be one that seeks to exploit the company's *old* technology far beyond its normal limits. But many death-march projects in this category are the ones that involve first-time usage of the new technologies. What really contributes to the death-march nature of such projects— beyond the obvious characteristics of size, schedule, and budget—is the attempt to use bleeding-edge technology for an industrial-strength application. Even if the technology is basically usable, it often does not scale up well for large-scale usage; and nobody knows how to exploit its strengths and avoid its weaknesses; and the vendors don't know how to support it properly; and on and on... It's important to remember that the younger technicians and project managers *prefer* these new technologies, precisely because they *are* new. And these are the same folks who are typically naively optimistic about the schedule and budget constraints within which they're working. Is it any wonder that things degenerate into a death-march project, with everyone working late nights and long weekends in order to coax the experimental new technology into some semblance of working order?

- *Intense pressure caused by unexpected government regulations*—As noted above, one of the reasons for death-march projects associated with globalization of markets is the decision by governmental authorities to reduce tariffs, eliminate import quotas, or other such decisions to "open" a previously closed market. However, there are also many instances of *increased* regulatory pressure from governmental authorities, which, as we'll discuss in the Paradigm Shifts section, is particularly relevant in the aftermath of the September 11th attacks. The particularly onerous thing about many of these government-mandated death-march projects is the deadline: The new system *must* be operational by some arbitrary date like January 1st, or fines of a million dollars a day will be imposed. There may be an opportunity to ask for an extension or a waiver, but in most cases, the deadline is absolute. And the consequences are usually as dire for the organization as those mentioned above: Layoffs, bankruptcy, or other calamities will occur if the new system isn't finished on time.

- *Unexpected and/or unplanned crises*—Your two best programmers have just marched into your office to inform you that (a) they're getting married, (b) they're joining the Peace Corps, and (c) today is their last day on the job. Or your legal department calls you to say that the company has been sued for ten zillion dollars because the company is not in compliance with some arcane tax code. Or it turns out that your company's computer center was located in the World Trade Center towers. As we discussed in Chapter 2, it's becoming more and more difficult to anticipate and plan for all the crazy things that can happen in the business world today. Indeed, even when we know *precisely* when a crisis will occur, it often leads to a death-march project—because management's tendency is to avoid dealing with the situation until the last possible moment. In the worst case, unforeseen crises create projects for which the deadline is "yesterday, if not sooner"—because the crisis has already occurred, and things will continue to get worse until a new system is installed to cope with the problem. In other cases, such as the unplanned departure of key project personnel, it can turn an otherwise rational project into a death-march exercise because of the shortage of manpower and the loss of key intellectual resources. For various reasons, these often turn out to be the worst kind of death-march projects, *because nobody anticipated that it would turn out this way.* For the Marine Corps situation discussed above, there are no surprises: everyone knows from the first day of the project that this one, like all previous projects, is going to require extraordinary effort. And for the startup companies, the death-march project is anticipated with excitement; not only will it be exciting and challenging, but its success could make everyone rich.

Why do people participate in death-march projects?

Before the dot-com era, the common reaction of many IT professionals to the prospect of participating in a death-march project was, "Are you crazy? No way!" The dot-com era tended to glorify the notion of wild, crazy death-march projects; and the popular perception was that if you were willing and able to tolerate such an assault on your body, soul, and peace of mind, you would be rewarded with vast quantities of stock options that could be cashed in for millions of dollars.

Well, the dot-com craze has come and gone, but death-march projects are still here—and people are still participating in them, just as they did in the years before the dot-com era. Here are the most common reasons:

- *The risks are high, but so are the rewards*—The dot-com craze may have disappeared, but there are still startup companies, and there are still stock options, and there are still opportunities to make vast sums of money with the right combination of innovative products, good management, extraordinarily hard work, and a certain amount of luck. There were fewer opportunities during the period this book was being written, because of the economic recession and the backlash from venture capitalists, financial "angels" and ordinary investors who were burned by the dot-com hype. But as the economy recovers, and as the next stage of technological innovation unfolds, there will be a new generation of investors, innovators, and adventurous young IT professionals hoping to make their fortune.

- *The "Mt. Everest" syndrome*—Why do people run a marathon and drive themselves to the point of physical collapse in triathlons? Because of the challenge. And so it is with death-march software projects. From this perspective, even the death-march projects that fail can be *noble* failures; even though they fail so badly that entire companies go bankrupt, and though they cause divorces, ulcers, and nervous breakdowns, the people who work on those projects still speak of their experiences in hushed tones. However, it's important to remember that senior management *knows* that IT techies can be seduced by the Mr. Everest syndrome—so watch out for the possibility that the challenge being described by your management is not such a big deal after all. A worse form of Mt. Everest project is the one where the challenge matters *enormously* to corporate management, but not at all to anyone who stops and thinks about the situation for a second. But the very worst death-march projects are the ones where the boss deliberately manipulates the innocent project team into believing that a Mt. Everest-style challenge is involved, when the boss knows full well that it's not.

- *The naiveté and optimism of youth*—Many of the most exciting and challenging IT projects are being performed by, and led by, people in their twenties—i.e., people who are young, idealistic, and absolutely convinced that they can do *anything*. The naiveté and optimism of youth are usually combined with enormous energy, single-minded focus, and freedom from such distractions as family relationships. Obviously, youth doesn't have a monopoly on any of this, but it's a lot more common to see an unmarried 22-year-old programmer willing and able to focus on the technical demands of a death-march project for 100+ hours per week, continuously for a year or two, than a 35-year-old programmer with a spouse and two children and a moderate passion for mountain climbing. The young programmer who signs up for a death march—as well as the relatively young project manager who optimistically promises success to the corporate chieftains—is implicitly saying, "Of *course* I'll succeed with this project; I'll overwhelm the obstacles with sheer energy!"

- *The alternative is unemployment*—At the time this book was being written, there was still an official shortage of experienced technical people in the computer field—but that only means that jobs in some areas (e.g., the computer security field discussed in Chapter 2) are increasing more rapidly than other jobs (e.g., entry-level HTML coders) are declining. Meanwhile, because of the recession, many of the large IT shops that expanded into bureaucracies of several thousand people during the 1990s have begun downsizing in order to reduce costs. All of this becomes a factor in death-march projects: the reason your project team has only half as many people as it should have is that management has cut the entire software organization in half. And the reason that your project schedule is twice as demanding as it should be is that management is attempting reengineering by edict: they've announced that the entire organization needs to be twice as productive as before, which translates into simple commands of, "Work harder! Work faster!"

- *It's required in order to be considered for future advancement*—As noted above, there are times when the "invitation" to join a death-march project carries with it a threat that future promotions and raises will be contingent upon (a) acceptance, and (b) success in the project. This is often associated with a reengineering initiative—e.g., "The people who lead the Megalith Bank into the 21st century will be the ones who lead us through this incredibly complex and challenging Total System 2000 reengineering project!" In the majority of cases I've observed, the threat of withholding promotions and raises is part of the "Marine Corps" culture discussed earlier in this chapter. Whether it's right or wrong doesn't matter at this point; what counts is that it's fairly consistent. If you receive such threats on your first death-march project, you'll probably get them on your second, third, and fourth. You may have been too naive to contemplate the long-term implications of such a policy when you first joined the company, but sooner or later it will sink in. There are really only two options in this case: Accept it, or quit.

- *The alternative is bankruptcy or some other calamity*—As mentioned earlier, some death-march projects have been caused by the reengineering, downsizing, and outsourcing decisions made by senior management, which in turn have often been caused by global competition, unexpected government regulations, etc. Whatever the cause, the results are the same: The employee signs up for the project because he sincerely believes that the alternative is bankruptcy or some other dire calamity. And the situation is often exacerbated by blunt statements from management that anyone unwilling to participate in the death march should resign forthwith, so that those who remain can concentrate on saving the company.

- *It's an opportunity to escape the "normal" bureaucracy*—Technical staffers and project managers often complain that their corporate bureaucracy stifles productivity and introduces unnecessary delays into the software development process. Death-march projects often provide the opportunity to circumvent some, if not all, of the bureaucracy—and this is reason enough for frustrated software developers to sign up for such projects. In the extreme case, the effort takes on the characteristics of a "skunk works" project: The project team moves out of the corporate facility into a separate building, where they can carry out their work without the distractions of the normal bureaucracy. But even in a less extreme situation, a death-march project can often get permission to use its own tools and programming languages, to try new technologies like object-oriented programming, and to short-circuit much of the ponderous procedures and documentation that would otherwise be required. Equally important, the death-march project manager is often given far greater latitude when selecting team members than would normally be the case.

- *Revenge*—Revenge may not seem like a rational explanation for working on a death-march project, but it's real nonetheless. The success of the death-march project might be sufficient to wrest power away from an incompetent Vice President, or it might serve to humiliate an obnoxious critic who continually tells you "it can't be done" within the schedule and budget constraints of the death-march project. Revenge is a powerful emotion, and it is particularly evident in the senior management ranks of large organizations, where insults are remembered forever, and where crafty politicians will sometimes wait months or years to wreak revenge upon their enemies; in the rare cases where revenge is a motivator for technical project personnel, it's usually caused by a more recent insult or injury—e.g., something that happened on the previous project.

Techniques and Technologies_____

If death-march projects were a rare anomaly, they wouldn't be worth discussing in detail. An observer looking across the entire industry might be able to identify some common characteristics of both successful and unsuccessful death-march projects, but if the typical IT professional believed that his involvement in a death-march project was an aberration never to be repeated, then he probably wouldn't pay much attention. Indeed, many IT professionals and managers *do* believe that death-march projects are an aberration, and their only strategy for success is massive amounts of overtime.

When *Death March* was published in 1997, I believed that such projects had become so common that they were the norm rather than the exception. I still believe that to be true, as this book is being written—though, as we'll discuss, there are some paradigm shifts in terms of the nature and causes of death-march projects. In any case, if they are now common, then it makes sense to look for strategies above and beyond the brute-force approach of working until one drops from exhaustion. There are four major strategies for succeeding on a death-march project:

- negotiating an achievable set of objectives
- recruiting and motivating individuals and teams on the project
- adopting and practicing sensible software processes
- monitoring progress to an accurate determination of the project status

Negotiations

Because of the politics inevitably associated with death-march projects, it's crucial to know who the key "stakeholders" are; in particular, who has the authority, power, and responsibility to declare success? And who, if anyone, stands to benefit from the project's failure? As part of that determination, it's equally important to define, in precise terms, what constitutes "success" and "failure." All of these seem like obvious, common-sense points; but since many IT project managers and technicians are political neophytes, it's all too common to see enormously ambitious projects launched where nobody really knows who's in charge, or what has to be accomplished in order to declare success.

Once you know who's in charge, and what has to be accomplished, then the next—and most difficult—step is to negotiate a set of conditions that will create at least a reasonable chance of success. This may involve negotiating for more time, or more money, or more people; but that doesn't usually work, so the critical negotiation involves *tradeoffs* between people, resources, money, functionality, and any other relevant issues (e.g., the issue of good-enough quality, which we discussed in Chapter 7). As most IT professionals know, these tradeoffs are not "linear" in nature: You can't develop a system in half the time by simply doubling the number of people on the team. This tends to complicate the negotiations, especially if the conversations between the developers and the stakeholders have become emotional or confrontational: It's not easy persuading a technologically inexperienced end-user that cutting the project schedule in half would require three times, or four times, as many people.

In a large percentage of death-march projects, most of the relevant project-planning "variables" have already been determined, and are considered non-negotiable. Thus, the project manager is told that the schedule/deadline is fixed, the budget is fixed, the "head-count" is fixed, and the quality is assumed to be perfect ("What?!? You want us to pay you for putting bugs in the software?"). Thus, the *only* negotiable variable turns out to be functionality, which means that the concept of *triage* is crucial. If the project manager has been given an "impossible" deadline, budget, head-count, and quality objective, then it's essential to get the stakeholders to clearly identify those functions, features, and capabilities that are essential; those that are important but not absolutely essential; and those that are merely cosmetic or "nice." This has to be reflected in the official criteria for project success, too: if the team can successfully deliver at least the "essential" features, then the project has to be judged at least a moderate success; if it delivers the essential features and a reasonable percentage of the "important" features, then it should be judged a major success.

In my experience, death-march projects succeed or fail at this initial stage of negotiations; among other things, this means that the ultimate success or failure is usually visible at a very early point in time, months (sometimes years) before the ultimate deadline. And that raises an obvious point for the project manager and everyone else on the project team: What should be done if the negotiations fail? If the key stakeholders adamantly refuse to discuss the concept of triage, if they refuse to negotiate a realistic set of tradeoffs between the various project-planning variables, and if they insist on imposing an "impossible" deadline, budget, head-count, quality and functional requirements—then what?

One option is to hope for miracles, and to forge ahead; Hollywood loves to produce movies in which miracles do occur, and everyone lives happily ever after. But there are other alternatives, and they need to be considered by ratio-nal, mature adults: Quitting, and appealing to higher authorities, are the two most obvious alternatives. The third alternative is to determine whether there are administra-tive/bureaucratic rules that can be bent, circumvented, or ignored in order to remove costs and obstacles; a simple (though not always successful) strategy is to let the project team work at home, in order to avoid the distractions and interruptions normally found in an office environment.

Peopleware

As mentioned above, the initial negotiations have to pro-duce a set of conditions in which project success is possible; otherwise, it's not worth paying much attention to people-ware issues, software processes, or even the monitoring of progress. But assuming that the negotiations have suc-ceeded, then one of the important ingredients for success—if not *the* most important ingredient—is the collection of techniques and approaches collectively referred to as "peo-pleware."[1]

In the best of all worlds, a project manager would have the authority to: hire as many people as he needed, and to have the freedom to choose *which* people he hired; pay them as much money as the marketplace required (and perhaps even a premium, in order to reduce the chances of turn-over); spend whatever money was required to train them, equip them with good offices and working conditions; and take whatever steps were necessary to ensure that they were well-motivated, undistracted, and fully aware of the project's objectives. Such conditions may exist for elite mili-tary forces like the Green Berets and the Navy SEALS; but they are often missing in the average corporate environ-ment. Indeed, it often takes extraordinary effort and deter-mination by the project manager to prevent a "worst-case" combination of peopleware factors from occurring.

---

1. This buzzword may have existed for many years, but it was popular-ized and legitimized by a classic book, *Peopleware*, by Tom DeMarco and Tim Lister. The book first appeared in 1987; a revised and expanded second edition appeared in 1999.

Realistically, the tight budgets and fixed head-counts associated with death-march projects means that the project managers probably won't be able to hire as many people as they need, and may not be able to pay them as much as they deserve. However, it's crucial to ensure that they have veto power over the assignment of individuals to the project team, in order to avoid being stuck with one or more "losers" that have been foisted on the team for political or bureaucratic reasons. Similarly, it may not be possible to provide effective offices, tools, and equipment; but an effective manager can usually find a way to circumvent these problems (e.g., by letting the team work at home) or to minimize the impact of a less-than-adequate working environment. As for providing motivation, focus, and an absence of distractions: This usually requires great effort, charm, determination, and other personal characteristics that distinguish the truly effective project managers from the merely average ones.

Here again, there are circumstances where it's clear from the outset that the death-march project is doomed to failure—because the project manager is given no choice about the members assigned to the project team; or because they have no training or experience in the necessary skills for performing the project; or because their working conditions are so miserable that it's virtually impossible to get any work done; or because the combination of these factors and related political issues has so completely demoralized the team that it simply doesn't care whether the project succeeds or not. In that case, the options are the same as the ones mentioned above: Hope for miracles, appeal to a higher authority, quit before things get worse, or find a way to "break the rules" in such a way that success becomes possible.

Processes

IT project teams frequently use words like *process*, *procedure*, and *methodology* to describe "the way we do things around here"—particularly with regard to such activities as requirements-analysis, design, coding, and testing. There is a great deal of debate about whether it's better to have a formal, disciplined process, or an informal, ad hoc process; but that tradeoff must not be confused with the tradeoff between "heavy" (excruciatingly detailed) versus "light" processes. There is a tendency for "formal" processes to be "heavy," and for "informal" processes to be "light," but that need not always be the case.

Thus, one can imagine a project manager who says, "I have only a few rules about the way things will be done on this project; but those rules *will* be enforced." And one can imagine a project manager who says, "I'm only going to provide some general guidelines about how we'll carry out activities X and Y on this project; but activity Z is *so* crucial, and *so* difficult, that I'm going to provide extremely detailed procedures and checklists, and I'm going to insist that all of the activity-Z work be reviewed by two other people."

Because death-march projects typically have severe constraints on the available time and available personnel, there is usually a strong desire to have a "light" software process—so much so that the team sometimes degenerates into anarchy, with everyone frantically doing whatever appears to need doing at any given moment. But it's possible to conduct a death-march project with software processes that are both "light" (and thus devoid of time-wasting, resource-consuming bureaucracy) but also extremely "formal." Ideally, the choice of formality versus informality (which is not a binary all-or-nothing choice, but rather a continuous spectrum of choices) should be based on the degree to which the project and the surrounding environment are orderly and predictable, versus chaotic and unpredictable. As we discussed in Chapter 5, a chaotic and unpredictable environment calls for *emergent* systems; and by the same argument, it favors emergent processes. Thus, the manager might say to the project team, "We have a standard approach for testing software systems—but this project is so crazy and unpredictable that we need to be prepared to modify and adapt our testing process on a continuous basis throughout the project."

One last point about processes: Because death-march projects are, by their very nature, much riskier than "ordinary" projects, the processes associated with *risk management* are correspondingly more important. The concepts and strategies discussed in Chapter 4 are *generally* more important in the post-9/11 world than they were before; but they are of extreme importance for death-march projects.

Monitoring progress

Because death-march projects are faced with such aggressive deadlines and pressures, it's imperative to have a credible, frequent measure of progress and status. This may sound obvious, but traditional measures of project progress and status are neither credible nor frequent. Milestones, deliverables, reviews, and approvals are sometimes more ceremonial and political than substantive; and the *real* indications of project status—e.g., being able operate some of the desired functionality of the system—sometimes occur so late that nothing can be done to remedy any problems that may be discovered.

A variety of strategies have emerged over the past several years to help provide more frequent and credible measures of progress, e.g., prototyping, time-boxing, iterative/ spiral lifecycles, mini-post mortems, and a "daily build" approach. Such strategies work, and provide significant benefit, on almost any kind of IT project, but they are almost mandatory on a death-march project.

Paradigm Shifts _____

As noted earlier, death-march projects have existed for years, arguably since the beginning of the computer industry in the late 1940s and early 1950s. What, if anything, is different about them in this first decade of the 21st century? I believe that the differences are based on two factors: the recession, and the events of September 11th.

The impact of September 11th

As mentioned earlier, one of the depressing characteristics of some death-march projects is that they are portrayed as

life-and-death struggles by a project sponsor or senior executive—but it ultimately becomes clear that nobody else
cares about the project, and nobody will long remember
whether it succeeded or failed. Those who are swept up in
the Sturm and Drang of the project are not always astute
enough, or brave enough, to ask the appropriate questions
about the justification for the project; but an epiphany
sometimes occurs a year or two after the project was ended,
when a disillusioned project team member notices that the
"successful" project he worked on resulted in a system that
was abandoned by the users after a month, because they
never really wanted it in the first place. "Was *this* why I
worked nights and weekends for the past two years?" the
programmer will ask himself. "Was *this* why I ruined my
marriage and missed all those important events in my children's lives?"

Perhaps there will be similar opinions about some of the
death-march projects emanating from the September 11th
attacks; no doubt there will be corporate initiatives which
use that event as a rallying point for projects that would
otherwise have been ignored or cancelled. But there are also
9/11-related projects that *are* important, and that literally
have life-and-death consequences, on a scale we've not seen
for several generations. The World War II effort to build an
atomic bomb was, for all practical purposes, a death-march
project; and it's quite possible that there are equivalent
projects underway today to find a way to cope with the
threat of anthrax, smallpox, chemical, and nuclear attacks.
In the greater scheme of things, nobody really cares about a
death-march project whose purpose is to increase XYZ
Corp.'s earnings-per-share by $0.13; but *lots* of people will
care if the Centers for Disease Control succeeds in building
a system to coordinate and manage the distribution of 300
million units of smallpox vaccine to medical facilities across
the country.

The Manhattan Project was an isolated, secretive project
involving only a few thousand people; very few people
knew that it was taking place, and consequently it didn't
affect the rest of the country until the bombs were dropped
on Hiroshima and Nagasaki. Similarly, there may be

national-security projects underway in today's post-9/11 world that most of us will never see or hear about—unless they are revealed as part of a subsequent terrorist activity.

But outside of the secretive world of military/government projects, there are also 9/11-related projects going on in hundreds, if not thousands, of private-sector corporations and mundane government agencies at the local, state, and federal levels. Many of these projects involve security issues discussed in Chapter 3; others involve disaster-recovery and contingency-planning issues of the sort discussed in Chapter 4. And many of them have the kind of deadline associated with extreme death-march projects—i.e., "yesterday, if not sooner!" The reason is straightforward: The projects have been launched to cope with potential hacker/ terrorist attacks that could occur today, tomorrow, or at any point in the future.[2]

The impact of the recession

As we saw in the Basic Concepts section, there are many common justifications for creating a death-march project; but during the latter half of the 1990s, one of the most common justifications was the expectation of instant wealth in dot-com companies. For many IT professionals in the twenty-something age bracket, it was the *only* reason for participating in a death-march project; most of them are too young to have experienced the death-march projects caused by the recession of 1990-91, or the recession of 1982-83.

Thus, for many of today's IT professionals and managers, a death-march project caused by economic recession is a paradigm shift of mind-boggling proportions. The objective of today's death-march projects is not to get rich, but to stay in business and remain employed. The alternative to the death-march project is not an equally lucrative death-march

---

2. It's not as if these are all *new* vulnerabilities, which were just created yesterday. Indeed, some of them have existed for years—which means that the organizations were subject to attack yesterday, last month, and last year. But death-march projects are largely a political phenomenon, and sometimes represent an over-reaction to a problem that could have been solved in a more straightforward way if resources had been allocated earlier.

project at some other dot-com company, but rather the unemployment line. And instead of being pampered with free lunches, company-paid massages, and other frills, today's death-march participant finds that frills and luxuries have been eliminated, and the corporate "bean-counters" are questioning every expenditure.

Strategic Implications

The strategic implications for this new wave of death-march projects are most likely to affect IT professionals and mid-level IT managers; however, I'll offer a few suggestions for government leaders, senior executives, and citizens as well:

Government leaders

- *Beware of the temptation to impose deadlines by decree.* If you have launched a death-march project—either directly or by the indirect mechanism of enacting legislation with aggressive deadlines—it's important that you recognize that you can't make miracles occur by executive fiat. In late November of 2001, it became apparent that the Congress, Senate, and Executive branch of government had done just that by passing a highly political airport security bill whose provisions simply cannot be implemented within the aggressive schedule that had been mandated. No doubt there will be similar temptations to launch high-pressured IT projects in a similar vein, particularly because most lawmakers don't have the slightest understanding of what software development is all about.

- *Acknowledge the concept of non-linear tradeoffs between time, resources, budget, functionality, and quality.* Senior government officials who have access to virtually unlimited resources may believe that a large, complex software project can be accomplished within an arbitrarily aggressive schedule by simply throwing more money and people at it. "If a hundred programmers isn't enough to get the job done by the deadline, then we'll get two hundred," a frustrated official might decree. "And if two hundred isn't enough, by God, then we'll get a thousand!" Unfortunately, such brute-force techniques run afoul of a time-honored principle in the IT field known as "Brooks' Law," which states that adding more programmers to a late software project just makes it later.[3] The details of the non-linear tradeoffs between the various "parameters" of time, money, functionality, etc., have been carefully studied, and can be modeled with a reasonable degree of accuracy in several commercially available products. Unfortunately, the results are almost always politically controversial: Nobody wants to hear that it takes substantially *more* than twice as many people to produce a system in half the time.

- *Look for ways to define the objectives of the death-march project in terms of a compelling "vision."* IT professionals are willing and able to work as hard as the people in any other profession—but like everyone else, they need to have a sense that they are investing their blood, sweat, and tears for something meaningful. Projects that have a direct, urgent, vital impact on the security of the country, or the health of the public, are obvious candidates. Unfortunately, we're also likely to see some death-march projects where the "vision" of importance and relevance is not so obvious—and may be lacking altogether. Imagine, for example, that you are a programmer who has just been told by your boss: "I need you to volunteer to work 80-hour weeks for the next year in order to build a system that will allow Senators and Congressmen to send email messages to each other more quickly and efficiently!" But if the programmers observes that Congress spends less time "in session" than out of session, and that half of them don't even have an email account, he's not

---

3. Dr. Fred Brooks, now the Chairman of the Computer Science Department at the University of North Carolina, was the project manager of IBM's famous OS/360 software development effort in the 1960s. The lessons from that project, including his famous law, are captured in a book called *The Mythical Man-Month* (20th anniversary edition, Addison-Wesley, 1995).

likely to be strongly motivated to make the sacrifice that has just been asked of him.

- *Don't penny-pinch when asking people to make the kind of sacrifices required for a death-march project.* The programmer who is being asked to work 80-hour weeks for the next year would probably be a lot happier if he was being paid overtime for the extra hours, or if he believed he would earn a large bonus at the end of the project. But most IT professionals understand that they aren't entitled to overtime pay, and that a large bonus is probably out of the question, too. What drives them crazy, though, is having a $10 expense-account voucher rejected by the accounting department, because they worked until midnight and then decided to take a taxi home rather than public transportation, because they live or work in a dangerous neighborhood. It takes a very powerful "vision" statement, and a very charismatic manager, to overcome this kind of narrow-minded behavior; and if the vision is fuzzy and the manager is uninspiring, it's only a matter of time before the programmer decides that he's no longer willing to work more than a token amount of overtime.

- *Don't procrastinate and compound the problems of a death-march project with bureaucratic delays.* Imagine the programmer who is told that he will be part of a project team that *must* deliver a complex system in a year—a task that would only be feasible if everyone works the proverbial 80-hour week—but that it will take three months to go through the requisition process to acquire desks, chairs, and a PC to work on. While government does not have an exclusive monopoly on this kind of bureaucratic nonsense, it is famous for practicing it with a stubbornness that would make the most ornery mule gasp in admiration. If it really is a death-march project, and if the system really does have to be finished in a year, then someone at an appropriately high level of command—whether it's a General, a Senator, or a Cabinet secretary—has to be willing and able to pick up the phone and cut through the delays.

Senior corporate executives

The suggestions for government officials applies, in large measure, to senior corporate executives as well. Of course, one difference is that a corporate executive—especially in a medium- or small-sized company—is less likely to have access to the vast resources that a senior government official does. The CEO of IBM or General Motors could, if he or she chose to, assign a thousand programmers to work on a crash project; but the CEO of a $100 million/year company could not.

While high-level government officials come and go whenever an election changes the balance of power, managers in a corporate environment have an opportunity to create a "corporate culture" that can be used to communicate and share an overall sense of values, strategies, and priorities. Obviously, this can involve a broad range of issues, many of which are entirely outside the realm of this book; but one of the relevant issues today *is* the notion of death-march projects. If senior management sincerely believes that death-march projects are more likely to be the norm than the exception in the future, then they need to communicate that fact to their employees, and explain why it's necessary.

That was an easy task during the dot-com era, and senior executives could glorify the concept as they implicitly (and sometimes explicitly) promised financial rewards to their employees. Now the task is much more difficult; but for precisely that reason, it needs to be addressed openly and honestly by senior management. There is a common tendency for senior management to characterize the death-march environment as a short-term, or temporary, situation; but sooner or later, employees come to the realization that it has become a way of life. Without open, frank, and sincere communication from senior management, it's only a matter of time before they begin looking for another job.

Mid-level IT managers

The mid-level IT managers are usually the ones directly responsible for making a death-march project succeed. They are given the demands and constraints associated with schedule, budget, and manpower allocation—and then they are expected to somehow lead their team to victory.

The techniques and strategies summarized in Techniques and Technologies are aimed directly at this category of managers. All of those techniques and strategies are important; but if I had to pick one to emphasize, it would be the area of *negotiations*. As a consultant who has reviewed IT projects in hundreds of companies, my experience has been that the majority of death-march projects sow the seeds of success or failure during the first few days or weeks: If the developers and the stakeholders can negotiate a reasonable combination of project-planning variables, then success is possible. But if the negotiations collapse, or if the stakeholders bully the project manager into accepting an impossible set of demands, then it will be almost impossible to succeed—even with the best people, the best tools, and the best processes.

Since this book is being written during a time of corporate belt-tightening caused by a recession, it's also worth reminding mid-level managers that their IT professionals have long memories. If they are pushed too hard, or generally treated badly, they may decide that the prudent thing is to keep their mouths shut and endure the discomfort. But they won't forget the long hours, the penny-pinching, the lack of appreciation, and the fact that they are being asked to make substantial personal sacrifices for some business/ political purpose that has no meaning to them. When the economy eventually recovers—as it eventually did after the recessions of 1991, 1982, and 1973—they will exact their revenge by quitting as quickly and abruptly as they can.

Even though this is an entirely predictable aspect of human behavior, it inevitably takes many mid-level IT managers by surprise. "Why is Dilbert quitting?" the pointy-haired manager in Scott Adams' cartoon strip might be heard to exclaim. "Times are better now—and we're only asking people to work 60 hours a week! Why would anyone quit?"

IT professionals

- *Realize that the game has changed.* As noted earlier in the Basic Concepts section, IT professionals volunteer for death-march projects more often than one would expect—and for reasons that are not always rational or realistic. With the collapse of the dot-com industry, it *is* true that many IT professionals are more jaded and cynical than they were before; but they still get sucked into far too many death-march projects because of naiveté, over-confidence, or dreams of glory. True, there may be some glory associated with a death-march project that helps to prevent an otherwise-deadly terrorist attack, or that helps to bring about a significant improvement in the nation's public-health system; but it's also likely that the majority of death-march projects are going to be downright mean, nasty, and unpleasant. *C'est la vie.*

- *Assess the situation realistically in advance.* Even during the height of the dot-com craze, there were some IT professionals who realized that the chances of real financial wealth (as opposed to "paper" stock options that might become worthless overnight) were slim; but many of them signed up for the startup-company death-march projects anyway, saying, "The technology is exciting, the people are fun, and they throw wild office parties every Friday night. If we go public and make a bunch of money, too, that's just an extra bonus!" But in today's environment, the IT professional needs to realistically assess not only the chances of success, but also the relative degrees of pain and pleasure that will be experienced *during* the project. The wild office parties have disappeared, the people are no longer as much fun, and the technology for this year's death-march project might be downright mundane.

- *Recognize that there may not be alternatives in the short term.* If the office parties have disappeared, the people are boring, the technology is mediocre, and the promise of lucrative stock options have disappeared, why would anyone sign up for a death-march project today? The simple answer, as we suggested in Basic Concepts, is: there may not be an immediate alternative. Thus, while a common response to an unpleasant death-march project throughout the 1990s was to say, "Hell, no! I quit!", the prudent strategy for many IT professionals today is to bide one's time and wait for things to improve.

Citizens

The ordinary citizen may be aware that death-march projects are taking place all around him, but is unlikely to be directly affected—unless, of course, the *outcome* of the death-march project is something that has direct, personal consequences. In that case, a citizen needs to make his own assessment, as realistically as possible, of the chances that the death-march project will succeed. Imagine, for example, a citizen so terrified about air-travel security and the threat of bio/chemical/nuclear attacks that he has to decide whether to (a) trust that the government's "crash" programs will succeed within the next 6-12 months, or (b) take matters into his own hands by finding alternative means of travel, and personal strategies for protection against bio/chemical/nuclear attack. Every person has to make his own assessment of the risks and the tradeoffs; but at the very least, it's important not to put blind faith in the government's commitment to provide a solution to the problem by carrying out a death-march project with an overly aggressive schedule.[4]

Part of the assessment, though, has to include a realistic evaluation of one's own personal resources, abilities, and choices. Many citizens, for example, feel that they must continue traveling by plane, because their job depends on it; others are willing to change careers, or make the sacrifice of time, money, and energy to travel by train, car, or bus.

---

4. The same strategy holds true for assessing death-march projects undertaken by private-sector companies. Death-march IT projects are intrinsically risky, and have a high likelihood of being late, over budget, riddled with bugs, or outright failures—regardless of whether they are carried out by government or private-sector organizations.

A final piece of advice: If the person involved in a death-march project is your spouse, sibling, parent, or someone else you care about, then *you* may be the one who has to provide some much-needed perspective by asking, gently but persistently: "Do you understand why you are doing this? Are you sure it's worth the sacrifice you're making?" Alas, some manipulative politicians, corporations, and managers will use September 11th to create the illusion of "patriotic" death-march projects for no other reason than to squeeze out a few more pennies of profit; and in those cases, we can help our loved ones understand that they are being bamboozled.

On the other hand, September 11th has created some critical challenges, and some unavoidable death-march projects that somebody, somewhere, has to sign up for. Inevitably, some of us will find that the volunteers for such projects turn out to be the husband or wife who should have been home putting his or her child to sleep, or the brother or sister who should have been able to join us for the Thanksgiving holidays, or the boyfriend or girlfriend who should have been there for that quiet evening in front of a roaring fireplace. For those situations, we citizens can offer support, love, and an abiding presence; after all, they would do no less for us.

CONCLUSIONS

What we imagine is order is merely the prevailing
form of chaos. ■

—Kerry Thornley, Principia Discordia, 5th edition

A Summary of the Paradigm Shifts_____

Security-related paradigm shifts

As we saw in Chapter 3, the paradigm shifts associated
with security include the following:

- *IT systems are part of the "critical infrastructure"*—and as
  such, require a much more thorough and robust form
  of security than was typically expected in the 1970s or
  1980s. Computer systems, networks, and databases
  are part of the nation's critical infrastructure —which
  was arguably *not* the case a decade ago. And most
  technology experts warn that the phenomenon will
  continue for the foreseeable future—as the nation
  becomes increasingly "wired," increasingly automated, and increasingly dependent on highly reliable
  computer systems. The other part of the paradigm

shift is that the attacks on the computer-related components of the nation's infrastructure have changed, from infrequent and amateurish, to frequent and persistent and increasingly malevolent.

- *Threats exist from various levels of players*—In the good old days, computer security personnel typically expected the "bad guys" to fall into a relatively small number of categories, all of whom were technologically sophisticated. But in addition to these traditional "players," today's security experts must also cope with the attacks from technologically naïve end-users, "script kiddies," and stateless terrorists.

- *Security must now deal with software <u>development</u>, as well as <u>operation</u> of software systems*—Traditionally, it has been assumed that computer systems are designed and developed in a "safe" way, and that when placed in operational status, they carry out the functionality they were programmed to carry out—nothing more and nothing less. The security problems were assumed to be external attacks upon a properly functioning system—or, in rare cases, an attack perpetrated by, or enabled by, an "insider." But today, we have to focus just as hard on the possibility of security being compromised or circumvented during the *development* of critical systems, the existence of which may not be known until months or years after the system has been placed into operational status.

- *Security has changed because of miniaturization*—The transition from mainframes to minis to PCs to PDAs means that security officers can no longer accomplish *physical* security as easily and effectively. Putting a computer system in a locked room, protected by armed guards, isn't very effective if computers can be taken into and out of the building in one's purse or briefcase.

- *Security has changed because the Internet is now being used as an indirect weapon to support terrorism*—the very tools and technologies created by IT professionals are being used to help organize and coordinate terrorist attacks against them. This is something separate from the usual concern of "direct" attacks on one's computer systems; for example, the Internet search engines which are such a boon to researchers, scientists, business professionals, and ordinary men and women are also being used by hackers and terrorists to track down crucial information and security flaws.

Risk management paradigm shifts

As we saw in Chapter 4, the paradigm shifts related to risk management include the following:

- *High-tech can be threatened by low-tech*—Thus, IT professionals and risk-management professionals will need to remember that attacks on their systems may involve techniques more like the *MacGyver* television show than the James Bond movies.

- *The re-emergence of kamikaze players*—Risk-management and security strategies of many companies have been predicated on the notion that individuals and organizations behave in a "rational" way; thus, if we make it more dangerous and unpleasant to attack our systems than *we* would be willing to tolerate, we assume that it will also be too dangerous and unpleasant for anyone else. That's no longer true today.

- *The rise of the "stateless" power*—In more and more cases, we find ourselves facing risks caused by loosely-organized, difficult-to-identify groups like the drug cartels from South America and Asia; the terrorist groups of Hamaz and Al Qaeda; the new-generation spinoffs from the Mafia and Cosa Nostra; and ephemeral hacker groups that communicate and collaborate with one another on the Internet. Just as the American government finds it difficult to decide who to declare war against, and who to drop bombs on, many organizations have a difficult time identifying whom they should "attack" in order to eliminate their risks.

- *The rapid pace of change* —In today's fast-paced environment, neither individuals nor organizations are likely to have time to *create* a risk-mitigation strategy between the time the first warning is received and the time the risk actually materializes. Thus, for risks that are "ordinary" and repeatable, individuals and organizations need to have pre-organized risk-management strategies that can be invoked on a moment's notice. And for risks that emerge at a rapid pace, and which are *not* ordinary or repeatable, we need some form of *emergent systems* that was discussed in Chapter 5.

Emergent-systems paradigm shifts

As we saw in Chapter 5, the paradigm shifts associated with emergent systems involve the following:

- *The rapidity and degree of changes in our environment*— Business, government, and society have experienced a paradigm shift at least once each decade from the 1970s through the current time. Life is moving at 10 times the speed that we experienced in the early 1990s, the changes from one "state" or "scenario" to the next occurs 10 times faster; and the degree of the change is 10 times greater. And correspondingly, the need for an emergent-systems approach is 10 times greater, while the ability of a traditional top-down, hierarchically-managed organization to cope with the situation is 10 times less than before.

- *The degree of awareness of emergence*—The message that is slowly sinking into American government, business, and society is: It's a new world out there. It's a world that changes abruptly, unexpectedly, without warning, and in ways that are sometimes dangerous and threatening. And we have to be prepared for the possibility that "they" won't be able to control the situation, and might not even know what the situation is. We have to be prepared to take matters into our own hands and cope with the changes by ourselves, or with our immediate family, friends, and co-workers.

Resiliency paradigm shifts

As we saw in Chapter 6, the paradigm shift associated with resiliency has to do with the *rationale* for encouraging it, versus the rationale that one might have heard a generation ago. Our systems and our critical infrastructures are intrinsically more reliable than before, but now they are exposed to attack by hostile terrorists, hostile competitors, or hostile governments. The disruptive shocks to our organizations are no longer accidental, benign, or acts of nature; now they are deliberate and malevolent.

Meanwhile, the pace of business, technology, communication, and social change is much faster than it was a generation ago. It's easier to be resilient when you have time to fully assimilate one set of changes before the next one arrives. In today's environment, the "storm of a century" disruptions are occurring, one right after the other, so quickly that we're still reeling in shock from one disruption when the next one arrives.

Good-enough paradigm shifts

As we saw in Chapter 7, the paradigm shifts associated with the "good-enough" theme involve the following:

- *Malevolent threats*—In today's world of terrorists and hackers, we must assume that at least some of our users make a deliberate effort to *find* the defects—not to write a critical review in a computer trade magazine, but to exploit the defect to circumvent the systems security and protection mechanisms, or to cause a system crash, or to cause the destruction or corruption of the system's database. Thus, the determination of a good-enough balance between functionality, cost, speed of development, and defects must now take into account the likelihood that some of the users will deliberately and aggressively look for ways to *mis*-use the system.

- *Life and death circumstances*—While the debates in the 1990s about good-enough systems sometimes touched on life-and-death issues, the scale of potential disaster was measured in terms of a single life, or the lives of a relatively small group of people. As part of the paradigm shift in today's world, the good-enough strategies of IT developers have to contemplate the possibility of much larger-scale disasters: biological,

chemical, and nuclear attacks as well as the more traditional terrorist acts of bombing, shooting, and flying
airplanes into buildings. IT plays a critical role in
many of these areas: We need computer systems to
organize and deploy vaccines and health-care teams in
the event of a biological attack, and we need computer
systems to monitor the purchase, shipments, and disposal of chemical and nuclear wastes that might
become terrorist weapons. And if used to their maximum capabilities, such weapons could conceivably
kill not just thousands, but millions of citizens.

Death-march paradigm shifts

As we saw in Chapter 8, the paradigm shifts associated
with death-march projects consist of the following:

- *The recession of 2001*—For many of today's IT professionals and managers, a death-march project caused
  by economic recession is a paradigm shift of mind-
  boggling proportions. The objective of today's death-
  march projects is not to get rich, but to stay in business
  and remain employed. The alternative to the death-
  march project is not an equally lucrative death-march
  project at some other dot-com company, but rather the
  unemployment line. And instead of being pampered
  with free lunches, company-paid massages, and other
  frills, today's death-march participant finds that frills
  and luxuries have been eliminated, and the corporate
  "bean-counters" are questioning every expenditure.

- *The events of September 11*—The Manhattan Project was
  an isolated, secretive project involving only a few
  thousand people; very few people knew that it was
  taking place, and consequently it didn't affect the rest
  of the country until the bombs were dropped on
  Hiroshima and Nagasaki. It's reasonable to assume
  that there are already one or more national-security
  projects underway in today's post-9/11 world that
  will rival the World War II Manhattan Project in terms
  of scale and importance. And outside of the secretive
  world of military and government projects, there are

also 9/11-related projects going on in hundreds, if not thousands, of private-sector corporations. Many of them have the kind of deadline associated with extreme death-march projects—i.e., "yesterday, if not sooner!" The reason is straightforward: The projects have been launched to cope with potential hacker/terrorist attacks that could occur today, tomorrow, or at any point in the future.

A Summary of the Strategic Implications _____

Government officials

As we saw in the various chapters of the book, the implications of today's world of high-tech, rapidly-changing, unpredictable, disruptive events for government officials include the following:

- Balance the need for security with the right to privacy.
- Make your *existing* security mechanisms work effectively before launching a plethora of new mechanisms.
- Monitor yourself at least as diligently as you monitor companies, groups, and individuals.
- Remember that hardly anyone watches the programmers.
- Hire "white-hat" security experts and then *listen* to their advice.
- Educate and inform the public about security.
- Withhold risk-related information if you must, but don't lie to the public.
- Provide a central source of information about risks and threats.
- Provide opportunities for citizens to report risks.
- Recognize that risks may change too quickly to be *controlled* in a top-down fashion; endorse emergent systems.
- Publicly acknowledge those parts of the hierarchical control system that are broken.

- Encourage bottom-level citizens, individuals, and groups to devise their own emergent-systems approaches.
- Eliminate obstacles to peer-to-peer communication and collaboration mechanisms.
- Identify those parts of the critical infrastructure that are not resilient.
- Invest in resiliency.
- Invest in early warning systems.
- Encourage citizens to develop their own resiliency.
- Be candid and honest with the public about good-enough tradeoffs.
- Recognize that an effective strategy requires an *overt* discussion of quality.
- Recognize the short-term/long-term tradeoffs for death-march projects.
- Beware of the temptation, in a death-march project, to impose deadlines by decree.
- Acknowledge the concept of non-linear tradeoffs between time, resources, budget, functionality, and quality.
- Look for ways to define the objectives of the death-march project in terms of a compelling "vision."
- Don't penny-pinch when asking people to make the kind of sacrifices required for a death-march project.
- Don't procrastinate and compound the problems of a death-march project with bureaucratic delays.

Senior corporate executives

As we saw in the various chapters of the book, the implications of today's world of high-tech, rapidly-changing, unpredictable, disruptive events for senior corporate executives include the following:

- Get the basics in place before you spend enormous sums of money on fancy high-tech security gadgets.
- Get a periodic audit of your company's security status.

- Obtain regular *external* briefings of major IT security threats.
- Tell your mid-level managers that they need to look at security from a "business imperative" perspective, not just an ROI/IRR perspective.
- Remember that nobody is watching your programmers.
- Prepare for a substantial increase in the number of viruses, DoS attacks, and other forms of cyber-attacks.
- Prepare for a substantial increase in the amount of security-related legislation from local, state, and Federal government agencies.
- Withhold risk-related information if you must, but don't lie to the public.
- Provide a central source of information about risks and threats.
- Provide opportunities for citizens to report risks.
- Recognize that risks may change too quickly to be *controlled* in a top-down fashion; endorse emergent systems.
- Publicly acknowledge those parts of the hierarchical control system that are broken.
- Encourage bottom-level citizens, individuals, and groups to devise their own emergent-systems approaches.
- Eliminate obstacles to peer-to-peer communication and collaboration mechanisms.
- Develop a set of policies, procedures, rules, and strategies that correspond to the Defense Department's strategy for military personnel who are incommunicado and stranded in enemy territory.
- Assess the degree of brittleness in your existing systems; invest in additional resiliency.
- Invest in early-warning systems.
- Encourage your employees to become personally resilient in terms of their day-to-day work.
- Initiate "resiliency drills," and practice them on a regular basis.

- Be candid and honest with the public about good-enough tradeoffs.
- Recognize that an effective strategy requires an <u>overt</u> discussion of quality.
- Delegate as many of the good-enough decisions and strategies as possible <u>downward</u> in the hierarchy, as low as possible.
- Recognize the short-term/long-term tradeoffs for death-march projects.
- Beware the temptation, in a death-march project, to impose deadlines by decree.
- Acknowledge the concept of non-linear tradeoffs between time, resources, budget, functionality, and quality.
- Look for ways to define the objectives of the death-march project in terms of a compelling "vision."
- Don't penny-pinch when asking people to make the kind of sacrifices required for a death-march project.
- Don't procrastinate and compound the problems of a death-march project with bureaucratic delays.
- If senior management sincerely believes that death-march projects are more likely to be the norm than the exception in the future, then they need to communicate that fact to their employees, and explain why it's necessary.

Mid-level IT managers

As we saw in the various chapters of the book, the implications of today's world of high-tech, rapidly-changing, unpredictable, disruptive events for mid-level IT managers include the following:

- Make your own assessment of your company's security status.
- Remember that *you* are probably the one who will have to impose configuration management practices, and monitor the code written by programmers who report to you.

- In a software development project, make sure that security issues are properly aligned with the appropriate life-cycle activity.
- Don't lie about risks.
- Provide access to risk-related information.
- Provide a mechanism for your subordinates to report risks without falling victim to the "shoot the messenger" syndrome.
- Whenever you're unsure of the situation, "share" the risk with your boss.
- Recognize that risks may change too quickly to be *controlled* in a top-down fashion; endorse emergent systems.
- Publicly acknowledge those parts of the hierarchical control system that are broken.
- Encourage bottom-level citizens, individuals, and groups to devise their own emergent-systems approaches.
- Eliminate obstacles to peer-to-peer communication and collaboration mechanisms.
- Study the various books of the "extreme programming" (XP) and "agile-development" IT community for possible application to your company's project.
- Assess the degree of brittleness in your existing systems; invest in additional resiliency.
- Invest in early-warning systems.
- Encourage your employees to become personally resilient in terms of their day-to-day work.
- Recognize that brittleness in the organization can be associated with critically-important personnel.
- Ensure that resiliency is identified as one of the important "ilities"—along with maintainability, portability, flexibility, usability, etc.—when developing new systems.
- Insist that senior managers articulate specifically what they mean by "good-enough" in today's troubled times.

- Reassess your own personal values and ethics in the years ahead with regard to good-enough systems.
- Enable the success of death-march projects by insisting that a reasonable combination of project-planning variables be negotiated.
- Recognize that if IT professionals are pushed too hard, or generally treated badly, they will exact their revenge by quitting as quickly and abruptly as they can when the economy recovers.

IT professionals

As we saw in the various chapters of the book, the implications of today's world of high-tech, rapidly-changing, unpredictable, disruptive events for IT professionals include the following:

- Perform your own security assessment.
- Consider specializing in security as a new career.
- Be prepared to be watched more closely in the future.
- Be prepared for increased security to slow down your work.
- Don't lie about risks.
- Provide access to risk-related information.
- Whenever you're unsure of the situation, "share" the risk with your boss.
- Recognize that in today's environment, the risks are sometimes serious enough that one must make a fuss, regardless of whether anyone wants to listen.
- Recognize that you and your fellow IT professional programmers may effectively operate in a world of anarchy—simply because management doesn't understand what you are doing, and/or finds itself unable to keep up with the pace of change.
- If a rigid control structure is mandated and enforced ruthlessly, then ask yourself whether it works effectively; if not, look for opportunities to overtly or covertly begin introducing some of the emergent-systems concepts—by practicing an extreme programming approach.

- Begin building your own peer-to-peer networks for communication and collaboration, so that you can "invoke" them in circumstances of chaotic disruption.
- Advise your superiors of any significant brittleness in the systems you are involved in developing or maintaining.
- Raise this issue and discuss it openly with the end-user, customer, and stakeholders in the project
- Advise the end-user about the brittleness of the business processes, in addition to whatever assessment needs to be made about incorporating resiliency into the hardware/software environment.
- Recognize that people are part of any system, and people with critical skills or business knowledge may represent part of the overall brittleness of the system.
- Recognize that you may be the source of brittleness in a system or organization—for all of the reasons articulated above.
- Insist that your project managers articulate what they mean by "good enough."
- If you don't like the good-enough choice that has been made by your manager and/or customers, then you should find yourself a new customer to work for—a customer whose appreciation for technical quality matches your own.
- Recognize that the malevolent exploitation of system defects means that you and your managers need to re-examine your testing strategy as they decide how to apply their limited resources to identify and remove as many defects as possible.
- Realize that the death-march game has changed.
- Assess the death-march situation realistically in advance.
- Recognize that there may not be alternatives to death-march projects in the short term.

Citizens

As we saw in the various chapters of the book, the implications of today's world of high-tech, rapidly-changing, unpredictable, disruptive events for ordinary citizens include the following:

- Examine your philosophical attitude about the trend toward more security and less privacy.

- Examine the *practical* impact of increased security and decreased privacy on your life.

- Make your *own* computing devices more secure.

- Ensure that you have the relevant phone numbers, fax numbers, email addresses, and/or Web sites of the organizations to which you might reasonably expect to report suspicious occurrences or dangerous risks.

- When given information about potentially serious risks, look for alternate, independent sources of information before reaching a conclusion about what to do.

- Take a look at the hierarchical control structures that govern your day-to-day activities, and ask yourself whether they really work. If not, see whether the control-hierarchy actually pays attention to what you're doing, and ask yourself whether you're willing to take the risks associated with circumventing the hierarchy to do what you believe is the right thing to do.

- Build your own peer-to-peer collaborative communications network, and be ready to call upon it if you find yourself in a disruptive crisis that overwhelms the resources and capabilities of the existing top-down, hierarchical control system.

- Assess your own resilience, in terms of the systems and infrastructures they depend on to carry out your day-to-day life—taking into account a realistic assessment of the likelihood of various kinds of disruptions, and the consequences of such disruptions.

- Teach your children about resilience.

- Acknowledge the concept of good-enough systems, and articulate your expectations and preferences as clearly as possible, so that government leaders (as well as senior corporate executives) can make informed decisions.

- Assess the realistic chances of success of any government-sponsored or corporate-sponsored death-march project whose outcome might seriously affect you; don't put blind faith in the government's commitment to provide a solution to the problem by carrying out a death-march project with an overly aggressive schedule.

A Final Thought: When Will We Be Able to Abandon These Ideas?

We have now arrived at the end of a book about concepts and strategies that have been bubbling and brewing for several years, but which boiled over in a thunderous roar on September 11th. Security and risk management hardly have to be explained or justified to anyone in the IT field; but concepts like emergence, resilience, good-enough systems, and death-march projects may seem extreme, objectionable, and downright dangerous to others.

If this book was based *only* on the awful experiences of September 11th, then one might agree with the comments of the German physicist and philosopher, G.C. Lichtenberg, who asked at the end of the 18th century:

> What is the good of drawing conclusions from experience? I don't deny we sometimes draw the right conclusions, but don't we just as often draw the wrong ones?[1]

But the September 11th terrorist attacks were just one of the unanticipated disruptions with which we have been confronted in recent years, at what appears to be a steadily increasing pace. Some of these disruptions might be characterized as "good," because they take the form of technological innovations like cell phones or the Internet; but invariably they cause upheavals and seismic shocks in

---

1. G. C. Lichtenberg, *Aphorisms*, "Notebook F," aphorism 123 (written 1765–99; translated by R. J. Hollingdale, 1990).

terms of lifestyles, government regulations, and intense competition within industries, across industries, and around the world. Other disruptions are more commonly characterized as "bad": bankruptcies of corporate giants like Enron; bond defaults of countries like Argentina; hurricanes, floods, earthquakes, wildfires, and other environmental disasters; and, of course, war and terrorism. While many of these disruptions were localized and self-contained a decade or two ago, they now have a tendency to ripple around the world, with secondary and tertiary consequences that can have a global impact.

Whether the strategies discussed in this book turn out to be the most effective ones for coping with such disruptions may well be a discussion of great debate. As suggested at the beginning of this chapter, disruptions and paradigm shifts don't occur everywhere at once. Terrorism issues that we are facing in the United States today are similar to what Ireland and Israel encountered several years ago; and relatively peaceful, stable countries like Australia and Brazil may be able to ignore them until/unless they encounter similar problems years from now. Disruptions that plague advanced countries may not be relevant for developing nations, and vice versa. Some countries may experience devastating consequences from global warming or El Nino, while others escape it. And so forth. . .

If there is some part of the world that has escaped all of these problems, and manages to live in idyllic harmony (New Zealand and Tahiti come to mind), perhaps a few of us will be lucky enough to move there, and ignore everything in this book. But to the extent that everywhere else in the world, *all* of us are finding ourselves buffeted by one or more of these disruptive perturbations, it seems inevitable to me that we will have to embrace some, if not all, of the concepts of emergent systems, resilience, good-enough systems, death-march projects, aggressive risk management, and heightened security—*at least for the time being.*

Which leaves us with one major question, the question our children should be asking us: *How long will this go on?* Clearly, if disruptions of the sort discussed in this book were one-time, short-term phenomena, or events that recur only once every 20,000 years,[2] then we could grit our teeth, do whatever was necessary, and then return to normalcy. But the U.S. has suffered increasingly serious terrorist attacks, on roughly an annual basis, since 1993; the global economy has suffered major defaults, panics, bankruptcies, and depressions[3] on a steady basis for a decade or more; and on the positive side, the order-of-magnitude technology-based disruptions that we've experienced for the past 40 years are forecast to continued for at least another decade into the future.

The recession that was pummeling the United States economy when this book was being written may well end in 2002 or 2003, depending on how optimistic you are; but it's just as reasonable to assume that there will be more Enron-style bankruptcies, and more Argentina-style defaults as it is to assume that we'll return to some simpler world where everything is prosperous and stable and predictable.

---

2. An example is the 1,000-foot-wide asteroid that hurtled past Earth at 68,000 miles per hour on Jan. 7, 2002, missing us by only 375,000 miles. Astronomers estimate that an asteroid of that size and speed could destroy an area the size of Texas—or, as Benny Peiser, of Great Britain's Royal Astronomical Society, put it, "It could essentially wipe out a medium-sized country. The environmental consequences would be regional but the social and economic consequences would be global." The asteroid was spotted less than two weeks before it zoomed past Earth; thus, if it had followed a direct, head-on course, there would have been no time or way to stop it; nor would there have been time for very much in the way of risk management. Fortunately, the chances of a direct hit are small—perhaps one every 20,000 years—so having miraculously avoided the January 2001 collision, we can go back to whatever we were doing before. See "Earth escapes brush with killer asteroid," by Richard Stenge, *CNN.com*, January 7, 2002.
3. Americans have such grim memories of the Great Depression of the 1930s that, even two or three generations later, they tend to reject the use of such words as "alarmist" and "extremist." Perhaps it is when discussing the American economy; but in November 2001, the renowned economist Paul Krugman used just such a word to describe what appears to be happening in Japan. See "Japan may slip into depression, warns Krugman: Tokyo is running out of options to fend off a downward spiral similar to 1930s Great Depression, he says," *The Straits Times Interactive*, Nov. 29, 2001.

As for terrorism: It's possible that the American government will announce that it has killed or jailed every known member of the Al Qaeda movement by the time this book is published. It's theoretically possible that Jews and Palestinians will grow tired of their murderous battles, and that Protestants and Catholics in Ireland will decide to join hands in peace. Miracles are certainly possible. But given what we know about the situation, it's probably a more realistic bet that the various forms of terrorism around the world will continue to be a major factor for the remainder of this decade, if not longer. It was sobering to note, for example, that as this chapter was being finished in mid-January 2002, the U.S. Defense Department was drawing up budgets and plans on the assumption that the struggle against Al Qaeda and other international terrorist groups would last until at least 2008—even if Osama bin Laden was found and eliminated at an early stage in the struggle.[4]

Thus, the pragmatic conclusion is to assume that we have now officially recognized and acknowledged a new, *permanent* way of life that has been creeping up on us since the mid-1990s, if not earlier. For better or worse, this is it: *This* is the new normalcy.

Does that mean we should abandon all hope, sacrifice all that was meaningful and pleasurable in our lives, and hide in our barricaded homes for the rest of our lives? Well, it depends: There are middle-class Argentinean citizens who now swear that they will never put another peso in a bank, for the rest of their lives, after the government devalued and their currency and froze their bank accounts. Every time a "killer hurricane" passes through Florida, there are citizens who lose their homes and belongings—and swear they'll never again return to the state. In the aftermath of September 11th, there are people who swear they will never again fly in a commercial airline, or enter an office tower more than three stories high. And so on …

But most of us will, I am convinced, adopt one or more of the strategies outlined in this book—for today, tomorrow,

---

4. See "Pentagon warns of war lasting six years," by David Wastell, *New.telegraph.co.uk*, Jan. 13, 2002..

and the rest of our lives. We do this so that we can maintain as much of our pre-9/11 normalcy as possible, while maintaining the power to overcome those unpredictable disruptions as effectively as possible. And we do it for one other reason: to maintain the optimism that makes life worth living. Winston Churchill put it best, after leading his country through disruptive shocks at least as severe as anything our citizens are likely to see in the coming decade:

"For myself I am an optimist—it does not seem to be much use being anything else."[5]

---

5. Sir Winston S. Churchill, speech at the Lord Mayor's banquet, London, November 9, 1954.

BIBLIOGRAPHY

1. Andrews, Dorine C., and Susan K. Stalick. *Business Reengineering: The Survival Guide.* (Prentice-Hall, 1994).

2. Bartholomew, Mel. *Square Foot Gardening.* (Rodale Press, 1981).

3. Beck, Kent. *eXtreme Programming eXplained: Embrace Change.* (Addison-Wesley, 2000).

4. Beck, Kent, Martin Fowler, and Jennifer Kohnke. *Planning eXtreme Programming.* (Addison-Wesley, 2000).

5. Benson, Ragnar, with Devon Christensen. *Live off the Land in the City and Country.* (Paladin Press, 1982).

6. Berman, Morris. *The Twilight of American Culture.* (W.W. Norton, 2001).

7. Bingham, Rita, James Talmage Stevens, Esther Dickey, and Clair C. Bingham. *The NEW Passport to Survival: 12 Steps to Self-Sufficient Living,* (Natural Meals Publishing, 1999).

8. Boehm, Barry. *Tutorial: Software Risk Management.* (IEEE Computer Society Press, 1989).

9. Brooks, Fred. *The Mythical Man-Month*. (20th anniversary edition, Addison-Wesley, 1995).

10. Charette, Robert, *Application Strategies for Risk Analysis*. (McGraw-Hill, 1990).

11. Charette, Robert S. *Software Engineering Risk Analysis and Management*. (McGraw-Hill, 1989).

12. Covey, Stephen R., A. Roger Merrill, and Rebecca R. Merrill. *First Things First: to Live, to Love, to Learn, to Leave a Legacy*. (Fireside, 1996).

13. DeMarco, Tom. *Why Does Software Cost So Much? and other puzzles of the information age*. (Dorset House, 1995).

14. DeMarco, Tom, and Timothy Lister. *Peopleware*. (Revised edition, Dorset House, 1999).

15. DeMarco, Tom. *Slack: getting past burnout, busywork, and the myth of total efficiency*. (Broadway Books, 2001).

16. Dickson, Murray. *Where There Is No Dentist*. (The Hesperian Foundation, 1983).

17. Emery, Carla. *The Encyclopedia of Country Living*. (9th edition, Sasquatch Books, 1994).

18. Fisher, R.A., J.H. Bennett (editor), and Henry Bennett (editor). *The Genetical Theory of Natural Selection*. (Oxford University Press, 2000).

19. Fowler, Martin, with Kent Beck and John Brant. *Refactoring: Improving the Design of Existing Code*. (Addison-Wesley, 1999).

20. Garfinkel, Simson. *Database Nation: The Death of Privacy in the 21st Century*. (O'Reilly, Jan. 2000).

21. Gilder, George. *Telecosm: How Infinite Bandwidth Will Revolutionize Our World*. (Free Press, 2000).

22. Hammer, Michael. *The Agenda: What Every Business Must Do to Dominate the Decade*. (Crown Business, 2001).

23. Hall, Elaine M. *Managing Risk: Methods for Software Systems Development*. (Addison-Wesley, 1998).

24. Highsmith, James A. *Adaptive Software Development: A Collaborative Approach to Managing Complex Systems*. (Dorset House, 2000).

25. Holland, John H. *Hidden Order: How Adaptation Builds Complexity* (Perseus Books, 1995).

26. Holland, John H. *Emergence: from Chaos to Order*. (Perseus Books, 1998).

27. Honeynet Project. *Know Your Enemy: Revealing the Security Tools, Tactics, and Motives of the Blackhat Community.* (Addison-Wesley, 2002).

28. Jeffries, Ron, Ann Anderson, and Jennifer Kohnke. *eXtreme Programming Installed.* (Addison-Wesley, 2000).

29. Jenning, Chris, Lori Fena, and Esther Dyson. *The Hundredth Window: Protecting Your Privacy and Security in the Age of the Internet.* (Free Press, 2000).

30. Jones, Capers. *Assessment and Control of Software Risks.* (Prentice Hall, 1994).

31. Kuhn, Thomas S. *The Structure of Scientific Revolutions.* (Third edition, University of Chicago Press, 1996).

32. Lessig, Lawrence. *Code, and Other Laws of Cyberspace.* (Basic Books,1999).

33. McCarthy, Jim. *Dynamics of Software Development.* (Microsoft Press, 1995).

34. Mead, Margaret. *Commitment and Culture: the new relationships between the generations in the 1970s.* (Columbia University Press, updated and revised edition, 1978).

35. Neumann, Peter G. *Computer-Related Risks.* (Addison-Wesley, 1995).

36. Nichols, Randall K., Daniel J. Ryan, Julie J. C. H. Ryan, and William E. Baugh, Jr. , *Defending Your Digital Assets Against Hackers, Crackers, Spies, and Thieves.* (McGraw-Hill,1999).

37. Perrow, Charles. *Ordinary Accidents: Living with High-Risk Technologies.* (Princeton University Press, 1999).

38. Petroski, H. *To Engineer Is Human: The Role of Failure in Successful Design.* (Vintage Books, 1992).

39. Putnam, Larry, and Ware Myers. *Measures for Excellence: Reliable Software on Time, Within Budget.* (Prentice Hall, 1992).

40. Resnick, Mitchel. *Turtles, Termites, and Traffic Jams: Explorations in Massively Parallel Microworlds.* (MIT Press, 1994).

41. Sacks, Peter. *Generation X Goes to College: An Eye-Opening Account of Teaching in Postmodern America.* (Open Court Publishing, 1996).

42. Schrage, Michael. *No More Teams! Mastering the Dynamics of Creative Collaboration.* (Doubleday-Dell Publishing Company, 1995).

43. Schrage, Michael, and Tom Peters. *Serious Play: How the World's Best Companies Simulate to Innovate.* (Harvard Business School Press, Dec. 1999).

44. Schwartau, Winn, and John Draper. *Cybershock: Surviving Hackers, Phreakers, Identity Thieves, Internet Terrorists and Weapons of Mass Destruction.* (Thunder's Mouth Press, 2000).

45. Senge, Peter M. *The Fifth Discipline: The Art and Practice of the Learning Organization.* (Doubleday, 1990).

46. Senge, Peter M., Charlotte Roberts, Richard B. Ross, Bryan J. Smith, and Art Kleiner. *The Fifth Discipline Fieldbook: Strategies and Tools for Building a Learning Organization.* (Doubleday, 1994).

47. Stevens, James Talmage. *Making the Best of Basics: Family Preparedness Handbook.* (Tenth edition, Gold Leaf Press, 1997).

48. Voltaire, Francois-Marie Arouet, and Theodore Besterman (editor), *aaa Philosophical Dictionary.* (Viking Press, 1984).

49. Waldrop, M. Mitchell. *Complexity: The Emerging Science at the Edge of Order and Chaos.* (Simon & Schuster, 1992).

50. Werner, David, with Carol Thuman and Jane Maxwell. *Where There Is No Doctor: A Village Health Care Handbook.*(Revised English Edition, The Hesperian Foundation, 1992).

51. Yourdon, Edward. *Rise and Resurrection of the American Programmer.* (Prentice Hall, 1996).

52. Yourdon, Edward. *Death March.* (Prentice Hall, 1997).

53. Yourdon, Edward. *Managing High-Intensity Internet Projects.* (Prentice Hall, 2001).

54. ——. *Back to Basics: How to Learn and Enjoy Traditional American Skills.* (Readers Digest, 1997).

Index

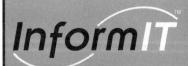

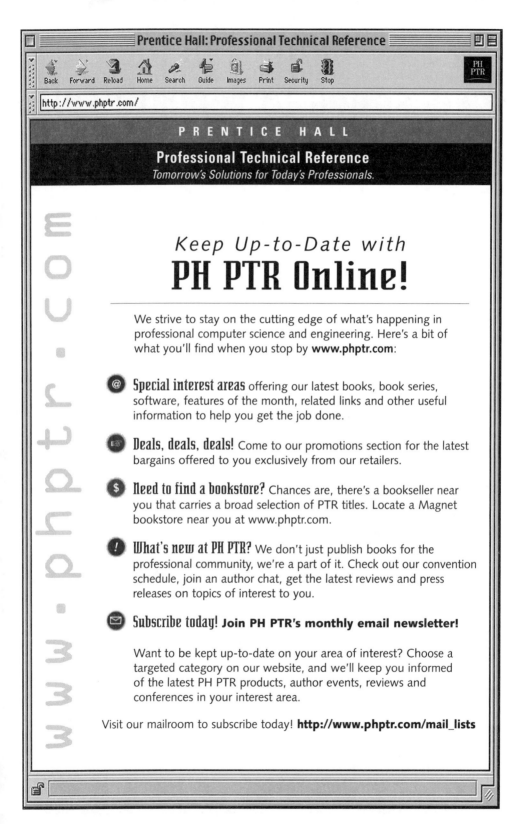